Young people and health

Health behaviour in school-aged children

A report of the 1997 findings

Authors
Lucy Haselden – BMRB
Helen Angle – BMRB
Mary Hickman – HEA

Acknowledgements
This study was commissioned by the Health Education Authority (HEA) and carried out by a team of researchers at BMRB International. Thanks are due to all of the BMRB staff who worked on this project and to the field staff who administered the survey in the schools. Thanks are also due to Antony Morgan at the HEA for his support of the project and valuable contribution to the final text.
Above all, we would like to thank all of the schools that found time in their already busy schedules to participate in the survey, and the pupils themselves for taking part.

A summary of this report, published by the Health Education Authority, is available to order. Contact Marston Book Services for more details, quoting ISBN 0 7521 1309 7.

Health Education Authority
Trevelyan House
30 Great Peter Street
London SW1P 2HW

www.hea.org.uk

Printed in Great Britain
0.5m 3/99

ISBN 0 7521 1308 9

Contents

Foreword

I welcome this second report of the Health Behaviour in School-aged Children survey, carried out in England in 1997. This initiative, a collaborative programme with the WHO Regional Office for Europe initiated in 1982. The survey has the important function of monitoring the health of young people in 28 countries and regions in Europe as well as in Canada and the United States. The survey is carried out internationally every four years.

Monitoring the health of young people is increasingly seen by WHO as an essential feature for informing country policy development on child and adolescent health. Research of this sort has always been an important part of the work of the Health Education Authority (HEA). Building on a continuing programme of research, WHO was delighted that the HEA had carried out the Health Behaviour in School-Aged Children Survey (HBSC) in England for the first time in 1995. The report from this survey was published in 1997 as *Young people and health: the behaviour of school-aged children.*

The current survey interviewed young people in schools. Although the initial survey gathers information about health behaviour, it also looks at the school as a learning environment, the role of the family and socio-eonomic inequalities. These social and economic factors are crucial determinants of health. Countries which concentrate action on protecting the health of young people need to take seriously the whole life experience of the young person, so gathering data about young people's educational experience is very important. The survey is instrumental in supporting the new WHO health policy for Europe, Health 21. It is also my hope that the emerging trends found in the data from the English survey will find resonance in the health agenda of the present government and be utilized in informed policy decisions.

Erio Ziglio
Regional Advisor for Health Promotion and Investment
WHO Regional Office for Europe

Introduction

BACKGROUND

Work with young people has always been an important part of the programme of work carried out by the Health Education Authority (HEA) for England. Monitoring the health of young people has been an integral part of this programme. In 1989 the HEA carried out two national studies of young people, 'Today's Young Adults' and 'Tomorrow's Young Adults'.[1,2] These two studies provided the major national source of information within the HEA for the development and direction of health promotion activity aimed at young people. By 1995 there was a need for more up-to-date information and the HEA applied to become an associate member of the Health Behaviour in School-aged Children Survey (HBSC). They become a full member of the survey when they have successfully completed one main wave. The HEA joined the survey for two main reasons:

- to update the knowledge base on the issues and concerns relating to young people's health in England;

- to gain a pan-European perspective on young people's health, as this was becoming increasingly important.

The HBSC is a World Health Organization (WHO) sponsored Cross-national Survey initiated in 1982. The study has three main aims:

1   to gain insights into and increase understanding of young people's health attitudes and behaviour, and the context in which they develop so that appropriate health promotion and health education initiatives can be undertaken;

2   to increase understanding of how young people perceive health itself;

3   to develop national information systems on the health and lifestyles of each country's young people.

The HBSC survey is administered to school-aged young people at regular intervals, at least every four years, in a growing number of countries. This latest survey was conducted during the 1997–98 school year in a sample of schools in nearly 30 countries in Western and Eastern Europe, Israel, Canada, the United States and Greenland.

The HEA carried out the first HBSC survey in the autumn of 1995,[3] based on the questionnaire and protocol used by other member countries during the 1993–94 school year. This present study has been carried out to the international protocol set for the 1997–98 international study and was undertaken in the autumn of 1997. As with the 1995 survey, British Market Research Bureau (BMRB) International was commissioned by the HEA to carry out the work.

The theoretical orientation of the study is towards the behavioural and social sciences; the 'dependent' variables of the study are health behaviours, and young people's perceptions of health. The 'predictors' are primarily the characteristics of the young people themselves and of their perceived environment. It is not an epidemiological study, and its primary aims are not to shed light on the relationship between risk factors and long-term consequences for disease and death.

In 1992 the government published *The Health of the Nation*.[4] Subtitled *A strategy for health in England*, the White Paper identified key areas where there was both the greatest need and the greatest scope for making cost-effective improvements in the overall health of people in England. The White Paper also recognised the contribution of health promotion to achieving its targets. This document formed the framework for the 1997 HBSC survey in England.

Since the fieldwork for this survey, the government has published the Green Paper, *Our Healthier Nation*.[5] This document gives greater recognition to the wider determinants of health. It legitimises the need to look not only at individual behaviour but also at the influences of the social environment and of the wider community on health. The HBSC has long recognised these wider determinants and has addressed them where possible when surveying young people.

THE QUESTIONNAIRE

The international standard questionnaire is made up of two components: the core section that remains largely unchanged over time, and the special focus that changes every four years. Individual members can then include additional questions, according to national needs. There is also the opportunity for groups of member countries to develop comparable questions, based on a common interest. Each participating country carries out its survey using the methodology prescribed in the international protocol. This sets out the rules for sample selection and for the design and administration of the self-completion questionnaires.

Topics included in the 1997–98 survey included: demographic information, behavioural questions relating to major health problems (including smoking, drinking, physical activity and nutrition), psycho-social aspects of health, the school as a work environment and social inequality. England collaborated with other member countries to include questions on accident and injury. Fourteen- and fifteen-year-olds in England were also asked questions on sexual health and the use of illegal substances.

SELECTION OF SCHOOLS

The sample universe consisted of pupils in the maintained and non-maintained sectors, with the exception of special and hospital schools. The aim of the sampling process was to be able to select an equal number of pupils in each year that the school covered between Years 7 and 11. This entailed selecting with a probability proportionate to the number of pupils in the year. The sample frame was stratified both explicitly and implicitly in order to ensure that a representative sample was drawn.

The sampling of schools was undertaken by the Office for National Statistics (ONS) using the Department for Education and Employment (DfEE) database of schools. The Teenage Smoking survey which was conducted by ONS took place at the same time as the HBSC survey, and a co-ordinated sampling approach avoided the same school being selected for the two surveys, with potential impact on willingness to participate. Schools which had recently taken part in similar surveys were flagged so that they were not selected, although they remained in the database so they would contribute towards pupil totals in their strata.

The sample was stratified by the number of years covered by the school (within the Year 7–11 range), and within those covering five years it was further stratified by the type of school (local authority, grant-maintained and independent). Within these strata there was implicit stratification by the actual years covered (e.g. within those schools covering two years, those covering Years 10 and 11 were grouped together first, with those covering Years 7 and 8 grouped at the end of the stratum). The list was also ordered by region (North, Midlands, London, South, based on local education authority) and by size of school.

A sample of 100 schools was selected, with a matched sample of schools as a reserve sample. If the school in the first sample refused to participate then the matched school was approached. If they also refused then no further substitute was approached.

Based on previous experience, 75 schools were expected to participate in the survey (50% of the initial sample of schools and 50% of the reserve 50 schools). Also based on experience, an 84% response rate was expected among the pupils selected to participate. Using this information the number of schools and pupils to be selected, and the expected weighting factor required to adjust the achieved sample to make it representative, could be calculated. This is outlined below.

No. of years covered by school	Type of school	Percentage of pupils attending	No. of pupils to be selected from this type of school	No. of pupils selected per school (assuming 36 per year)	No. of schools to participate	Schools actually sampled	No. of pupils selected	Weighting factor
5	LEA	64.8	10800	180	60.00	60	10800	1.00
5	GM	16.5	2750	180	15.28	15	2700	1.02
5	Ind	6.6	1100	180	6.11	6	1080	1.02
4		4.3	717	144	4.98	5	720	1.00
3		6.7	1117	108	10.34	11	1188	0.94
2		1.1	183	72	2.55	3	216	0.85
Total		100	16667		99	100	16704	

If a school was selected with fewer than the necessary number of pupils (shown in the fifth column in the table above) it was replaced with the closest school in the stratum with the required number of pupils. This happened in five cases in both the main and the matched samples.

RECRUITMENT OF SCHOOLS

Recruitment procedure

Following the selection of the schools, their co-operation needed to be sought. A letter was sent to all the headteachers of the initial sample, explaining the purpose of the survey and asking if they would be willing for their school to participate. They were then telephoned to check that they would be willing to participate and to check details such as the number of years covered at the school. Incentives were not offered, but any costs incurred (e.g. photocopying and postage costs) were reimbursed. In addition a copy of the summary report of the survey was also offered.

From the initial sample 51 schools agreed to take part; 48 refused and 1 was ineligible because it covered only Years 3–6. The substitutes were then approached and 25 of the 49 matched sample agreed to take part. However, of these 76 schools, 9 dropped out at a later stage for circumstantial reasons and it was possible to recruit substitutes from the matched sample in 3 cases. Thus a total of 70 schools actually participated in the survey.

Reasons for refusal

Despite the efforts to avoid selecting schools known to have participated in recent surveys, the main reason for refusal was 'survey fatigue'. Schools felt they had too many demands on their time to set aside the time to participate in this survey. The sampling procedure which selects pupils at random across the year rather than taking a whole class at one time was considered to be disruptive, but it is unclear what effect on response a simpler pupil-selection procedure would have had. Other circumstantial reasons were given for non-participation, such as

OFSTED (Office for Standards in Education) inspections, building work and a fire in the school.

SELECTION OF PUPILS

The schools which had agreed to participate were visited by a fieldwork supervisor who selected the pupils who were to take part in the survey. Pupils were selected at random from a list of all pupils in the year. Those selected were given a letter explaining the purpose of the survey. A letter was also provided to be sent to parents if the school wished to notify parents. Schools were reimbursed for the costs incurred.

COMPLETION OF QUESTIONNAIRES

The selected pupils completed the questionnaires under the supervision of an interviewer. Interviewers followed the international protocol in administering the questionnaires. The questionnaire took around one hour to complete.

Details of the number of pupils selected, the number who completed the questionnaire and reasons for non-attendance (where known) were recorded; 67 questionnaires returned were unusable. From this, response rates were calculated. Overall, a response rate for the usable questionnaires of 84% was achieved, as shown below.

	Year 7	Year 8	Year 9	Year 10	Year 11	Total
Selected	2557	2465	2440	2532	2306	12300
Completed	2209	2080	2112	2118	1899	10418
Refused	35	35	15	38	24	147
Ill	127	132	126	140	102	627
Absent (other)	37	19	41	41	62	200
Absent (unknown)	149	199	146	195	219	908
Usable	2193	2063	2102	2102	1891	10351
Completed	86%	84%	87%	84%	82%	85%
Usable	86%	84%	86%	83%	82%	84%

WEIGHTING

At the analysis stage, the data were subjected to corrective weighting to ensure that the respondents are representative. Details of the weighting are set out below.

Number of years covered by school	Type of school	Number responded	Percentage of total	Target percentage of sample	Weighting factor
2	All	136	1	1	0.989509
3	All	656	6	7	1.128282
4	All	169	2	4	2.654305
5	Local authority	7047	68	65	0.954827
5	Grant-maintained	1758	17	16	0.956863
5	Independent	641	6	6	1.049714

NOTES ON THIS REPORT

Because of the wide variety of topics covered by the survey, an overall summary chapter has not been included in this report. Instead, each individual chapter is prefaced by a box summarising the key findings for that section of the survey.

When a question has ranked answers (e.g. 'agree strongly', 'agree slightly', 'disagree slightly', 'disagree strongly'), in certain cases a mean score has been calculated. When this is done, each rank is assigned a score between 0 and 100, with equal increments. For example, 'disagree strongly' would score zero, 'disagree slightly' would score 25, 'neither agree nor disagree' would be 50, 'agree slightly' 75 and 'agree strongly' 100. It is the mean value of these numbers over all responses which is taken as the mean score. These means provide a fairly crude but quick and easy comparison across subgroups for the same question.

On occasion, nets and other summed percentages are used in the report. These are always calculated by adding the original frequencies and recalculating the percentage in order to avoid any rounding errors that would be incurred by simply adding the percentage figures.

In the tables, a percentage given as '*' represents less than 0.5, but not zero; '–' represents zero.

The numbers in the tables have been rounded off to the nearest per cent for convenience. In some cases, this means that columns in the tables do not add to 100%, due to cumulative rounding errors; however, each individual number is correct. Similarly, results mentioned in the text based on combinations of rows from tables may appear to give a slightly different answer to that formed by simply adding the relevant figures in the table (again due to cumulative rounding). In such cases, the figure given in the text is the recalculated figure.

For all the questions on the survey, some of the young people either did not answer the question or answered the question with 'don't know'. In most cases the proportion of such answers was very small. However, in some tables where these 'non-response' categories were thought particularly relevant, a 'don't know'/'not stated' row has been included.

Certain questions asked the young people to give more than one answer, if appropriate. This means that the cumulative total over all answers might be higher than 100%. Tables based on these 'multi-coded' questions have been marked as such.

For tables showing comparisons with the previous wave, 1995 figures are given in brackets.

The table below shows how large the difference between two proportions needs to be to be significant at the 95% confidence level. When comparing two groups of the same size the size of the difference required will depend on the proportions being examined. For example, when comparing figures that are close to 10%, one should look in the first column; when comparing figures that are close to 30%, one should look in the second column, etc. The table assumes that the sample size of the proportions being compared are the same or similar. If the sample size is about 2000 (as for school year) and the percentages being compared are about 10%, a difference of 1.2% between the two groups is required in order to be significant.

Sample size	10%/90%	30%/70%	50%/50%
10000	0.0%	0.0%	0.0%
5000	0.6%	0.9%	1.0%
4000	0.7%	1.1%	1.2%
3000	0.9%	1.4%	1.5%
2000	1.2%	1.8%	2.0%
1000	1.8%	2.7%	2.9%
500	2.6%	3.9%	4.3%

REFERENCES

1   Health Education Authority (1992) *Today's young adults*. London: HEA.

2   Health Education Authority (1992) *Tomorrow's young adults*. London: HEA.

3   Turtle, J., Jones, A. and Hickman, M. (1997) *Young people and health: the health behaviour of school-aged children*. London: HEA.

4   Department of Health (1992) *The health of the nation: a strategy for health in England*. London: HMSO.

5   Department of Health (1998) *Our healthier nation: a contract for health*. London: The Stationery Office.

1 The young people and their families

Key findings

- The sample was evenly split between boys and girls (49% boys and 50% girls). (Section 1.1)

- The majority of the sample (77%) attended schools maintained by the local education authority. A further 16% of the sample went to grant-maintained schools and 6% went to independent or voluntary schools. (Section 1.2)

- 86% of the sample described themselves as white and 11% as from another ethnic group. (Section 1.3)

- Most of the young people (67%) lived with both natural parents and 12% lived with just one natural parent – in nearly nine cases out of ten this was the mother. Thirteen per cent of the young people had a step-parent – nearly always a stepfather. (Section 1.4)

- 33% of respondents were classified as belonging to the ABC1 social grade and 47% to C2DE social grade. (Section 1.5)

- Girls were slightly more likely than boys to have their own bedroom but in each case the proportion rose with school year. Only 71% of those in Year 7 had their own bedrooms; by Year 11 82% did so. (Section 1.6)

- Based on pocket money and earned income, young people can be grouped into three broad income bands – those with an income of less than £5 per week (29%), those with an income of between £5 and £9.99 (28%) and those with an income of £10 or over (36%). Boys tended to have a slightly higher income than girls. (Section 1.7)

This first chapter gives demographic details of the sample of young people in terms of such key characteristics as sex, age, ethnicity and household structure, and also covers types of schools and areas. It includes information on such household issues as car ownership, young people's rooms and their incomes.

1.1   SEX, AGE AND SCHOOL YEAR

The sample was more or less evenly split between girls and boys (49% boys and 50% girls with 1% not stated) and between each of the five school years with approximately 20% of the sample in each (Table 1a).

Table 1a   **Sex, age and school year (%)**

	Total	Sex	
		Boys	Girls
Age			
11	15	14	15
12	20	20	20
13	20	21	20
14	20	20	21
15	19	19	19
16	4	4	4
School year			
7	21	21	21
8	20	20	20
9	20	21	20
10	20	20	21
11	18	18	19
Base	*10407*	*5063*	*5241*

Unweighted base: all respondents

1.2   AREA AND SCHOOL CHARACTERISTICS

Of all the young people in the weighted sample 6% went to school in Greater London with a further 19% attending schools in other metropolitan areas. The remainder were split between the northern and southern counties, with 44% being pupils in the former and 31% in the latter. The pupils were then asked what type of area they lived in and according to these perceptions – which may or may not reflect more objective measures – only 17% said that they lived in a city or large town, including the suburbs. Nearly three in five (55%) said they lived in a town, nearly a quarter (22%) said they lived in a village and 5% said they lived in the countryside. There was, not surprisingly, a high correlation between the areas in which young people said they lived and the areas in which their schools were situated. Thus young people who attended school in Greater London, and to a lesser extent in other metropolitan areas, were more likely to say that they lived in a city, although in both these cases more than half said they lived in a town and a fifth of those going to school in a metropolitan area said they lived in a village or countryside (Table 1b).

Table 1b   Location of home by location of school

	School location				
	Total	Greater London	Metro-politan	Northern counties	Southern counties
Area type					
City/large town	17	40	23	15	12
Town	55	54	55	52	60
Village	22	3	19	25	23
Countryside	5	1	1	7	4
Not stated	2	3	2	1	1
Base	*10407*	*671*	*2040*	*4387*	*3309*

Unweighted base: all respondents

The vast majority of the sample (77%) attended schools maintained by the local education authority. A further 16% of the sample went to grant-maintained schools and 6% went to independent or voluntary-aided schools. The profile of those attending the latter was different in that there was a higher proportion of girls (79%) and respondents were more likely to say they lived in a village or the countryside than were those in the rest of the sample (Table 1c and Figure 1).

Table 1c   Sex and location of home, by type of school (%)

	Total	Local authority	Grant-maintained	Independent/ voluntary-aided
Sex				
Boys	49	51	51	21
Girls	50	49	48	79
Area type				
City/large town	17	19	12	10
Town	55	54	63	46
Village	22	22	20	30
Countryside	5	4	4	14
Base	*10407*	*8008*	*1758*	*641*

Unweighted base: all respondents

Figure 1   **Type of school**

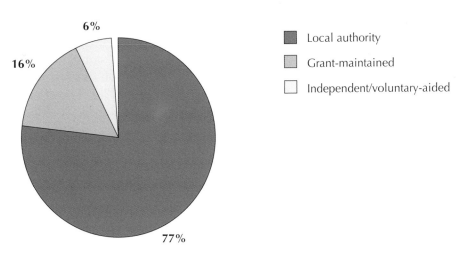

Base: all respondents (10407)

1.3   ETHNICITY

Of the young people in the sample, 86% described themselves as white and 11% as from another ethnic group. The remainder did not answer this question. The proportion of non-white pupils varied somewhat by area, as shown in Table 1d.

Table 1d   **Ethnicity by school location (%)**

		School location			
	Total	Greater London	Metro-politan	Northern counties	Southern counties
White	86	69	85	90	85
Black – Caribbean	1	4	2	*	1
Black – African	*	2	*	*	*
Black – Other	*	1	*	*	*
Indian	3	9	2	1	6
Pakistani	1	1	4	*	2
Bangladeshi	*	1	1	*	*
Chinese	*	1	*	*	*
Mixed race	2	4	2	2	2
Other	1	4	1	1	1
Not stated	4	4	5	4	4
Base	*10407*	*671*	*2040*	*4387*	*3309*

Unweighted base: all respondents

The ethnic mix of the sample taken from Greater London schools differed substantially from that taken in other schools. The proportion of young people describing themselves as Indian (9%) or black (8%) was higher than in any other area, and the proportion describing themselves as white was correspondingly lower (69%). Other metropolitan areas reflected the total sample more closely with the most notable difference being the higher proportion of young people of Pakistani origin (4% compared to the national average of 1%). The ethnic mixes of the northern and southern counties were fairly similar and reflected the sample as a whole, although there was a higher proportion of those of Indian origin in the southern counties.

1.4   FAMILIES AND HOUSEHOLDS

Most of the young people (67%) lived with both their natural parents and a further 12% lived with just one natural parent – in nearly nine cases out of ten this was the mother; 13% of young people had a step-parent – nearly always a stepfather. A high proportion of the sample (82%) had a brother or sister living with them, 4% lived in households containing at least one grandparent and 5% had some other person living in their house. Most young people lived in households containing between two and four people other than themselves, although 15% of the young people interviewed lived with five or more people. Household size varied somewhat with ethnicity so that non-white children tended to live in larger households (Table 1e and Figure 2).

Table 1e   Household type (%)

	Total
Household includes	
Both natural parents	67
One natural parent	12
Step-parent	13
Brother/sister	82
Grandparent(s)	4
Other people	5
Base	*10407*

Unweighted base: all respondents

Figure 2 **Household type**

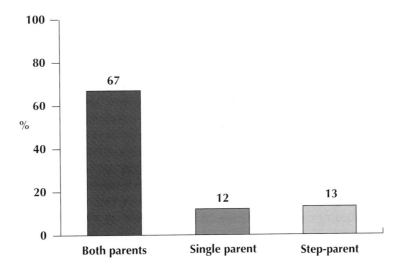

Base: all respondents (10407)

1.5   SOCIAL GRADE

Social grade of the household was derived either from the young person's description of the father's or stepfather's occupation or – where the father was unemployed or the information was missing – from the occupation of the young person's mother. Therefore only a very broad classification into ABC1 social grade (non-manual occupations) and C2DE social grade (manual occupations) has been possible, with unemployed parents included in the latter category: 33% of respondents were classified as belonging to the ABC1 social grade and 47% to C2DE social grade. One-fifth of the sample did not provide sufficient information for even this broad classification which makes it difficult to draw conclusions from these data (Table 1f).

Table 1f   **Social grade (%)**

	Total
Social grade	
ABC1	33
C2DE	47
Insufficient information	20
Base	*10407*

Unweighted base: all respondents

1.6   HOUSEHOLD AMENITIES

A number of questions were asked about household amenities and other aspects of the young people's lives which might indicate the relative affluence of their families. These aspects are discussed below.

Girls were slightly more likely than boys to have their own bedroom but in each case the proportion rose with school year so that whilst only 71% of those in Year 7 had their own bedrooms, by Year 11 82% did so (Table 1g). The proportion of young people having their own bedroom also varied with social grade so that 86% of those classified as ABC1s had their own bedroom compared with 74% of C2DEs (Table 1h).

Table 1g   Young people with their own bedroom, by school year (%)

	Total	School location				
		7	8	9	10	11
Boys with own bedroom	75	68	71	75	78	82
Girls with own bedroom	78	73	74	78	81	83
Total	76	71	72	77	80	82
Base	*10407*	*2193*	*2063*	*2102*	*2102*	*1891*

Unweighted base: all respondents

Respondents were asked how many times they had travelled away on holiday with their families in the last year. Those classified as ABC1s showed markedly different frequencies of going on holiday than those classified as C2DEs: a fifth (20%) of those classified as ABC1 went away on holiday three times or more in the last year compared with 15% of those classified as C2DEs. Conversely 13% of ABC1s did not go away on holiday with their families at all compared with 20% of C2DEs (Table 1h).

There was also a fairly strong relationship between car ownership and socio-economic group. Whilst more than one in ten of those classified as C2DE did not have a car, the proportion of those classified as ABC1 was much lower at 3%. Conversely whilst more than three-fifths (62%) of those classified as ABC1 had two or more cars, this compared with just under two-fifths (39%) of C2DEs (Table 1h).

The tenure of the young people's homes was another powerful discriminator between those classified as ABC1 and those classified as C2DEs. Whilst nearly nine out of ten of those classified as ABC1 lived in homes that their parents or guardians owned, only seven out of ten of those classified as C2DE did so (Table 1h).

Table 1h   Measures of affluence, by social grade (%)

	Total	ABC1	C2DE
Young person has own bedroom	76	86	74
No. of holidays away with family in past year			
0	18	13	20
1	37	37	39
2	25	30	24
3 +	17	20	15
No. of cars/vans in household			
0	9	3	11
1	42	34	48
2+	45	62	39
Tenure of house			
Owned	71	88	68
Rented	17	7	21
Don't know	8	4	9
How well off			
Very well off	12	11	12
Quite well off	35	45	31
Average	41	38	46
Not very well off	6	5	7
Not at all well off	2	1	2
Mean score	62.85	65.33	61.36
Base	10407	3713	5232

Unweighted base: all respondents

Young people were asked how well off they thought their families were and their answers were recorded on a five-point scale so that 100 points were given to respondents who said they thought their families were very well off, 75 points were given to those who described themselves as quite well off, 50 points to those who described themselves as average, 25 points to those who said they were not very well off and 0 points to those who said they were not at all well off. Mean scores could then be calculated for any sub-group. The mean score for those falling in the ABC1 social grade was 65.33 compared with 61.36 for those in the C2DE social grade (Table 1h).

1.7   YOUNG PEOPLE'S WEEKLY INCOME

The pupils were asked to say how much money they usually got each week, including pocket money and money they earned, but not money they were given for travel or school dinners. Answers were grouped into ranges as shown in Table 1i.

Table 1i   **Weekly income by sex and school year (%)**

	Total	School location				
		7	8	9	10	11
Boys						
None	3	5	4	2	3	4
Less than £2.50	10	21	14	7	5	3
£2.50–£4.99	12	20	19	11	7	5
£5.00–£9.99	27	24	27	33	27	22
£10.00–£14.99	17	10	13	18	22	21
£15.00–£19.99	8	2	4	8	12	13
£20.00 or over	14	5	8	13	18	28
Not stated	9	13	10	8	6	5
Base	*5063*	*1073*	*1011*	*1051*	*1009*	*917*
Girls						
None	4	5	4	4	3	4
Less than £2.50	13	29	15	9	6	3
£2.50–£4.99	15	21	21	17	9	6
£5.00–£9.99	29	24	30	34	30	25
£10.00–£14.99	16	7	15	17	21	22
£15.00–£19.99	7	2	3	6	12	12
£20.00 or over	11	3	5	8	14	26
Not stated	6	9	7	5	4	2
Base	*5241*	*1105*	*1040*	*1042*	*1087*	*967*
Total						
None	4	5	4	3	3	4
Less than £2.50	11	25	15	8	5	3
£2.50–£4.99	14	20	20	14	8	5
£5.00–£9.99	28	24	28	33	29	24
£10.00–£14.99	16	8	14	17	22	22
£15.00–£19.99	7	2	4	7	12	12
£20.00 or over	13	4	7	11	16	27
Not stated	7	11	9	6	5	4
Base	*10407*	*2193*	*2063*	*2102*	*2102*	*1891*

Unweighted base: all respondents

Young people can be divided into three broad income groups – those with an income of less than £5 per week (29%), those with an income between £5 and £9.99 (28%) and those with an income of £10 or over (36%). (About 7% did not give a classifiable answer to this question.) Boys tended to have a slightly higher weekly income than girls. Those in different types of household and in different types of area received very similar amounts. The main factor affecting income was age. Half (50%) of those in Year 7 received an income of less than £5 a week, compared with a quarter (26%) in Year 9 and 12% in Year 11. At the other end of the scale, only 14% of those in Year 7 received an income above £10. This rose to 35% of those in Year 9 and 61% of those in Year 11 – 27% of the latter group were receiving at least £20 per week (Table 1i).

1.8 COMPARISON WITH 1995 WAVE

The profile of the young people interviewed in the 1997 wave was very similar to that of 1995. In 1997 there was a slight decline in the number of households containing both natural parents but there was no corresponding increase in the number of single-parent and step-parent households. This may suggest that this might have been partly as a result of incomplete questionnaires.

2 General health

- The majority of young people described themselves as 'quite healthy'. One in five saw themselves as very healthy. The youngest respondents were the most positive: 27% of Year 7 saw themselves as very healthy compared with 17% of Year 11. (Section 2.1)

- Young people who disliked school were less likely than those who liked school to see themselves as very healthy. (Section 2.1)

- Those who displayed signs of low self-esteem, as determined by how they answered questions about whether they felt lonely, left out of things, helpless or confident in themselves, were less likely than average to describe themselves as being 'very healthy' and more likely to suffer at least once a week from a variety of symptoms asked about in the survey. (Section 2.2)

- Headaches were the most common symptom asked about for which young people took medication – 53% of the young people had done so within the last month. (Section 2.3)

- Those who disliked school were more likely than those who liked school to have taken medication for any of the symptoms listed. (Section 2.3)

- Those showing signs of low self-esteem were more likely to have taken some form of medication than those with higher levels of self-esteem. (Section 2.3)

- Just over two out of five young people (43%) felt tired at least once a week when setting off for school in the morning, and nearly a fifth felt tired at least four mornings a week. (Section 2.4)

- Those who disliked school were more likely than those who liked school to feel tired when setting off for school in the morning. (Section 2.4)

This chapter deals with young people's assessments of their own health, and asks which, if any, symptoms of ill health they have experienced recently and whether or not they have taken any medication for them. Tiredness in the morning is also discussed.

2.1 SELF-ASSESSMENT OF HEALTH

The majority of young people (73%) described themselves as 'quite healthy'. However, one in five (20%) saw themselves as very healthy with boys being much more likely to say this than girls. The youngest respondents were the most positive: 27% of Year 7 saw themselves as very healthy, compared with only 17% of Year 11 (Table 2a and Figure 3).

Table 2a   **Self-assessment of health, by sex and school year (%)**

	Total	School year				
		7	8	9	10	11
Boys						
Very healthy	27	34	26	26	25	26
Quite healthy	67	62	70	67	68	68
Not very healthy	5	5	4	6	6	6
Not stated	*	*	*	*	–	*
Base	*5063*	*1073*	*1011*	*1051*	*1009*	*917*
Girls						
Very healthy	14	21	18	12	9	9
Quite healthy	79	77	77	80	82	79
Not very healthy	7	2	5	8	9	11
Not stated	*	*	*	*	–	–
Base	*5241*	*1105*	*1040*	*1042*	*1087*	*967*
Total						
Very healthy	20	27	22	19	17	17
Quite healthy	73	69	74	74	76	74
Not very healthy	6	3	4	7	8	9
Not stated	1	*	*	*	*	*
Base	*10407*	*2193*	*2063*	*2102*	*2102*	*1891*

Unweighted base: all respondents

Figure 3   Self-assessment of health

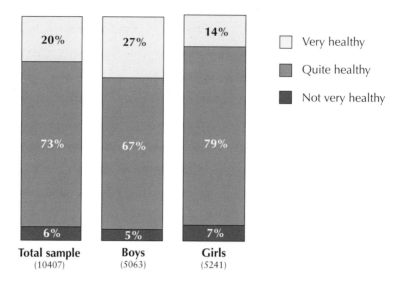

	Total sample (10407)	Boys (5063)	Girls (5241)
Very healthy	20%	27%	14%
Quite healthy	73%	67%	79%
Not very healthy	6%	5%	7%

Base: all respondents (10407)

Six per cent of young people described themselves as 'not very healthy'. Young people who smoked and tried drugs were much more likely to say this, as were those who did not do much exercise.

Young people who disliked school were less likely to see themselves as very healthy than those who were happy at school. (Only 15% of those who disliked school described themselves as very healthy compared with 22% of those who liked school.) Whether young people had ever been bullied or had taken part in bullying at school did not appear to affect their perceived health status as much as their attitude to school (Table 2b).

Table 2b   Self-assessment of health, by psycho-social factors (%)

	Attitudes to school		Bullying	
	Like school	Dislike school	Bullied	Bullied others
Very healthy	22	15	17	19
Quite healthy	73	73	75	72
Not very healthy	4	11	7	9
Not stated	1	1	1	1
Base	*7472*	*2767*	*5087*	*2906*

Unweighted base: all respondents

In addition those showing signs of low self esteem (as shown in Table 2c), were also much less likely to describe themselves as very healthy. In particular those who described themselves as often or always feeling confident in themselves were nearly twice as likely to describe themselves as being very healthy as those who rarely or never felt confident.

Table 2c   Self-assessment of health, by measures of self-esteem (%)

	Ever lonely		Ever left out of things		Ever helpless		Confident in yourself	
	Yes	No	Always/ often	Rarely/ never	Always/ often	Rarely/ never	Always/ often	Rarely/ never
Very healthy	15	26	14	24	16	23	26	14
Quite healthy	77	64	76	70	72	72	70	75
Not very healthy	7	6	9	5	11	5	4	10
Not stated	1	1	1	1	1	1	1	1
Base	*4972*	*4994*	*1361*	*5647*	*1010*	*6599*	*5815*	*1591*

Unweighted base: all respondents

Young people living with both natural parents were slightly more likely to have a positive view of their own health than those who lived with one natural parent only or whose family included a step-parent. The household's social grade had no significant effect on how young people rated their health.

2.2   SYMPTOMS EXPERIENCED

The young people were asked to say how often they had experienced a range of symptoms in the last six months. The most common symptoms of ill health reported by young people were more closely linked to emotional distress than to physical illness; 42% confessed to feeling irritable or bad-tempered at least once a week. A smaller proportion, just under a third (31%) in each case, claimed to feel nervous or have difficulties getting to sleep on a weekly basis. Over a quarter (28%) felt low at least once a week (Table 2d).

Headaches were experienced at least once a week by 30% of the sample. Girls of all ages were much more likely to suffer from them and whilst young people in Year 11 of both sexes were generally more likely to experience headaches, this was much more pronounced amongst girls. A smaller number of young people – no more than one in five overall – reported suffering from other problems at least once a week. These included stomachache, feeling dizzy and backache (Table 2d).

Girls of all ages were more likely than boys to experience most of the symptoms listed, especially headaches, stomachaches and feeling low, which may all be related to menstruation. They were also more likely to feel nervous and have difficulties getting to sleep (Table 2d).

Most of the symptoms, especially headache, backache and irritability or bad temper were more likely to be experienced by older respondents. However, stomachache was more commonly experienced by younger pupils. Although there was little difference across the years in the proportions of girls saying they felt nervous, there were fewer boys experiencing this symptom in Year 11 than in the lower years (Table 2d).

Table 2d **Symptoms experienced at least once a week, by sex and school year (%)**

		School year				
	Total	7	8	9	10	11
Boys						
Headache	23	23	25	21	23	26
Stomachache	15	20	14	15	13	11
Backache	13	11	11	12	16	17
Feeling low	23	26	22	24	22	24
Irritability or bad temper	42	38	40	44	42	44
Feeling nervous	28	32	27	31	27	25
Difficulties in getting to sleep	29	32	32	28	24	30
Feeling dizzy	15	14	15	15	16	16
Base	*5063*	*1073*	*1011*	*1051*	*1009*	*917*
Girls						
Headache	35	27	32	38	39	42
Stomachache	23	27	25	22	20	20
Backache	14	11	12	13	17	18
Feeling low	31	26	29	33	34	40
Irritability or bad temper	43	38	41	42	43	48
Feeling nervous	34	35	33	35	34	34
Difficulties in getting to sleep	33	32	30	32	35	37
Feeling dizzy	17	13	16	17	19	20
Base	*5241*	*1105*	*1040*	*1042*	*1087*	*967*
Total						
Headache	30	25	29	29	32	34
Stomachache	19	24	20	18	17	301
Backache	13	11	12	12	16	17
Feeling low	28	26	25	28	28	33
Irritability or bad temper	42	39	41	43	42	46
Feeling nervous	31	33	30	33	31	30
Difficulties in getting to sleep	31	32	31	30	30	
Feeling dizzy	16	14	15	16	17	18
Base	*10407*	*2193*	*2063*	*2102*	*2102*	*1891*

Unweighted base: all respondents; multi-coding possible

It is clear that the symptoms complained of, whether emotional or physical, were correlated with the attitude of the young person towards school. For example, only about one-quarter (23%) of those who said they liked school felt low at least once a week, compared with just over two in five (42%) of those who disliked school. Both young people who had ever been bullied at school and those who had ever bullied others said they experienced more symptoms on a weekly basis than other young people. This was particularly true of irritability or bad temper (Table 2e and Figure 4).

Table 2e   **Symptoms experienced at least once a week, by psycho-social factors (%)**

	Attitudes to school		Bullying	
	Like school	Dislike school	Bullied	Bullied others
Experiencing symptoms at least once a week				
Headache	26	38	34	33
Stomachache	17	24	21	21
Backache	12	18	16	15
Feeling low	23	42	35	36
Irritability or bad temper	37	56	48	55
Feeling nervous	29	37	37	36
Difficulties in getting to sleep	28	40	37	36
Feeling dizzy	13	23	19	21
Base	*7472*	*2767*	*5087*	*2906*

Unweighted base: all respondents

Figure 4   **Symptoms experienced at least once a week**

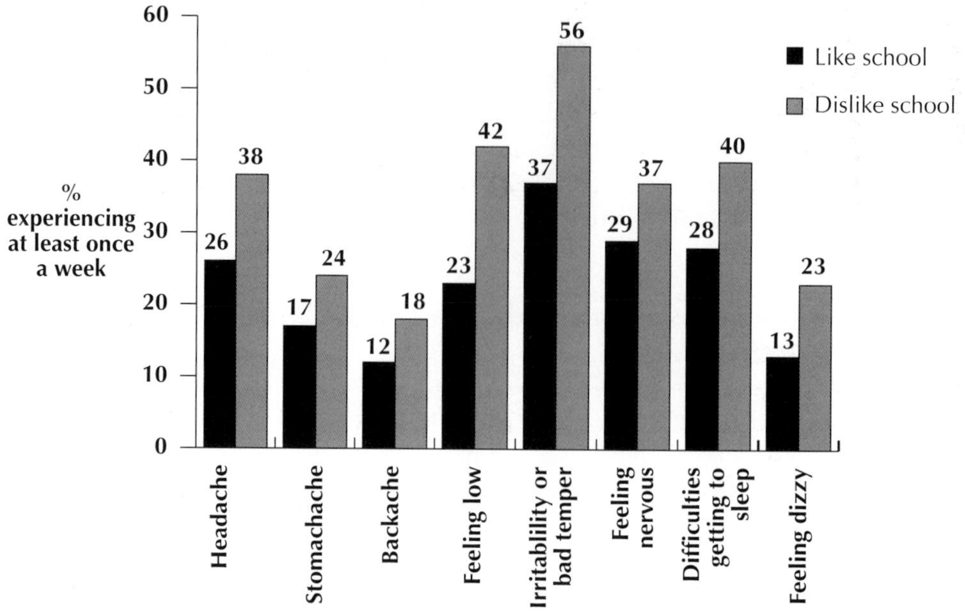

Base: all respondents (10407)

Those who displayed signs of low self-esteem, as determined by how they answered questions about whether they felt lonely, left out of things, helpless or confident in themselves, were more likely to have suffered from any of the symptoms listed at least once a week than those with higher self-esteem (Table 2f).

Table 2f   **Symptoms experienced at least once a week, by measures of self-esteem (%)**

	Ever lonely		Ever left out of things		Ever helpless		Confident in yourself	
	Yes	No	Always/ often	Rarely/ never	Always/ often	Rarely/ never	Always/ often	Rarely/ never
Experiencing symptoms at least once a week								
Headache	35	24	41	25	41	25	26	39
Stomach-ache	22	14	29	15	29	15	16	25
Backache	16	10	22	10	25	11	12	19
Feeling low	38	17	50	18	58	19	19	42
Irritability or bad temper	50	34	60	35	64	36	39	51
Feeling nervous	40	22	49	24	50	25	25	44
Difficulties in getting to sleep	39	22	50	25	27	42	27	38
Feeling dizzy	11	19	25	12	29	12	13	21
Base	*4972*	*4994*	*1361*	*5647*	*1010*	*6599*	*5815*	*1591*

Unweighted base: all respondents

Young people living with both natural parents were less likely to report any type of symptom than those living with only one natural parent or with a step-parent. This was particularly true for headaches, feeling low, irritability or bad temper and difficulties getting to sleep, which are all related to emotional well-being. However, those in single-parent households or who lived with a step-parent were no more likely to feel nervous than those who lived with both natural parents. Social grade did not affect the frequency with which young people suffered from any of the symptoms (Table 2g).

Table 2g **Symptoms experienced at least once a week, by household type and social grade** (%)

	Social grade		Household type		
	ABC1	**C2DE**	**Both natural parents**	**One natural parent**	**Step-parent**
Headache	29	30	29	33	31
Stomachache	17	19	18	21	21
Backache	14	13	13	14	14
Feeling low	28	28	26	32	32
Irritability or bad temper	42	43	41	44	47
Feeling nervous	29	33	31	32	32
Difficulties in getting to sleep	31	31	30	34	34
Feeling dizzy	13	17	15	18	18
Base	*3713*	*5232*	*7023*	*1213*	*1354*

Unweighted base: all respondents; multi-coding possible

2.3 RECENT ILLNESS

Young people were asked whether they had taken any medicines or tablets for a range of specified illnesses. Headaches most frequently made young people take medication, with over half of the sample (53%) having taken some form of medication for them in the past month. Medication was taken for stomachache by nearly a quarter (22%) of the sample. Only a very small minority had taken medication for sleeping difficulties (5%) or nervousness (3%) (Table 2h).

Girls were more likely to have taken medication than boys, especially for headaches and stomachache, the symptoms common to menstruation. The incidence of taking medication for a headache became higher with school year for both boys and girls. Whilst older girls were more likely to take medication for stomachache than their younger counterparts, the opposite was true for boys (Table 2h).

Table 2h **Ailments for which tablets or medicine were taken in the last month, by sex and school year (%)**

| | Total | School year | | | | |
		7	8	9	10	11
Boys						
Headache	47	42	44	46	50	52
Stomachache	12	16	14	12	10	10
Difficulties getting to sleep	5	6	5	4	6	4
Nervousness	4	5	4	3	3	3
Base	*5063*	*1073*	*1011*	*1051*	*1009*	*917*
Girls						
Headache	59	46	55	61	65	67
Stomachache	32	19	25	33	43	43
Difficulties getting to sleep	5	6	5	5	4	5
Nervousness	3	5	2	2	3	3
Base	*5241*	*1105*	*1040*	*1042*	*1087*	*967*
Total						
Headache	53	44	50	54	58	60
Stomachache	22	17	19	23	27	27
Difficulties getting to sleep	5	6	5	4	5	4
Nervousness	3	5	3	3	3	3
Base	*10407*	*2193*	*2063*	*2102*	*2102*	*1891*

Unweighted base: all respondents; multi-coding possible

Those who disliked school were more likely than those who liked school to have taken medication for any of the symptoms listed. In particular those who disliked school were more likely to take medicine for headaches (Table 2i).

Table 2i   **Ailments for which tablets or medicines were taken in the last month, by psycho-social factors (%)**

	Attitudes to school		Bullying	
	Like school	Dislike school	Bullied	Bullied others
Headache	51	59	56	57
Stomachache	21	26	25	24
Difficulty getting to sleep	4	6	6	6
Nervousness	3	4	4	4
Base	*7472*	*2767*	*5087*	*2906*

Unweighted base: all respondents

Those showing signs of low self-esteem were more likely to have taken some form of medication for the four symptoms described than those with higher levels of self-esteem (Table 2j).

Table 2j   **Ailments for which tablets or medicines were taken in the last month, by measures of self-esteem (%)**

	Ever lonely		Ever left out of things		Ever helpless		Confident in yourself	
	Yes	No	Always/ often	Rarely/ never	Always/ often	Rarely/ never	Always/ often	Rarely/ never
Headache	57	48	58	50	59	50	51	57
Stomachache	27	18	29	20	30	19	74	63
Feeling nervous	2	1	6	3	8	2	3	5
Difficulties in getting to sleep	6	4	10	4	11	4	4	7
Base	*4972*	*4994*	*1361*	*5647*	*1010*	*6599*	*5815*	*1591*

Unweighted base: all respondents

2.4   TIREDNESS

Just over two out of five young people (43%) felt tired at least once a week when going off to school in the morning, and nearly a fifth (19%) felt tired nearly every school morning. Boys were more likely to feel tired four or more days a week but girls were more likely to feel tired occasionally or one to three times a week (Table 2k).

Those who disliked school were more likely than those who liked school to feel tired when setting off for school in the morning. Those who had been bullied were also slightly more likely to feel tired in the morning than pupils generally. Most notable though is that those who had bullied other young people were much more likely to feel tired and on a regular basis (Table 2l and Figure 5).

Table 2k **Frequency of feeling tired when setting off for school in the morning, by sex and school year (%)**

		School year				
	Total	7	8	9	10	11
Boys						
Rarely or never	15	21	16	14	11	11
Occasionally	42	40	43	45	43	38
1–3 times a week	22	20	21	24	22	24
4 times a week	21	19	19	17	24	26
Base	*5063*	*1073*	*1011*	*1051*	*1009*	*917*
Girls						
Rarely or never	10	16	14	8	6	4
Occasionally	46	51	49	49	41	39
1–3 times a week	26	21	23	25	30	29
4 times a week	18	12	13	17	23	27
Base	*5241*	*1105*	*1040*	*1042*	*1087*	*967*
Total						
Rarely or never	12	18	15	11	8	8
Occasionally	44	45	46	47	42	39
1–3 times a week	24	20	22	25	26	27
4 times a week	19	15	16	17	23	27
Base	*10407*	*2193*	*2063*	*2102*	*2102*	*1891*

Unweighted base: all respondents; multicoding possible

Figure 5 **Tiredness when setting off for school**

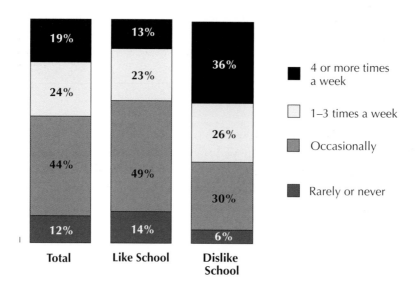

Base: all respondents (10407)

Table 2l **Frequency of feeling tired when setting off for school in the morning, by psycho-social factors (%)**

	Attitudes to school		Bullying	
	Like school	Dislike school	Bullied	Bullied others
Rarely or never	14	6	11	9
Occasionally	49	30	41	37
1–3 times a week	23	26	25	25
4 times a week	13	36	22	27
Not stated	*	1	*	1
Base	*7472*	*2767*	*5087*	*2906*

Unweighted base: all respondents

Similarly those showing signs of low self-esteem were more likely to say they felt tired when setting off for school in the morning. In particular, a third of those who said they always or often felt helpless were tired in the mornings four or more days a week compared to only 16% of those who said they rarely or never felt helpless (Table 2m).

Table 2m **Frequency of feeling tired, by measures of self-esteem (%)**

	Ever lonely		Ever left out of things		Ever helpless		Confident in yourself	
	Yes	No	Always/ often	Rarely/ never	Always/ often	Rarely/ never	Always/ often	Rarely/ never
Rarely or never	8	15	9	14	9	14	14	11
Occasionally	41	48	36	47	32	47	48	34
1–3 times a week	27	21	25	21	25	22	21	27
4 times a week	24	15	29	17	33	16	16	27
Not stated	*	*	1	1	1	1	1	1
Base	*4972*	*4994*	*1361*	*5647*	*1010*	*6599*	*5815*	*1591*

Unweighted base: all respondents

2.5 COMPARISON WITH 1995 WAVE

Data collected concerning general health were broadly similar in the 1997 wave to those in 1995. This is to be expected as general measures of health take a relatively long time to change.

3 The school environment

Key findings

- Nearly three-quarters (72%) of young people said they liked school. Girls in Year 7 were much more likely than boys in the same year to say they liked school a lot but by Year 11 there was no difference between the sexes. (Section 3.1)

- More young people were positive about the school environment than were negative, but older pupils were more likely to be negative than the younger pupils. (Section 3.1)

- The majority of young people were positive about their teachers but attitudes became more negative with age. (Section 3.2)

- Half of all young people had been bullied at some time during their time at school and more than one in five had been bullied during the current term. (Section 3.4)

- Most young people who had been bullied in the current term had only experienced it once or twice but there was a small minority for whom it was a weekly occurrence. (Section 3.4)

- Boys were more likely to admit to bullying others than were girls. (Section 3.4)

- Those who disliked school were more likely to have bullied others than were those who liked it. (Section 3.4)

- About half of those who said they had bullied others had done so within the last term. (Section 3.4)

- There was a strong correlation between those who have bullied others and those who have themselves been bullied. (Section 3.4)

- The most common form of bullying was making fun of people because of the way they looked. (Section 3.4)

- Two-fifths of young people said they always felt safe at school. (Section 3.4)

- Almost four in five young people said that their parents always encouraged them to do well in school. (Section 3.5)

- Nearly seven out of ten young people said their parents were always ready to help if they had a problem. (Section 3.5)

- Boys were more likely to be bored at school than girls (47% of boys said they were bored often or very often compared with 41% of girls). (Section 3.6)

- One in ten young people had skipped more than one day of school in the current term and older pupils were more likely to play truant than younger ones. (Section 3.6)

- Approximately half the sample agreed that either their parents or their teachers expected too much of them. As young people got older they were more likely to agree that too much was expected of them by their parents or teachers. (Section 3.7)

- Half of all young people expected to go on to study for A levels at school or college when they reached age 16, with a further 15% expecting to be at school or college on some other type of course. (Section 3.8)

- Nearly two-thirds (64%) of those from ABC1 households expected to be studying A levels at school or college compared with under half (45%) of those in C2DE households. (Section 3.8)

Previous HBSC studies have shown that negative attitudes towards school are often associated with health behaviour. In this chapter we look both at overall attitudes and at detailed aspects of the school environment, as perceived by the young people who took part in this study.

3.1 ATTITUDES TO SCHOOL AND SCHOOL RULES

Nearly three-quarters (72%) of young people said they liked school, with a quarter (25%) saying they liked it a lot. There was a marked decline in positive attitudes as pupils got older, with 82% of Year 7 pupils saying they liked school, compared with 73% of Year 9 pupils and only 62% of those in Year 11. Girls were marginally more likely than boys to say they liked school a lot (27% compared to 22% of boys) but this difference varied a great deal with school year – in Year 7, girls were substantially more likely than boys to say they liked school a lot (48% compared with 35% of boys); by Year 9 the difference of opinion between girls and boys had diminished so that 24% of girls said they liked school a lot compared to 18% of boys; by Year 11 there was very little difference between the sexes so that 16% of girls compared with 15% of boys liked school a lot (Table 3a and Figure 6).

Table 3a   General attitude towards school, by sex and school year (%)

				School year		
	Total	7	8	9	10	11
Boys						
Like it a lot	22	35	24	18	17	15
Like it a bit	48	45	46	53	48	47
Don't like it very much	17	10	15	17	20	24
Don't like it at all	10	7	11	8	13	13
Not stated	2	4	3	3	2	1
Base	*5063*	*1073*	*1011*	*1051*	*1009*	*917*
Girls						
Like it a lot	27	48	29	24	17	16
Like it a bit	46	37	47	50	49	47
Don't like it very much	18	10	16	17	24	25
Don't like it at all	8	4	7	8	10	12
Not stated	1	2	1	1	*	*
Base	*5241*	*1105*	*1040*	*1042*	*1087*	*967*
Total						
Like it a lot	25	42	27	21	17	16
Like it a bit	47	41	47	52	49	47
Don't like it very much	18	10	15	17	22	24
Don't like it at all	9	5	9	8	11	13
Not stated	2	3	2	2	1	1
Base	*10407*	*2193*	*2063*	*2102*	*2102*	*1891*

Unweighted base: all respondents

Figure 6   Attitude towards school

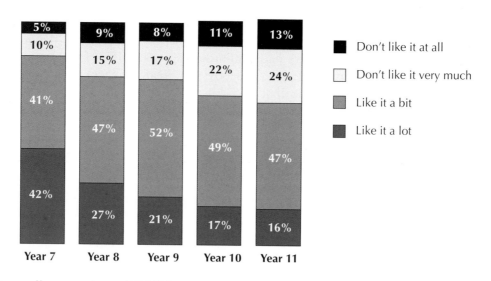

Base: all respondents (10407)

There were some differences between young people at independent or voluntary-aided schools, 29% of whom said they liked school a lot, and those at schools maintained by the local authorities (25%) or by direct grant (22%).

To explore young people's attitudes towards school in greater detail, a series of statements about school, teachers and other pupils was presented. Young people were asked to indicate their reaction to these statements using a five-point scale ranging from 'agree strongly' to 'disagree strongly', so that 100 points were given to respondents who agreed strongly with the statement, 75 points were given to those who agreed slightly, 50 points to those who neither agreed nor disagreed, 25 points to those who disagreed slightly and 0 points to those who said they disagreed strongly. Mean scores could then be calculated for any sub-group.

In Table 3b, overall responses to five statements about school organisation and discipline are presented. Substantially more young people agreed than disagreed that they felt they belonged to their school, that their school was a nice place and that the rules were fair; about one-third disagreed (27% agreed) that the pupils were treated too severely. Only 31% agreed with the statement 'In our school the pupils take part in making the rules' compared with 38% who disagreed (Table 3b and Figure 7).

Table 3b   **Attitudes to school rules (%)**

	Agree strongly (100)	Agree (75)	Neither agree or disagree (50)	Disagree (25)	Disagree strongly (0)	Not stated	Mean score
In our school the pupils take part in making the rules	5	25	29	25	13	2	46.23
The pupils are treated too severely/strictly in this school	7	20	37	27	6	3	48.61
Our school is a nice place to be	10	38	31	11	8	3	58.15
The rules in this school are fair	11	43	24	14	6	3	59.79
I feel I belong at this school	15	43	25	8	7	3	62.74

Unweighted base: all respondents

Figure 7   **Agreement with statements about school and school rules**

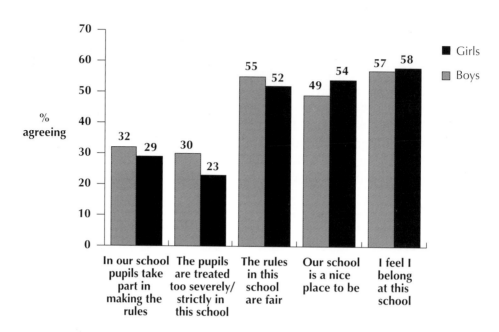

Base: all respondents (10407)

Boys and girls gave similar responses to all the statements. Analysis by year suggests a growing alienation as young people progress through school, illustrated most clearly by the decrease in the proportion agreeing that the school rules are fair (70% in Year 7 compared to 43% in Year 11) and that school is a nice place to be (63% in Year 7 compared to 41% in Year 11) (Table 3c).

Again there was also some difference between pupils from different types of schools. Those at independent or voluntary-aided schools were much more likely than average to agree that their school was a nice place to be (63% agreeing, 15% strongly), and that they felt they belonged to their school (67% agreeing, 20% strongly). However, they were less likely to agree that 'in our school the pupils take part in making the rules' or that 'the rules in this school are fair'.

3.2   RELATIONSHIP WITH TEACHERS

A further four statements related specifically to the help and encouragement provided to young people by their teachers. For these statements (shown in Table 13d) the balance of opinion was more positive than when young people were considering the school in the abstract, as an organisation. Seven out of ten young people said they could get extra help when they needed it, 59% said that they were encouraged to express their own views in class and a similar number (56%) said that their teachers treated them fairly. However, less than two in five (39%) thought their teachers were interested in them as a person.

Table 3c   Attitudes to school and school rules, by sex and school year (% agreeing)

	Total	School year				
		7	8	9	10	11
Boys						
In our school pupils take part in making the rules	32	42	32	34	29	23
The pupils are treated too severely/strictly in this school	30	31	35	31	26	27
The rules in this school are fair	55	67	58	55	49	44
Our school is a nice place to be	47	60	49	45	42	38
I feel I belong at this school	57	62	57	57	55	52
Base	*5063*	*1073*	*1011*	*1051*	*1009*	*917*
Girls						
In our school pupils take part in making the rules	29	41	32	27	23	20
The pupils are treated too severely/strictly in this school	23	20	25	26	25	21
The rules in this school are fair	52	72	57	47	42	42
Our school is a nice place to be	49	65	53	45	39	43
I feel I belong at this school	58	68	59	56	52	54
Base	*5241*	*1105*	*1040*	*1042*	*1087*	*967*
Total						
In our school pupils take part in making the rules	31	42	32	31	26	22
The pupils are treated too severely/strictly in this school	27	26	30	28	26	24
The rules in this school are fair	54	70	58	51	45	43
Our school is a nice place to be	48	63	51	45	41	41
I feel I belong at this school	57	65	58	56	53	53
Base	*10407*	*2193*	*2063*	*2102*	*2102*	*1891*

Unweighted base: all respondents

Again, there was a strong relationship between some of the attitudes that the young people expressed and their age. Those in Year 7 were much more likely to agree that their teachers treated them fairly (74% compared to 46% in Year 11) and that their teachers were interested in them as people (48% compared to 38% in Year 11). Agreement with the other statements was much less strongly related to school year, although it seems that as pupils got older they were more likely to be encouraged to express their own views in class (Table 3e).

Table 3d   **Relationship with teachers (%)**

	Agree strongly (100)	Agree (75)	Neither agree or disagree (50)	Disagree (25)	Disagree strongly (0)	Not stated	Mean score
When I need extra help I can get it	19	51	17	9	3	2	68.89
My teacher is interested in me as a person	9	30	37	15	7	2	54.56
I am encouraged to express my own views in my classes	14	45	28	8	3	2	65.10
Our teachers treat us fairly	12	44	21	16	6	2	60.45

Unweighted base: all respondents; multi-coding possible

As might be expected, those who disliked school were much less likely to agree than those who generally liked school with any positive statements about their teachers. In particular, they were much less likely to agree that their teachers treated them fairly (37% compared with 64%) or that they could get extra help when they needed it (56% compared to 76%).

Table 3e   **Relationship with teachers, by sex and school year (% agreeing)**

	Total	School year				
		7	8	9	10	11
Boys						
When I need extra help I can get it	69	74	67	66	69	70
I am encouraged to express my own views in class	58	55	59	59	60	58
Our teachers treat us fairly	57	72	59	56	49	47
My teachers are interested in me as a person	38	46	36	33	38	37
Base	*5063*	*1073*	*1011*	*1051*	*1009*	*917*
Girls						
When I need extra help I can get it	70	77	70	65	66	74
I am encouraged to express my own views in class	61	58	62	61	60	63
Our teachers treat us fairly	55	75	58	50	47	45
My teachers are interested in me as a person	39	49	40	34	34	39
Base	*5241*	*1105*	*1040*	*1042*	*1087*	*967*
Total						
When I need extra help I can get it	70	76	68	66	67	72
I am encouraged to express my own views in class	59	57	60	60	60	60
Our teachers treat us fairly	56	74	58	53	48	46
My teachers are interested in me as a person	39	48	38	34	36	38
Base	*10407*	*2193*	*2063*	*2102*	*2102*	*1891*

Unweighted base: all respondents; multi-coding possible

3.3   RELATIONSHIP WITH OTHER PUPILS

Three further statements dealt with relationships between the pupils themselves, the scale in this case being the relative frequency with which young people felt pupils in their classes enjoyed being together, accepted other young people as individuals or were kind and helpful. Attitudes were most positive on 'the pupils in my class enjoy being together' and 'other pupils accept me as I am', with opinion much more evenly divided on the frequency with which others were kind and helpful – 15% thought this happened rarely or never (Table 3f).

Table 3f   Relationship with other pupils (%)

	Always (100)	Often (75)	Sometimes (50)	Rarely (25)	Never (0)	Not stated	Mean score
The pupils in my classes enjoy being together	28	43	23	3	1	2	73.45
Most of the pupils in my classes are kind and helpful	14	33	36	12	4	2	60.67
Other pupils accept me as I am	40	32	18	5	3	2	75.38

Unweighted base: all respondents

Generally the statements did not generate much difference of opinion between either girls and boys or between pupils in different years. However, girls were slightly more likely to agree that most of the pupils in their classes were always or often kind and helpful (50% compared with 44%) and younger respondents were more likely to agree with this statement than older ones (Table 3g).

Table 3g   **Relationship with other pupils, by sex and school year (%)**

	Total	School year				
		7	8	9	10	11
Saying always/often						
Boys						
The pupils in my class(es) enjoy being together	72	71	73	74	71	72
Most of the pupils in my class(es) are kind and helpful	44	52	46	41	38	40
Other pupils accept me as I am	71	70	72	70	71	73
Base	*5063*	*1073*	*1011*	*1051*	*1009*	*917*
Girls						
The pupils in my class(es) enjoy being together	69	73	71	72	64	68
Most of the pupils in my class(es) are kind and helpful	50	61	51	47	44	48
Other pupils accept me as I am	73	75	73	72	72	72
Base	*5241*	*1105*	*1040*	*1042*	*1087*	*967*
Total						
The pupils in my class(es) enjoy being together	71	72	72	73	67	70
Most of the pupils in my class(es) are kind and helpful	47	57	49	44	41	44
Other pupils accept me as I am	72	72	72	71	71	73
Base	*10407*	*2193*	*2063*	*2102*	*2102*	*1891*

Unweighted base: all respondents; multi-coding possible

3.4   BULLYING

Half of all young people had been bullied at some time during their time at school and more than one in five had been bullied during the current school term. In the survey, bullying was defined as:

> *A pupil is being bullied when another pupil, or group of pupils, say or do nasty and unpleasant things to him or her. It is also bullying when a pupil is teased repeatedly in a way he or she doesn't like. But it is not bullying when two pupils of about the same strength quarrel or fight.*

Girls were slightly more likely than boys to say they had been bullied in the past but there was little difference in the proportion of girls and boys who said they had been bullied this term. Similarly, although older pupils were generally more likely to have been bullied in the past but not this term, there was a definite pattern of younger pupils being more likely to have been bullied this term. Most young people who had been bullied in the current term had only experienced it once or twice but there was a small minority for whom it was at least a weekly occurrence (Table 3h).

Although half of all young people in the survey said they had been bullied at some time, fewer than one in three (28%) said that they had ever bullied anyone else. While just over one in five pupils had been bullied this term, just over one in ten (14%) had bullied others in that time (Table 3i).

While similar proportions of each sex admitted to bullying in the past, a greater proportion of boys had bullied people within the last term. Overall, therefore, boys were more likely to admit to bullying others than were girls (30% compared to 25%). Table 3i shows these results as well as the results by school year. As might be expected, older pupils were more likely to have ever been bullies than younger ones. However, older pupils were also more likely currently to be bullies (17% of Year 11 had bullied others in the last term compared with 10% of Year 7).

Those who disliked school were also more likely to have been bullies (38% compared to 25% of those who had a positive attitude towards school). Those who smoked, drank alcohol or had tried drugs were also more likely to have been bullies, although this might have resulted from the high correlation between these groups and those who disliked school (see Chapter 13). In all cases around half of those who had bullied others had done so within the last term.

Table 3h   **Experience of being bullied, by sex and school year (%)**

		School year				
	Total	7	8	9	10	11
Boys						
Never been bullied	51	48	51	49	54	54
Been bullied in the past but not this term	23	17	22	24	26	30
Been bullied this term:						
– once or twice	13	20	14	13	9	9
– sometimes	4	4	4	4	4	3
– about once a week	2	2	2	2	2	2
– several times a week	3	4	2	4	4	2
Not stated	4	5	5	4	2	1
Base	*5063*	*1073*	*1011*	*1051*	*1009*	*917*
Girls						
Never been bullied	47	51	47	46	42	47
Been bullied in the past but not this term	31	22	27	32	36	37
Been bullied this term:						
– once or twice	13	15	15	14	12	10
– sometimes	4	3	5	3	5	3
– about once a week	2	2	2	1	2	2
– several times a week	2	3	3	2	3	2
Not stated	1	2	2	1	*	*
Base	*5241*	*1105*	*1040*	*1042*	*1087*	*967*
Total						
Never been bullied	49	49	49	48	48	51
Been bullied in the past but not this term	27	20	25	28	31	33
Been bullied this term:						
– once or twice	13	18	15	14	11	9
– sometimes	4	4	4	4	4	3
– about once a week	2	2	2	2	2	2
– several times a week	3	3	3	3	3	2
Not stated	*	4	3	2	1	1
Base	*10407*	*2193*	*2063*	*2102*	*2102*	*1891*

Unweighted base: all respondents

Table 3i   **Experience of bullying other people at school, by sex and school year (%)**

	Total	School year				
		7	8	9	10	11
Boys						
Never bullied other people	65	69	67	64	64	60
Bullied others in the past but not this term	14	13	11	15	16	17
Bullied others this term:						
– once or twice	13	10	12	13	14	15
– sometimes	2	2	3	3	2	3
– about once a week	1	*	1	1	*	1
– several times a week	1	1	1	1	2	3
Not stated	4	6	6	4	2	2
Base	*5063*	*1073*	*1011*	*1051*	*1009*	*917*
Girls						
Never bullied other people	74	83	74	73	70	70
Bullied others in the past but not this term	13	9	10	15	17	16
Bullied others this term:						
– once or twice	8	5	11	7	10	9
– sometimes	2	1	2	2	3	3
– about once a week	*	–	*	*	*	*
– several times a week	*	–	1	*	*	1
Not stated	1	2	2	1	1	1
Base	*5241*	*1105*	*1040*	*1042*	*1087*	*967*
Total						
Never bullied other people	69	76	70	68	67	65
Bullied others in the past but not this term	14	10	11	15	16	17
Bullied others this term:						
– once or twice	11	8	11	10	12	12
– sometimes	2	2	2	3	2	3
– about once a week	*	*	1	1	*	1
– several times a week	1	*	1	1	1	2
Not stated	3	4	4	3	1	1
Base	*10407*	*2193*	*2063*	*2102*	*2102*	*1891*

Unweighted base: all respondents

In addition there was a strong correlation between those who have bullied others and those who have themselves been bullied. A quarter of those who had been bullied this term had themselves bullied others this term (compared with just 9% of those who had never been bullied and 15% of those who had been bullied in the past but not this term) (Table 3j and Figure 8).

Table 3j   **Experience of bullying other people at school, by experience of being bullied (%)**

	Have never been bullied	Have been bullied but not this term	Have been bullied this term
Never bullied other people	81	64	59
Bullied others in past but not this term	9	21	15
Bullied others this term:	9	15	25
– once or twice	7	11	19
– sometimes	1	2	5
– about once a week	*	1	1
– several times a week	1	1	1
Base	*5103*	*2809*	*2253*

Unweighted base: all respondents

Figure 8   **Experience of bullying and being bullied**

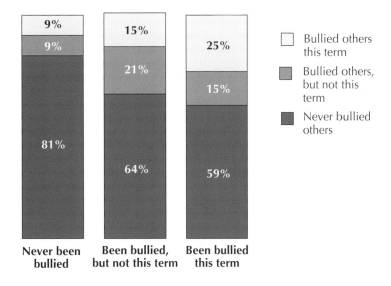

Base: all respondents (10407)

Pupils were also asked if they had been bullied in the last term in a number of specific ways. The results are shown in Table 3k. Two in five (41%) of the pupils had been made fun of in the last term because of the way they looked or talked, although most had had it happen to them only once or twice. A third (33%) had been slapped or pushed and a similar proportion (31%) had had rumours or mean lies spread about them. Only 8% had been made fun of because of their religion or race, although the proportion was substantially higher amongst non-white students (29%), suggesting that, not surprisingly, this was more of a problem for this particular subgroup.

Table 3k   Ways of being bullied by frequency of being bullied (%)

	Not this term (0)	Once or twice (25)	Sometimes (50)	About once a week (75)	More than once a week (100)	Not stated	Mean score
Spread rumours or mean lies about you	62	17	8	3	4	7	14.92
Made fun of you because of your religion or race	84	4	2	1	1	7	4.28
Made fun of you because of your looks or the way you talk	52	23	9	3	6	7	20.32
Hit, slapped or pushed you	60	19	7	3	4	7	15.69

Unweighted base: all respondents

Boys were much more likely than girls to have been slapped or pushed (41% compared to 26%) although there was little difference between the sexes for the other forms of bullying. There was very little correlation between school year and whether these events had occurred in the last term.

Young people were also asked how safe they felt at school. Two-fifths (40%) said they always felt safe at school. There was little correlation between how often they felt safe and either school year or sex, although the very youngest and the very oldest were the most likely to say they always felt safe. Not surprisingly those who had been bullied were less likely than respondents as a whole to say they always felt safe (67% compared with 74%) (Table 3l).

Table 3l   **How often respondents feel safe at school, by sex and school year (%)**

		School year				
	Total	7	8	9	10	11
Boys						
Always (100)	38	39	36	36	37	44
Often (75)	34	31	35	37	35	33
Sometimes (50)	16	16	14	17	16	13
Rarely (25)	5	5	5	4	6	5
Never (0)	4	4	5	4	5	3
Not stated	3	5	4	2	2	2
Mean score	75.21	75.17	74.54	74.73	73.89	78.04
Base	*5063*	*1073*	*1011*	*1051*	*1009*	*917*
Girls						
Always (100)	41	45	39	38	38	47
Often (75)	33	32	33	35	33	30
Sometimes (50)	17	16	20	18	19	14
Rarely (25)	4	3	4	6	5	3
Never (0)	3	2	3	3	4	3
Not stated	1	2	1	*	1	2
Mean score	76.56	79.20	75.01	75.22	74.49	79.10
Base	*5241*	*1105*	*1040*	*1042*	*1087*	*967*
Total						
Always (100)	40	42	37	37	37	46
Often (75)	33	31	34	36	34	31
Sometimes (50)	17	16	17	17	18	14
Rarely (25)	5	4	5	5	5	4
Never (0)	4	3	4	3	4	3
Not stated	2	3	2	1	1	2
Mean score	75.91	77.35	74.75	74.91	74.18	78.56
Base	*10407*	*2193*	*2063*	*2102*	*2102*	*1891*

Unweighted base: all respondents

3.5   PARENTS' INVOLVEMENT WITH SCHOOL

The young people were asked to indicate how frequently they received help and encouragement in their school life from their parents. In general, the results were encouragingly high, as shown in Table 3m.

Almost four in five young people said that their parents always encouraged them to do well at school, the results differing little by sex or school year. Young people from ABC1 households were slightly more likely than those from C2DE households to say this was the case (86% compared with 80%) (Table 3m and Figure 9).

Table 3m   **Parents' involvement with school (%)**

	Always (100)	Often (75)	Sometimes (50)	Rarely (25)	Never (0)	Not stated	Mean score
If I have a problem at school my parents are ready to help	68	14	7	3	3	4	86.98
My parents are willing to come to school and talk to teachers	63	17	9	4	3	5	84.90
My parents encourage me to do well at school	79	10	4	1	1	4	93.12

Unweighted base: all respondents

Figure 9   **Parents' involvement with school**

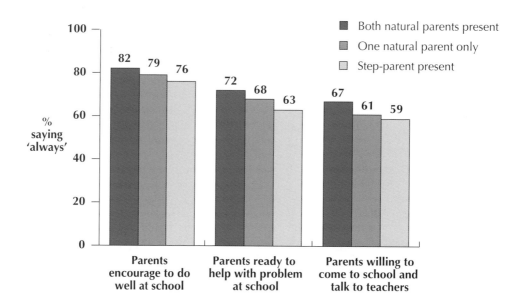

Base: all respondents (10407)

Nearly seven out of ten (68%) said their parents were always ready to help if they had a problem at school, with little difference in answers from girls and boys. This belief was strongest among Years 7 and 8 respondents (71% in each of these years said 'always') but by Year 11 it had weakened slightly so that only 65% of pupils in Year 11 said their parents were always ready to help. Young people who lived in households with both their natural parents were more likely to say that their parents were always ready to help than those who lived with just one natural parent. However, those with just one natural parent were more likely to feel that their parent was always willing to help than those who had a step-parent (Table 3n).

Over half of the young people thought that their parents would always be willing to come into school and talk to teachers (63%). Young people in ABC1 households were slightly more likely to think their parents would always or often be willing to come into school (86% compared with 81% of C2DEs saying always or often) (Table 3n).

Table 3n   **Parents' involvement with school, by household type and social grade (%)**

	Social grade		Household type		
	ABC1	**C2DE**	**Both natural parents**	**One natural parent**	**Step-parent**
Saying always or often					
My parents encourage me to do well at school	95	91	92	92	88
If I have a problem at school, my parents are ready to help	88	83	85	84	79
My parents are willing to come to school and talk to teachers	86	81	83	79	77
Base	*3713*	*5232*	*7023*	*1213*	*1354*

Unweighted base: all respondents; multi-coding possible

Another interesting correlation exists between the young person's attitude to school and the degree to which their parents were involved in school life. This might be linked to the household type as there is a correlation between this and a young person's attitude to school, but the strength of the relationship makes it worth noting. Those with a positive attitude to school were much more likely to agree with all of the statements than those with a negative attitude. In particular, only 57% of those who disliked school said that if they had a problem at school their parents were always willing to help, compared to 73% of those who liked school.

3.6   INTEREST IN SCHOOL

Most young people thought that school was boring at least sometimes (80%) and 44% thought it was boring often or very often. Boys were more likely to be bored at school than girls (47% of boys said they were bored often or very often compared with 41% of girls). Similarly older pupils were more likely than younger ones to say they were often or very often bored at school (31% of Year 7 pupils gave this response compared with 45% of Year 9 pupils and 52% of Year 11 pupils (Table 3o).

Table 3o   How often young people find school boring, by sex and school year (%)

| | Total | School year | | | | |
		7	8	9	10	11
Boys						
Very often	23	19	23	21	27	27
Often	24	18	24	25	25	27
Sometimes	33	33	32	36	32	33
Rarely	13	18	13	13	12	10
Never	4	8	4	3	3	2
Not stated	3	4	4	3	1	1
Base	*5063*	*1073*	*1011*	*1051*	*1009*	*917*
Girls						
Very often	19	12	17	18	24	25
Often	23	13	21	25	29	25
Sometimes	37	37	40	40	35	35
Rarely	15	23	16	14	10	12
Never	5	12	5	2	2	2
Not stated	1	2	1	1	1	1
Base	*5241*	*1105*	*1040*	*1042*	*1087*	*967*
Total						
Very often	21	16	20	20	25	26
Often	23	16	23	25	27	26
Sometimes	35	35	36	38	33	34
Rarely	14	21	15	13	11	11
Never	4	10	5	2	3	2
Not stated	2	3	2	2	1	1
Base	*10407*	*2193*	*2063*	*2102*	*2102*	*1891*

Unweighted base: all respondents

Young people in independent schools were much less likely than those in local authority or grant-maintained schools to find school boring (37% compared with 44% and 46% respectively). However, although, as stated above, a high percentage of these schools in this sample were attended by girls, the difference is still significant.

As would be expected, there was a big difference between those who generally liked school and those who disliked it. Over half (54%) of those who said they did not like school said it was very often boring compared with just one in ten (9%) of those who liked it. Similarly those who intended to stay on in education when they reached age 16 were less likely to find school boring than those who had no such intention.

Whilst there was little difference between pupils who had been bullied and the sample as a whole in terms of interest in school, those who bullied others were much more likely than the sample as a whole to find school boring (55% very often or often compared with 44% of the sample as a whole).

The young people were also asked how often they had skipped school this term. The vast majority (78%) had not done so at all but one in ten (11%) had missed more than one day. Girls and boys were equally likely to play truant but older pupils (particularly those in Years 10 and 11) were much more likely to do so than younger ones (Table 3p).

Table 3p **Frequency of skipping classes, by sex and school year (%)**

		School year				
	Total	7	8	9	10	11
Boys						
None this term	78	79	79	81	77	72
1 day	8	7	7	8	7	9
2 days	3	3	3	3	3	5
3 days	2	2	2	1	4	4
4 days or more	5	3	4	4	7	9
Not stated	3	5	5	2	2	2
Base	*5241*	*1105*	*1040*	*1042*	*1087*	*967*
Girls						
None this term	79	85	83	81	74	70
1 day	8	6	6	8	10	11
2 days	4	3	3	4	5	4
3 days	2	1	2	2	3	4
4 days or more	5	3	5	3	7	9
Not stated	2	2	1	1	2	2
Base	*5063*	*1073*	*1011*	*1051*	*1009*	*917*
Total						
None this term	78	82	81	81	75	71
1 day	8	7	7	8	9	10
2 days	4	3	3	3	4	5
3 days	2	2	2	2	4	4
4 days or more	5	3	5	4	7	9
Not stated	2	4	3	2	2	2
Base	*10407*	*2193*	*2063*	*2102*	*2102*	*1891*

Unweighted base: all respondents

As with finding school boring, those who disliked school were much more likely than those who liked it to skip classes. Although there was little difference between the general sample and those who had been bullied in their likelihood of skipping school, those who bullied other people were much more likely to do so.

3.7   PERFORMANCE AND PRESSURE AT SCHOOL

When asked the question, 'What does your class teacher(s) think about your school performance compared to your class mates?', over three-fifths of the respondents (62%) said their teacher considered their performance better than average (the most common response being 'good') and only 4% said their teacher thought them below average (Table 3q).

Those in Year 7 tended to place themselves slightly higher on the scale than those from other years: one in five (22%) of those in Year 7 expressed the opinion that their teacher thought them to be very good and just 2% thought they were below average. By Year 11 the corresponding results were 15% and 8%, respectively (Table 3q).

Table 3q   **Perceptions of what their class teacher thinks of school performance, by sex and school year (%)**

	Total	School year				
		7	8	9	10	11
Boys						
Very good	16	20	17	15	16	14
Good	43	44	42	42	46	40
Average	32	27	32	37	31	35
Below average	5	3	6	4	6	10
Not stated	3	5	4	3	2	2
Base	*5063*	*1073*	*1011*	*1051*	*1009*	*917*
Girls						
Very good	20	25	22	18	17	16
Good	45	46	42	48	46	44
Average	30	23	31	30	33	32
Below average	3	1	3	3	3	7
Not stated	2	4	2	2	1	1
Base	*5241*	*1105*	*1040*	*1042*	*1087*	*967*
Total						
Very good	18	22	19	16	16	15
Good	44	45	42	45	46	42
Average	31	25	31	33	32	33
Below average	4	2	4	3	4	8
Not stated	3	5	3	3	1	1
Base	*10407*	*2193*	*2063*	*2102*	*2102*	*1891*

Unweighted base: all respondents

Perception of their performance from the teacher's perspective was higher among young people from households where both natural parents were present (19% said 'very good') than among those from single-parent households (17%) which was in turn higher than young people from households where a step-parent was present (13%). Another key factor was attitude towards school: 21% of those who liked school gave the answer 'very good' compared with just 9% of those who disliked school, 12% of whom thought they were below average (Table 3r).

Table 3r   Pupils' perceptions of what their class teacher thinks of their performance, by household type and social grade (%)

	Social grade		Household type		
	ABC1	C2DE	Both natural parents	One natural parent	Step-parent
Very good	20	16	19	17	13
Good	48	43	46	40	41
Average	27	34	29	36	36
Below average	3	4	3	6	8
Not stated	2 '	2	2	2	2
Base	*3713*	*5232*	*7023*	*1213*	*1354*

Unweighted base: all respondents; multi-coding possible

There was a clear relationship between a young person's perception of their teacher's view and that young person's expectations for the future. Three-quarters (74%) of those who thought their teachers would rate them as very good expected to be studying at school or college when they were 16 (compared to 64% overall and 42% of those who thought they would be considered 'below average').

Next we consider the pressures put upon young people by school-work and the expectations of parents and teachers. The young people were asked whether they thought that too much was expected of them by their parents and their teachers (Table 3s). In each case less than half of the sample agreed that either their parents or their teachers expected too much of them. Boys were much more likely than girls to agree their parents expected too much of them and slightly more likely to agree that teachers expected too much of them. As young people got older, they were more likely to agree that both parents and teachers expected too much of them (Table 3s and Figure 10).

Table 3s **Pupils' view of whether too much is expected of them by parents and teachers, by sex and school year (%)**

		Base	By parents	By teachers
Agreeing that too much is expected				
Girls	Year 7	1105	24	23
	Year 8	1040	29	36
	Year 9	1042	30	36
	Year 10	1087	35	41
	Year 11	967	40	46
	Total girls	5241	32	36
Boys	Year 7	1073	37	35
	Year 8	1011	44	42
	Year 9	1081	40	40
	Year 10	1009	43	44
	Year 11	917	46	45
	Total boys	5063	42	41
Total	Year 7	2193	30	29
	Year 8	2063	37	39
	Year 9	2102	35	38
	Year 10	2102	39	42
	Year 11	1891	43	45
	Total	*10407*	*37*	*39*

Unweighted base: all respondents

Figure 10 **Pupils agreeing that too much is expected of them by parents and teachers**

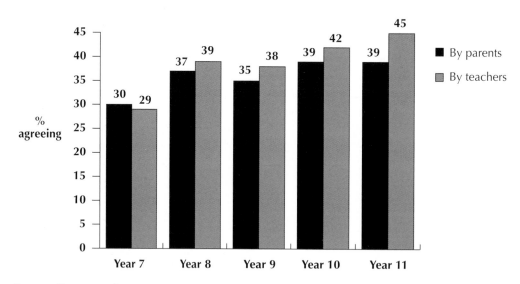

Base: all respondents (10407)

Agreement with both of these statements was higher among those who did not expect to be studying beyond 16. One in five of these young people agreed strongly that their teachers expected too much of them compared with just over one in ten of those who expected to be taking A levels or some other course at age 16. Nineteen per cent of those not expecting to study beyond 16 agreed strongly that their parents expected too much of them (compared with 14% of those expecting to continue).

As might be expected, different responses were also likely to be given by those who liked and those who disliked school. Amongst the former, only 9% agreed strongly that too much was expected by teachers and just 11% agreed that their parents expected too much. This compared with 23% of those who disliked school agreeing strongly that their parents expected too much of them and a similar proportion agreeing strongly that their teachers expected too much of them.

The respondents were then asked how pressurised they felt by the school-work they had to do. The most common response was 'a little', given by 45% of the young people. A further 36% felt more than a little pressured (either 'some' or 'a lot') by the work. This level rose sharply with school year from 24% of Year 7 to 57% of Year 11 (Table 3t).

Table 3t   How pressurised young people felt by school-work, by sex and school year (%)

| | Total | School year | | | | |
		7	8	9	10	11
Boys						
Not at all	18	25	21	18	14	9
A little	45	44	45	50	46	38
Some	22	16	19	20	24	30
A lot	12	8	10	10	13	22
Not stated	3	6	5	3	1	1
Base	*5063*	*1073*	*1011*	*1051*	*1009*	*917*
Girls						
Not at all	15	26	21	15	8	4
A little	45	47	51	51	45	32
Some	23	18	19	24	28	27
A lot	15	7	8	10	18	36
Not stated	1	2	1	1	1	1
Base	*5241*	*1105*	*1040*	*1042*	*1087*	*967*
Total						
Not at all	16	26	21	17	11	7
A little	45	46	48	50	46	35
Some	22	17	19	22	26	28
A lot	14	7	9	10	16	29
Not stated	2	4	3	2	1	2
Base	*10407*	*2193*	*2063*	*2102*	*2102*	*1891*

Unweighted base: all respondents

Although there was no real difference overall between the sexes on this issue, within Year 11 a difference appears – 36% of Year 11 girls felt a lot of pressure from the work they had to do, compared with just 22% of Year 11 boys (although this is still much higher than the overall result for boys of 12%) (Table 3t). Once again, the responses varied with attitude towards school: 25% of those with a negative attitude towards school felt under a lot of pressure from their work compared with only 10% of those who liked school.

3.8   EXPECTATIONS FOR AGE 16

Half of all the young people expected to go on to study A levels at school or college when they reached age 16, with a further 15% expecting to be at school or college studying some other type of course; 16% of pupils did not know what they expected to be doing at that age. As is to be expected this was very much a factor of school year. A quarter of the (mainly 11-year-old) pupils in Year 7 did not know what they would be doing when they were 16, falling to 6% of those in Year 11. Table 3u shows the detailed results.

Table 3u   **What respondents expect to be doing at age 16, by sex and school year (%)**

		School year				
	Total	7	8	9	10	11
Boys						
Doing A levels, either at school (6th form) or at college	46	46	46	49	44	43
Doing some other course at school (6th form) or at college	13	7	10	12	15	20
Getting a full-time job	10	10	11	9	11	8
Getting an apprenticeship/ training	8	4	4	8	10	16
Be unemployed	1	1	*	*	1	1
Going on an employment training course	1	1	1	1	1	2
Don't know	16	23	20	15	16	6
Not stated	6	9	7	5	3	4
Base	*5063*	*1073*	*1011*	*1051*	*1009*	*917*

Table 3u   **What respondents expect to be doing at age 16, by sex and school year (%) (continued)**

	Total	School year				
		7	8	9	10	11
Girls						
Doing A levels, either at school (6th form) or at college	54	51	55	57	51	57
Doing some other course at school (6th form) or at college	17	9	13	16	23	27
Getting a full-time job	5	5	5	4	5	3
Getting an apprenticeship/ training	3	2	2	2	4	5
Be unemployed	*	*	1	1	1	*
Going on an employment training course	1	1	1	2	1	2
Don't know	17	27	20	17	13	5
Not stated	3	6	4	3	2	2
Base	*5241*	*1105*	*1040*	*1042*	*1087*	*967*
Total						
Doing A levels, either at school (6th form) or at college	50	48	51	53	48	50
Doing some other course at school (6th form) or at college	15	8	11	14	19	23
Getting a full-time job	7	7	8	7	8	5
Getting an apprenticeship/ training	5	3	3	5	7	10
Be unemployed	1	1	*	*	1	1
Going on an employment training course	1	1	1	1	1	2
Don't know	16	25	20	16	14	6
Not stated	5	7	6	4	2	3
Base	*10407*	*2193*	*2063*	*2102*	*2102*	*1891*

Unweighted base: all respondents

Social grade of the young person's household was an important factor affecting response to this question, Nearly two-thirds (64%) of those from ABC1 households expected to be studying A levels at school or college, compared with under half (45%) of those from C2DE households. This latter group were more likely than average to expect to be in full-time work (9% compared with 4% of ABC1 respondents) and were also more likely not to have any clear expectations (19% compared with 12%).

3.9   COMPARISON WITH 1995 WAVE

Attitudinal questions about school rules and relationships with teachers tended to produce more neutral answers than in the previous wave. This was particularly noticeable for questions regarding relationships with teachers, as shown in Table 3v (1995 results are shown in brackets).

Table 3v   Relationship with teachers – comparison with 1995 wave (%)[†]

	Agree strongly	Agree	Neither agree or disagree	Disagree	Disagree strongly
When I need extra help I can get it	19 (43)	51 (32)	17 (7)	9 (11)	3 (7)
My teacher is interested in me as a person	9 (20)	30 (29)	37 (13)	15 (28)	7 (10)
I am encouraged to express my own views in my classes	14 (30)	45 (36)	28 (9)	8 (20)	3 (5)
Our teachers treat us fairly	12 (27)	44 (36)	21 (10)	16 (12)	6 (10)

Unweighted base: all respondents
[†]1995 figures shown in brackets

There was also a decrease in the proportion of pupils agreeing that too much was expected of them by their parents and their teachers, although there was no real change in the proportion of young people feeling pressurised by their school-work. The greatest change was in the proportion of young people feeling too much was expected of them by their parents (Table 3w).

Table 3w **Pupils' view of whether too much is expected of them, by parents and teachers – comparison with 1995 wave (%)[†]**

		Base	By parents	By teachers
Agreeing that too much is expected				
Boys	Year 7	1073 (1162)	37 (38)	35 (39)
	Year 9	1051 (1233)	40 (52)	40 (50)
	Year 11	917 (1001)	46 (57)	45 (52)
	Total boys	*3041 (3396)*	*42 (49)*	*41 (42)*
Girls	Year 7	1103 (1072)	24 (32)	23 (37)
	Year 9	1042 (1049)	30 (42)	36 (46)
	Year 11	967 (855)	40 (52)	46 (48)
	Total girls	*3114 (2976)*	*32 (46)*	*36 (46)*
Total	Year 7	2193 (2258)	30 (35)	29 (38)
	Year 9	2102 (2288)	35 (48)	38 (48)
	Year 11	1891 (1860)	43 (54)	45 (52)
	Total	*6186 (6406)*	*37 (46)*	*39 (46)*

Unweighted base: all respondents
[†] 1995 figures shown in brackets

4 Relationships outside school

Key findings

- Four out of five young people (78%) said they found it easy to make new friends. (Section 4.1)

- The vast majority of young people had at least three close friends. (Section 4.1)

- One in 20 young people said that other pupils did not want to spend time with them and they ended up alone at least once a week. (Section 4.1)

- Two out of five young people felt left out at least sometimes and this feeling was much more common amongst girls than boys and amongst older rather than younger pupils. (Section 4.1)

- Outside school, boys tended to spend time more frequently with their friends than did girls, both straight after school and in the evening. (Section 4.2)

- Most young people (74%) said it was easy to talk to friends of the same sex compared to only 45% who found it easy to talk to friends of the opposite sex. Girls found female friends much easier to talk to than boys found male friends (84% compared to 64% saying easy or very easy). (Section 4.3)

- It is clear that all young people were more at ease when talking to their mother than their father although those who had an elder sister also found her relatively easy to talk to. Fathers and elder brothers were much less approachable. (Section 4.4)

- There was an increase in the number of young people going out between four and six evenings a week between the 1995 and 1997 waves.

Results of previous HBSC studies in other countries provide evidence that young people who are socially well integrated and are able to interact effectively with other people report significantly better health than young people who are socially isolated. In this chapter, we examine the results of questions in the 1997 study about relationships with friends and the ease with which young people can communicate with other people.

4.1 MAKING AND KEEPING FRIENDS

Four out of five young people (78%) said they found it easy to make new friends, and over a quarter (26%) said it was very easy. These results were the same for both boys and girls. Pupils in Years 10 and 11 were slightly more likely than their younger counterparts to say that making friends was either quite or very easy (Table 4a).

Table 4a **How easy or difficult it is to make new friends, by sex and school year (%)**

| | Total | School year | | | | |
		7	8	9	10	11
Boys						
Very easy	25	27	26	24	24	25
Quite easy	53	44	49	55	57	58
Quite difficult	13	13	14	12	14	11
Very difficult	2	3	1	2	2	2
Not stated	7	12	10	7	3	3
Base	*5063*	*1073*	*1011*	*1051*	*1009*	*917*
Girls						
Very easy	26	30	30	25	23	24
Quite easy	53	47	49	54	58	57
Quite difficult	14	12	13	17	15	15
Very difficult	2	2	2	3	2	2
Not stated	4	9	6	2	2	1
Base	*5241*	*1105*	*1040*	*1042*	*1087*	*967*
Total						
Very easy	26	28	28	24	23	25
Quite easy	53	46	49	54	57	58
Quite difficult	14	12	13	15	15	13
Very difficult	2	3	2	2	2	2
Not stated	6	11	8	5	3	2
Base	*10407*	*2193*	*2063*	*2102*	*2102*	*1891*

Unweighted base: all respondents

Young people who had been bullied were more likely to find making friends difficult (22%) than respondents as a whole (16%). Those young people who disliked school were also more likely to find it difficult to make friends (21% compared to 14%).

Those young people displaying signs of low self-esteem tended to find making new friends much more difficult than those with higher levels of self-esteem (Table 4b).

Table 4b   **Ease of making friends, by measures of self-esteem (%)**

	Ever lonely		Ever left out of things		Ever helpless		Confident in yourself	
	Yes	No	Always/ often	Rarely/ never	Always/ often	Rarely/ never	Always/ often	Rarely/ never
Very easy	18	36	18	34	22	31	33	22
Quite easy	55	55	42	56	39	57	56	45
Quite difficult	22	7	28	8	26	10	9	25
Very difficult	4	1	10	1	11	1	1	7
Not stated	2	2	2	1	3	1	1	2
Base	*4972*	*4994*	*1361*	*5647*	*1010*	*6599*	*5815*	*1591*

Young people were also asked how many close friends they had at present. Their responses to this question showed much less variation, as the vast majority of young people had at least three close friends. There was no difference in answers from boys and girls, and the apparent difference between the years arose largely from the higher levels of non-response to this question from those in the younger age groups (Table 4c).

Table 4c   **Number of close friends, by sex and school year (%)**

	Total	School year				
		7	8	9	10	11
Boys						
None	3	2	2	3	4	2
One	5	7	5	4	4	4
Two	11	9	12	11	10	10
Three or more	73	66	71	74	77	80
Not stated	9	15	11	8	5	4
Base	*5063*	*1073*	*1011*	*1051*	*1009*	*917*
Girls						
None	1	1	1	1	1	2
One	6	8	7	5	4	6
Two	14	14	13	13	14	14
Three or more	75	68	73	77	79	78
Not stated	4	8	7	4	2	1
Base	*5241*	*1105*	*1040*	*1042*	*1087*	*967*
Total						
None	2	2	2	2	2	2
One	6	8	6	5	4	5
Two	12	12	12	12	12	12
Three or more	74	67	72	75	78	79
Not stated	6	12	9	6	3	2
Base	*10407*	*2193*	*2063*	*2102*	*2102*	*1891*

Unweighted base: all respondents

When asked how often other pupils did not want to spend time with them, so that they ended up alone, two-thirds of the young people said that it had not happened that term, and only 1 in 20 that it happened at least once a week. There were differences in responses from the various age groups, with young people in Year 7 the most likely, and those in Year 11 the least likely to believe they had suffered from this form of social ostracism (Table 4d).

Table 4d **How often other pupils did not want to spend time with the respondent by sex and school year (%)**

	Total	School year				
		7	8	9	10	11
Boys						
Hasn't happened this term	64	56	58	62	71	74
Once or twice	18	20	23	20	15	13
Sometimes	9	10	9	9	9	7
About once a week	3	4	3	3	1	2
Several times a week	3	4	3	3	5	2
Not stated	3	5	4	3	2	2
Base	*5063*	*1073*	*1011*	*1051*	*1009*	*917*
Girls						
Hasn't happened this term	67	57	60	69	72	76
Once or twice	17	23	19	17	14	11
Sometimes	10	10	13	9	8	7
About once a week	3	4	3	2	2	1
Several times a week	3	4	4	3	3	2
Not stated	1	2	1	1	1	2
Base	*5241*	*1105*	*1040*	*1042*	*1087*	*967*
Total						
Hasn't happened this term	65	57	59	66	71	75
Once or twice	18	21	21	18	15	12
Sometimes	9	10	11	9	9	7
About once a week	3	4	3	2	2	2
Several times a week	3	4	4	3	3	2
Not stated	2	4	3	2	2	2
Base	*10407*	*2193*	*2063*	*2102*	*2102*	*1891*

Unweighted base: all respondents

The young people were also asked a similar question: 'How often do you feel left out of things?' which produced rather different results, perhaps because the emphasis was on the young person's general feelings, rather than on the recall of specific occasions (Table 4e). Two out of five young people felt left out at least sometimes, and this feeling was more common amongst girls than boys and amongst older rather than younger pupils.

Table 4e   How often respondent felt left out of things, by sex and school year (%)

	Total	School year				
		7	8	9	10	11
Boys						
Always	3	4	3	3	2	1
Often	8	7	8	9	9	8
Sometimes	22	20	21	22	23	26
Rarely	36	30	32	37	39	43
Never	24	26	27	21	24	20
Not stated	7	13	9	7	3	3
Base	*5063*	*1073*	*1011*	*1051*	*1009*	*917*
Girls						
Always	3	3	3	4	3	3
Often	12	10	14	11	13	13
Sometimes	33	28	28	36	37	36
Rarely	34	34	33	34	34	35
Never	14	18	17	12	11	12
Not stated	4	8	6	3	1	1
Base	*5241*	*1105*	*1051*	*1042*	*1087*	*967*
Total						
Always	3	3	3	3	3	2
Often	10	8	11	10	11	10
Sometimes	28	24	24	29	30	31
Rarely	35	32	33	35	36	39
Never	19	22	22	17	17	16
Not stated	5	10	7	5	2	2
Base	*10407*	*2193*	*2063*	*2102*	*2102*	*1891*

Unweighted base: all respondents

Just under half (48%) of all young people said they felt lonely on occasions, the majority experiencing this feeling sometimes rather than often. Again, girls were more likely to experience this than boys, as were older pupils (53% of those in Year 11 said they felt lonely at least sometimes compared with only 46% of those in Year 7) (Table 4f and Figure 11).

Table 4f   **Frequency of feeling lonely, by sex and school year (%)**

	Total	School year				
		7	8	9	10	11
Boys						
Yes, very often	4	6	3	4	4	3
Yes, rather often	4	5	4	3	3	4
Yes, sometimes	31	31	30	30	29	36
No	55	48	55	56	61	56
Not stated	6	11	8	5	2	2
Base	*5063*	*1073*	*1011*	*1051*	*1009*	*917*
Girls						
Yes, very often	7	6	6	6	8	8
Yes, rather often	6	5	7	5	6	6
Yes, sometimes	44	40	37	45	50	48
No	40	43	44	42	36	37
Not stated	3	7	5	2	1	*
Base	*5241*	*1105*	*1040*	*1042*	*1087*	*967*
Total						
Yes, very often	5	6	5	5	6	5
Yes, rather often	5	5	5	4	5	5
Yes, sometimes	38	35	34	37	40	42
No	48	45	50	49	48	46
Not stated	4	9	6	4	1	1
Base	*10407*	*2193*	*2063*	*2102*	*2102*	*1891*

Unweighted base: all respondents

Figure 11   **Feeling lonely**

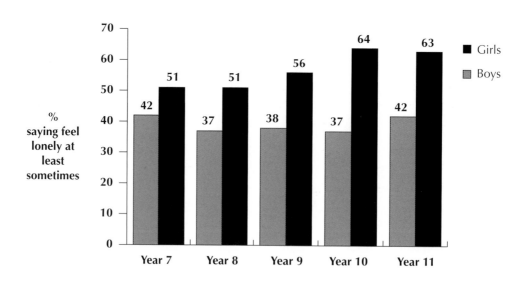

Base: all respondents (10407)

4.2   SPENDING TIME WITH FRIENDS OUTSIDE SCHOOL

Young people were asked how often they spent time with friends straight after school and how many evenings a week they spent out with friends.

About two-fifths (38%) went out with friends straight after school four or five days a week and about one-quarter (26%) said they went out straight after school once a week or less. The proportions of people going out in the evening were very similar, with about a quarter going out in the evening once a week or less (including 7% not allowed out in the evening at all) and as many as two-fifths (42%) going out more than four times a week in the evening. Almost one in six (15%) went out every evening (Tables 4g and 4h and Figure 12).

Table 4g   **Frequency of spending time with friends straight after school, by sex and school year (%)**

		School year				
	Total	7	8	9	10	11
Boys						
4–5 days a week	43	39	43	42	46	44
2–3 days a week	34	34	33	34	34	34
Once a week or less	21	24	20	21	17	20
Have no friends right now	1	2	2	1	2	1
Not stated	1	2	2	1	1	1
Base	*5063*	*1073*	*1011*	*1051*	*1009*	*917*
Girls						
4–5 days a week	33	29	32	31	38	34
2–3 days a week	34	34	37	36	29	32
Once a week or less	31	32	28	31	31	32
Have no friends right now	1	2	2	1	1	1
Not stated	1	2	1	1	1	1
Base	*5239*	*1105*	*1040*	*1042*	*1087*	*967*
Total						
4–5 days a week	38	34	38	37	42	39
2–3 days a week	34	34	35	35	32	33
Once a week or less	26	28	24	26	24	26
Have no friends right now	1	2	2	1	1	1
Not stated	1	2	1	1	1	1
Base	*10407*	*2193*	*2063*	*2102*	*2102*	*1891*

Unweighted base: all respondents

Table 4h   **Number of evenings per week usually spent with friends, by sex and school year (%)**

		School year				
	Total	7	8	9	10	11
Boys						
Not allowed out in the evening	5	9	6	4	2	2
None	6	7	8	6	6	6
1	10	12	9	10	8	
2	13	14	12	14	12	13
3	15	14	15	16	17	16
4–6	30	24	33	32	30	32
Every evening	18	16	15	17	22	21
Not stated	2	4	1	2	2	1
Base	*5063*	*1073*	*1011*	*1051*	*1009*	*917*
Girls						
Not allowed out in the evening	8	13	10	7	6	6
None	8	8	8	6	8	7
1	15	16	15	16	14	13
2	16	17	16	17	14	19
3	16	14	17	18	16	15
4–6	23	20	23	24	25	25
Every evening	13	9	11	12	17	14
Not stated	1	3	1	1	1	*
Base	*5241*	*1105*	*1040*	*1042*	*1087*	*967*
Total						
Not allowed out in the evening	7	11	8	5	4	4
None	7	8	8	6	7	6
1	12	14	12	13	11	11
2	15	15	14	15	13	16
3	16	14	16	17	16	15
4–6	27	22	28	28	27	29
Every evening	15	13	13	14	19	17
Not stated	2	3	1	1	1	1
Base	*10407*	*2193*	*2063*	*2102*	*2102*	*1891*

Unweighted base: all respondents

Figure 12   Going out straight after school at least four days a week

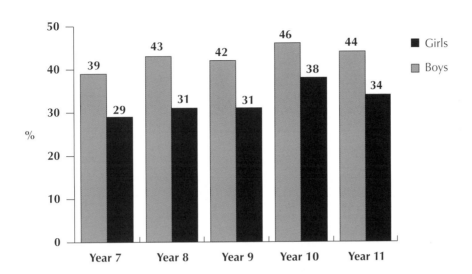

Base: all respondents (10407)

Outside school boys tended to spend time with their friends more frequently than girls, both straight after school and in the evening. Girls were more likely not to go out at all, or to limit themselves to one outing a week. The frequency of going out in the evening increased as pupils got older but young people in Year 10 were the age group most likely to go out with friends straight after school – perhaps because they were not yet too burdened with preparation for examinations (Tables 4g and 4h).

4.3   TALKING TO FRIENDS

Young people were asked how easy they found it to talk to different people – both friends and relatives – about things that really bothered them, using a four-point scale from 'very easy' to 'very difficult'.

Most young people (74%) said it was easy to talk to friends of the same sex compared to only 45% who found it easy to talk to friends of the opposite sex. Girls found female friends much easier to talk to than boys found male friends (84% compared to 64%), but both found it equally easy – or difficult – to talk to friends of the opposite sex (Table 4i).

Older pupils found communication with both same-sex and opposite-sex friends easier than younger pupils (Tables 4i and 4j).

Table 4i **How easy respondents found it to talk to friends of the same sex about things that really bothered them, by sex and school year (%)**

| | Total | School year | | | | |
		7	8	9	10	11
Boys						
Very easy	27	25	27	25	28	29
Easy	37	33	34	38	40	43
Difficult	16	14	14	17	17	17
Very difficult	8	7	10	8	7	6
Don't have friends of the same sex	3	6	3	2	2	2
Not stated	10	15	12	11	7	4
Base	*5063*	*1073*	*1011*	*1051*	*1009*	*917*
Girls						
Very easy	46	33	42	47	52	57
Easy	38	40	40	40	37	34
Difficult	8	12	9	7	7	7
Very difficult	2	3	2	2	1	1
Don't have friends of the same sex	1	2	1	1	1	*
Not stated	5	10	7	4	2	2
Base	*5241*	*1105*	*1040*	*1042*	*1087*	*967*
Total						
Very easy	36	29	34	36	41	43
Easy	38	36	37	39	38	38
Difficult	12	13	12	12	11	11
Very difficult	5	5	6	5	4	3
Don't have friends of the same sex	2	4	2	1	1	1
Not stated	8	13	10	7	5	3
Base	*10407*	*2193*	*2063*	*2102*	*2102*	*1891*

Unweighted base: all respondents

Table 4j **How easy respondents found it to talk to friends of the opposite sex about things that really bothered them, by sex and school year (%)**

	Total	School year				
		7	8	9	10	11
Boys						
Very easy	18	13	13	16	21	28
Easy	28	18	24	28	34	37
Difficult	22	20	21	24	23	20
Very difficult	14	18	19	16	11	7
Don't have friends of the opposite sex	7	12	10	5	4	3
Not stated	11	19	13	11	6	5
Base	*5063*	*1073*	*1011*	*1051*	*1009*	*917*
Girls						
Very easy	14	7	9	13	18	24
Easy	30	14	24	31	39	41
Difficult	28	31	30	32	27	21
Very difficult	16	26	22	15	10	8
Don't have friends of the opposite sex	5	9	7	5	3	3
Not stated	6	12	8	5	3	3
Base	*5241*	*1105*	*1040*	*1042*	*1087*	*967*
Total						
Very easy	16	10	11	14	19	26
Easy	29	16	24	30	37	39
Difficult	25	26	26	28	25	20
Very difficult	15	22	20	15	10	7
Don't have friends of the opposite sex	6	11	8	5	3	3
Not stated	9	16	11	8	5	4
Base	*10407*	*2193*	*2063*	*2102*	*2102*	*1891*

Unweighted base: all respondents

4.4 TALKING TO PARENTS AND OTHER RELATIVES

There were large differences in how easy young people found it to communicate with relatives, according to who they were talking to. Table 4k shows percentages together with mean scores calculated from the responses of young people who gave a rating to each type of relative they were in contact with. These scores enable comparisons to be made between different types of relative, regardless of how many young people gave a rating.

It is clear that all young people were most at ease when talking to their mother although those who had an elder sister also found her relatively easy to talk to. Fathers and elder brothers were seen as much less approachable, although better to talk to than step-parents (Table 4k).

Table 4k   **How easy respondents found it to talk to parents and other relatives about things that really bothered them (%)**

	Very easy (100)	Easy (66.6)	Difficult (33.3)	Very difficult (0)	Don't have or see this person	Not stated	Mean score
Mother	44	33	11	4	2	6	75.96
Elder sister	12	13	6	4	49	16	63.68
Father	20	32	25	9	8	6	57.39
Elder brother	8	11	9	8	48	15	52.12
Stepmother	2	3	2	2	70	21	48.09
Stepfather	2	5	4	4	66	20	45.83

Unweighted base: all respondents

Boys and girls found it equally easy to talk to their mother, but girls found fathers much more difficult to confide in than did boys (42% of girls said talking to their father was difficult, compared to 26% of boys). Those in the older age groups found it more difficult to communicate with their parents than did younger pupils. This contrasts with the results discussed above which indicated that older respondents found it easier to talk to their friends than did younger pupils.

4.5 COMPARISON WITH 1995 WAVE

As one would expect there were very few discernible changes in the two years since 1995 in the relationships young people had outside school. However, there is one area where changes appear to have occurred. The frequency with which young people go out in the evening has increased amongst all age groups but particularly amongst the older groups. The main increase occurred in the number of young people going out between four and six evenings a week (Table 4l).

Table 4l   **Number of evenings per week usually spent with friends, by sex and school year – comparison with 1995 wave (%)†**

| | | School year | | |
	Total	7	9	11
Boys				
Not allowed out in the evening	5 (6)	9 (10)	4 (6)	2 (2)
None	6 (11)	7 (15)	6 (11)	6 (8)
1	10 (14)	12 (15)	10 (14)	9 (13)
2	14 (16)	14 (12)	14 (15)	13 (21)
3	15 (15)	14 (13)	16 (14)	16 (17)
4–6	29 (20)	24 (18)	32 (20)	32 (20)
Every evening	18 (18)	16 (15)	17 (18)	21 (19)
Not stated				
Base 1997	*3041*	*1073*	*1051*	*917*
(Base 1995)	*(3396)*	*(1162)*	*(1233)*	*(1001)*
Girls				
Not allowed out in the evening	8 (9)	13 (15)	7 (6)	6 (5)
None	8 (9)	8 (13)	6 (12)	7 (8)
1	15 (11)	16 (16)	16 (15)	13 (16)
2	16 (16)	17 (14)	17 (14)	19 (19)
3	16 (16)	14 (13)	18 (15)	15 (14)
4–6	23 (14)	20 (15)	24 (18)	25 (21)
Every evening	12 (19)	9 (11)	12 (17)	14 (16)
Not stated				
Base 1997	*3114*	*1105*	*1042*	*967*
(Base 1995)	*(2976)*	*(1072)*	*(1049)*	*(855)*
Total				
Not allowed out in the evening	7(7)	11 (12)	5(6)	4(3)
None	7 (11)	8 (14)	6 (12)	6 (8)
1	12 (15)	14 (15)	13 (15)	11 (14)
2	15 (16)	15 (13)	15 (14)	16 (20)
3	16 (14)	14 (13)	17 (20)	15 (16)
4–6	27 (19)	22 (17)	28 (20)	28 (21)
Every evening	15 (16)	13 (14)	14 (18)	17 (18)
Not stated	2 (1)	3 (2)	1 (1)	1 (*)
Base 1997	*6186*	*2193*	*2102*	*1891*
(Base 1995)	*(6406)*	*(2258)*	*(2288)*	*(1860)*

Unweighted base: all respondents
†1995 figures shown in brackets

5 Psycho-social health

Key findings

- 91% of young people said they felt generally happy about their lives at present and more than one-third (35%) felt very happy. Three out of five (56%) always or often felt confident in themselves, nearly two-thirds (63%) rarely or never felt helpless and nearly half (48%) said they never felt lonely. Boys rated themselves more positively than girls. (Section 5.1)

- Those classified as ABC1s were slightly more likely to rate themselves more positively in terms of nearly all measures of social integration except for ease of making new friends. (Section 5.1)

- 44% of young people said they would like to change something about their own body. In each school year, this proportion was significantly higher for girls than boys and it also increased with age, rising from 24% of Year 7 boys to 70% of Year 11 girls. (Section 5.2)

- The change most young people wanted was in the overall size or shape of their bodies rather than any particular feature. (Section 5.2)

- In all five years about half the boys thought their bodies were about the right size. Year 7 girls were as likely as boys to say they were the right size (51%), falling to a third (36%) of Year 11 girls. (Section 5.2)

- Girls of all ages were less confident about their appearance than boys with the difference being particularly marked in Year 10, where 32% of girls said they were not good-looking compared to 12% of boys. (Section 5.2)

- There was some increase between the 1995 and 1997 waves in the proportion of young people who wanted to change some aspects of their bodies. This was especially true for girls. (Section 5.3)

In this chapter we look at young people's sense of happiness and confidence with their lives, and questions of self-image are dealt with – whether young people were happy with their bodies and, if not, what they would change.

5.1 GENERAL WELL-BEING AND SOCIAL INTEGRATION

The survey included a number of questions designed to measure well-being and social integration – the extent to which young people felt happy and confident about their lives and their social relationships, or (conversely) felt isolated, lonely and helpless.

Most young people (91%) said they felt generally happy about their lives at present and more than a third (35%) felt very happy. Three out of five (56%) always or often felt confident in themselves, nearly two-thirds (63%) rarely or never felt helpless and nearly half (48%) said they never felt lonely. On all these measures, boys rated themselves more positively than girls, particularly with regard to feeling confident. Whilst girls in Year 7 tended to rate themselves more positively than girls in other years, the same was not true for boys. Year 7 boys rated themselves more negatively on nearly every count than older boys (Table 5a).

Table 5a   **General well being of respondents, by sex and school year (%)**

		School year				
	Total	7	8	9	10	11
Boys						
Very/quite happy	94	94	94	94	93	92
Always/often feel confident	62	61	60	61	66	63
Rarely never feel helpless	67	60	66	67	71	73
Never feel lonely	55	48	55	56	61	56
Base	*5063*	*1073*	*1011*	*1051*	*1009*	*917*
Girls						
Very/quite happy	90	93	92	91	88	85
Always/often feel confident	49	56	54	51	43	43
Rarely never feel helpless	59	64	58	61	56	57
Never feel lonely	40	43	44	42	36	37
Base	*5241*	*1105*	*1040*	*1042*	*1087*	*967*
Total						
Very/quite happy	91	94	93	93	90	88
Always/often feel confident	56	59	57	56	54	53
Rarely never feel helpless	63	62	62	64	63	65
Never feel lonely	48	45	50	49	48	46
Base	*10407*	*2193*	*2063*	*2102*	*2102*	*1891*

Unweighted base: all respondents

Those who lived with both their natural parents were slightly more likely to rate themselves positively than those who lived with single or step-parents. Those living in ABC1 households were slightly more likely to rate themselves positively than those in C2DE households (Table 5b).

Table 5b   General well-being, by household type and social grade (%)

	Social grade		Household type		
	ABC1	C2DE	Both natural parents	One natural parent	Step-parent
Very/quite happy	92	91	93	88	88
Always/often feel confident	61	56	58	54	55
Never/rarely feel helpless	70	62	66	64	61
Never feel lonely	49	48	50	44	46
Base	*3713*	*5232*	*7023*	*1213*	*1354*

Unweighted base: all respondents

Measures of social integration included the number of close friends young people had, how often they felt excluded or left out of things by other pupils, whether they had been bullied and how easy they found it to make new friends.

Girls tended to rate themselves more highly on most of these things, although more girls sometimes 'felt left out of things'. Young people in Year 11 were most likely to have close friends, to feel other pupils want to spend time with them and to have had no recent experience of bullying (Table 5c).

Table 5c   **Social integration of young people, by sex and school year (%)**

		School year				
	Total	7	8	9	10	11
Boys						
Three or more close friends	73	66	71	74	77	80
Not been left alone by other pupils this term	64	56	58	62	71	74
Never been bullied at school	51	48	51	49	54	54
Not been bullied this term	23	17	22	24	26	30
Rarely/never felt left out of things	60	56	59	59	63	63
Very easy to make new friends	25	27	26	24	24	25
Base	5063	1073	1011	1051	1009	917
Girls						
Three or more close friends	75	68	73	77	79	78
Not been left alone by other pupils this term	67	57	60	69	42	76
Never been bullied at school	47	51	47	46	72	47
Not been bullied this term	31	22	27	32	36	37
Rarely/never felt left out of things	48	52	50	46	45	48
Very easy to make new friends	26	30	30	25	23	24
Base	5241	1105	1040	1042	1087	967
Total						
Three or more close friends	74	67	72	75	78	79
Not been left alone by other pupils this term	65	57	59	66	71	75
Never been bullied at school	49	49	49	48	48	51
Not been bullied this term	27	20	25	28	31	34
Rarely/never felt left out of things	54	54	55	52	54	55
Very easy to make new friends	26	28	28	24	23	25
Base	10407	2193	2063	2102	2102	1891

Unweighted base: all respondents

Those classified as ABC1s were slightly more likely to rate themselves more positively in terms of nearly all measures of social integration except for ease of making new friends. There was very little difference between young people living in various different household types although those who had a step-parent were more likely to find it very easy to make new friends (Table 5d).

Table 5d   **Social integration, by household type and social grade (%)**

	Social grade		Household type		
	ABC1	C2DE	Both natural parents	One natural parent	Step-parent
Three or more close friends	78	75	76	75	75
Not been left alone by other pupils this term	69	65	67	66	65
Not been bullied this term	30	27	28	28	29
Never been bullied at school	50	49	51	47	45
Hardly ever felt left out of things	57	54	56	55	53
Very easy to make new friends	25	27	26	25	29
Base	*3713*	*5232*	*7023*	*1213*	*1354*

Unweighted base: all respondents

5.2   SELF-IMAGE

Nearly half of the young people (44%) said they would like to change something about their own body. In each school year, this proportion was significantly higher for girls than boys, and it also increased with age, rising from 24% of Year 7 boys to 70% of Year 11 girls (Table 5e and Figure 13).

Table 5e   **Those wanting to change something about their body (%)**

Wanting to change something

		Base	*%*
Total		*10407*	*44*
Year 7	Boys	1073	24
	Girls	1105	37
	Total	2193	30
Year 8	Boys	1011	27
	Girls	1040	48
	Total	2063	38
Year 9	Boys	1051	34
	Girls	1042	59
	Total	2102	46
Year 10	Boys	1009	36
	Girls	1087	66
	Total	2102	52
Year 11	Boys	917	39
	Girls	967	70
	Total	1891	55

Unweighted base: all respondents

Figure 13   **Desire to change physical appearance**

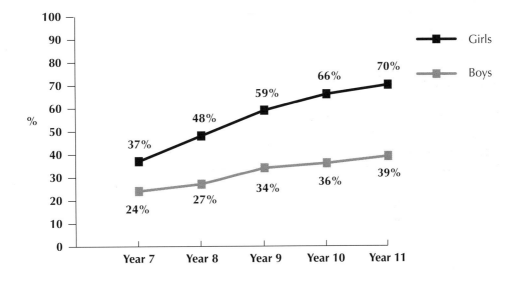

Base: all respondents (10407)

Those who disliked school were more likely to want to change something about their bodies than young people overall. Although those young people who claimed to do no half-hour physical activity sessions per week were less likely to want to change something about their bodies than the sample as a whole, those who did just a little were much more likely to want to change something than those who did a lot of exercise.

The change most young people wanted was in the overall size or shape of their bodies, rather than any particular feature. As might be expected girls were much more likely to mention this, and to refer to losing weight either generally or from specific parts of their anatomy. Girls were also keener than boys to want to change their faces and their legs. Boys mentioned a desire to be taller, to gain weight and to have more muscles or a bigger chest (Table 5f and Figure 14).

Table 5f   **Part of the body they would most like to change by sex (%)**

	Total	Boys	Girls
Lose weight	28	22	31
Face	12	8	15
Size/shape/weight/figure	12	7	15
Hair	10	10	10
Legs	10	2	14
Height/taller	8	9	7
Skin/spots/moles/freckles	7	7	6
Nose	7	4	8
Teeth	4	4	4
Everything	4	2	5
Eyes/eyesight/glasses	3	3	3
Feet/shoe size	3	2	3
Gain weight	3	3	2
More muscles/bigger chest	2	6	*
Bigger bust	2	*	3
Base	*4574*	*1615*	*2922*

Unweighted base: all respondents

Figure 14   **Aspect of appearance desired to be different**

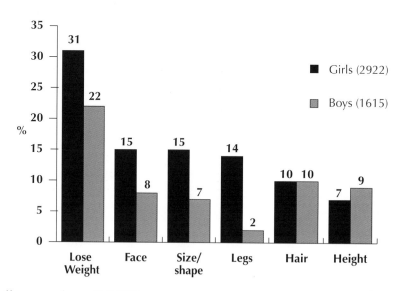

Base: all respondents (10407)

A further question asked young people directly whether they thought their body was too thin, too fat or about the right size. Table 5g shows how responses varied between girls and boys within each school year. In all five school years about half the boys thought their bodies were about the right size whilst between a tenth and a fifth said they were too thin and a slightly higher proportion said they were too fat. However, for girls the proportion thinking they were too fat increased from 23% in Year 7 to 51% in Year 11 with a corresponding decrease in the proportion thinking they were about the right size (Table 5g).

Table 5g **Self-assessment of weight, by sex and school year (%)**

	Total	7	8	9	10	11
Boys						
Much too thin	2	2	2	3	2	3
A bit too thin	12	9	10	12	13	15
About the right size	51	51	52	49	53	52
A bit too fat	18	16	18	21	17	18
Much too fat	2	2	1	3	2	3
I don't think about it	7	8	6	6	8	7
Not stated	7	13	10	7	4	2
Base	5063	1073	1011	1051	1009	917
Girls						
Much too thin	2	2	2	2	2	1
A bit too thin	10	9	10	12	9	9
About the right size	42	51	45	41	39	36
A bit too fat	32	20	26	31	38	44
Much too fat	6	3	5	8	8	7
I don't think about it	4	6	4	4	2	2
Not stated	4	9	7	3	2	1
Base	5241	1105	1040	1042	1087	967
Total						
Much too thin	2	2	2	2	2	2
A bit too thin	11	9	10	12	11	12
About the right size	47	51	48	45	46	43
A bit too fat	25	18	22	26	28	31
Much too fat	4	2	3	5	5	5
I don't think about it	5	7	6	5	5	5
Not stated	6	11	8	5	3	2
Base	10407	2193	2063	2102	2102	1891

Unweighted base: all respondents

Young people were also asked to rate themselves on a five-point scale ranging from 'very good-looking' to 'not at all good-looking'. Girls of all ages were again less confident about their appearance than boys with the difference being particularly marked in Year 10, where 32% of girls thought they were not good-looking compared to 12% of boys (Table 5h).

Table 5h   **Self-assessment of looks, by sex and school year (%)**

		School year				
	Total	7	8	9	10	11
Boys						
Very good-looking	9	12	9	8	9	8
Quite good-looking	17	15	16	16	19	22
About average	45	41	45	46	48	48
Not very good-looking	10	8	11	11	10	10
Not at all good-looking	3	3	2	3	2	2
I don't think about my looks	8	8	8	8	9	8
Not stated	8	13	10	7	4	2
Base	*5063*	*1073*	*1011*	*1051*	*1009*	*917*
Girls						
Very good-looking	2	4	3	2	2	1
Quite good-looking	15	16	15	13	14	14
About average	47	45	46	48	45	54
Not very good-looking	18	14	15	20	24	18
Not at all good-looking	7	5	8	9	8	7
I don't think about my looks	6	9	6	5	5	5
Not stated	4	9	7	3	2	1
Base	*5241*	*1105*	*1040*	*1042*	*1087*	*967*
Total						
Very good-looking	6	8	6	5	5	4
Quite good-looking	16	15	15	15	17	18
About average	46	43	46	47	46	51
Not very good-looking	14	11	13	16	17	14
Not at all good-looking	5	4	5	6	5	4
I don't think about my looks	7	8	7	7	7	7
Not stated	6	11	9	5	3	2
Base	*10407*	*2193*	*2063*	*2102*	*2102*	*1891*

Unweighted base: all respondents

5.3   COMPARISON WITH 1995 WAVE

There was some increase in the number of young people, especially girls, who wanted to change some aspect of their bodies (Table 5i).

Table 5i   **Young people wanting to change some aspect of their bodies, by age and sex – comparison with 1995 wave**

Wanting to change something

		1995 wave			1997 wave	
		Base	*%*		*Base*	*%*
Total		*6406*	*40*		*6186*	*43*
Year 7	Boys	1162	20	Boys	1073	24
	Girls	1072	32	Girls	1105	37
	Total	2258	25	Total	2193	30
Year 9	Boys	1233	36	Boys	1051	34
	Girls	1049	54	Girls	1042	59
	Total	2288	44	Total	2102	46
Year 11	Boys	1001	39	Boys	917	39
	Girls	855	65	Girls	967	70
	Total	1860	51	Total	1905	55

Unweighted base: all respondents

6 Food, diet and dental care

Key findings

- Six out of ten young people ate fruit, and one in three (36%) ate raw vegetables or salad daily. Almost two-thirds of the young people rarely, if ever, drank full-fat milk whilst seven out of ten drank skimmed or semi-skimmed every day. However, six out of ten in each case ate sweets or chocolate, or crisps, or drank cola every day and over three-quarters (77%) of the young people ate white bread daily. (Section 6.1)

- Two-thirds of young people were happy with their weight. One in ten was on a diet and one in five (22%) thought that they should lose weight. (Section 6.2)

- Young people who ate more unhealthy foods were more likely to agree with the statements 'As long as you are reasonably active you can eat what you like', 'I find healthy foods too boring', 'I don't know enough about which foods are good for you' and 'I just eat the foods I like and I don't worry about whether they are healthy or not'. (Section 6.3)

- Six out of ten young people (62%) ate breakfast every day before going to school although almost one in five (18%) rarely or never did so. Boys were more likely than girls to eat breakfast on a daily basis. However, among both sexes younger pupils were more likely to eat breakfast daily than older pupils. (Section 6.4)

- Seven out of ten young people had eaten snacks at least twice on the day prior to being interviewed and almost four out of ten (38%) had done so at least three times. Amongst all age groups boys ate more snacks than girls, with the proportion of boys who had eaten at least three snacks the previous day increasing with age. (Section 6.5)

- Seven out of ten young people brushed their teeth more than once a day, and almost all of them (96%) did so at least once a day. (Section 6.6)

A good diet is recognised by the government's Green Paper on health, *Our Healthier Nation*[1] as an important way of protecting health. The amount of fruit and vegetables that people eat is seen as an important influence on health. There is growing evidence to suggest that unhealthy diets, which tend to include too much fat and too little fruit and vegetables and starchy foods are linked to heart disease, stroke and some cancers in later life. The frequent consumption of sugary foods and drinks can contribute towards the development of tooth decay.

A number of diet-related disorders may begin to develop during childhood or young adulthood, but do not necessarily become apparent until later in life. These disorders include some slow-onset and chronic diseases such as coronary heart disease and some cancers. There is also some evidence that most young people find it difficult to take a long-term view of diet in relation to health.[2] Young people who are overweight in their early teens are more likely to be overweight as adults.[3]

Whilst young people are at an age where they can begin to make choices about the food they eat, they are exposed to many external influences, such as advertising, and fitting in with their peers. Making health choices is one factor that they juggle with other competing factors in selecting their overall diet. At the time of the survey there were no government guidelines on the nutritional content of school meals, which for many young people provide their main nourishment of the day.

This chapter looks at how frequently young people eat different types of food. The survey asked about how often they ate breakfast, the number of snacks such as chocolate, crisps and peanuts eaten the previous day, and attitudes towards dieting and weight. Young people's attitudes towards healthy eating were assessed, as were matters of oral hygiene. Young people were asked about the frequency with which they ate foods that they are encouraged to consume, such as fruit, bread, pasta and rice. Also assessed was their consumption of foods that they are advised to eat less frequently, including those high in sugar such as fizzy drinks and sweets, and those high in fat such as pies and crisps.

This survey does not, however, look at the dietary habits of young people in the same way as the Survey of the Diets of British School Children carried out by the Department of Health in the late 1980s.[4] The intention of this survey was to measure indicators of health-related lifestyles rather than to make comprehensive assessments of healthy or unhealthy diets.

6.1   FREQUENCY OF EATING DIFFERENT FOODS

The young people were asked how frequently they consumed each of several different types of food and drink, which were separated at the analysis stage into 'more healthy' and 'less healthy' foods. Whilst it is recognised that there are neither 'healthy' nor 'unhealthy' foods and it is the overall diet that is important, the methodology adopted by the survey internationally does not take account of overall diet. For the purposes of analysis, foods for which an increase in consumption is recommended, such as fruit, pasta and bread were called 'more healthy foods'. Those which are high in fat and/or sugar and which should not be consumed too frequently were termed 'less healthy' foods. These terms were adopted primarily for convenience of reference and, because the methodology adopted cannot measure the constituents of a balanced diet. The young people were rated on two scales of 0–4, one based on a selection of the 'more healthy' and one on how many of a selection of 'less healthy' foods they ate at least once a day.

Table 6a lists the 'more healthy' and 'less healthy' foods upon which the scales were based. Table 6b compares the two scales against each other.

Table 6a   **'More healthy' and 'less healthy' foods used to calculate scales**

'More healthy'	'Less healthy'
Fruit	Sweets or chocolate
Raw vegetables or salad	Chips
Cooked vegetables	Crisps
Wholemeal or rye bread	Cakes or biscuits

Table 6b   **Number of 'less healthy' foods eaten at least once a day, by number of 'more healthy' foods eaten at least once a day (%)**

'Less healthy' foods eaten daily:	'More healthy' foods eaten daily:				
	0	1	2	3	4
0	16	15	16	18	25
1	20	19	21	22	23
2	23	26	24	24	20
3	25	25	24	23	17
4	16	15	15	14	14
Base	*2201*	*2777*	*2439*	*1978*	*1012*

Unweighted base: all respondents

Six out of ten young people (60%) said that they ate fruit at least once a day. Approximately one in three (36%) ate raw vegetables or salad on a daily basis. Cooked vegetables were consumed daily by about half (47%) of all young people. Just over three-quarters (77%) of young people ate white bread at least once a day and nine out of ten (91%) ate it at least once a week. Less than a third ate wholemeal or rye bread at least once a day and just over half (53%) of young people rarely or never ate wholemeal or rye bread (Tables 6c and 6d).

Cola or drinks containing sugar, sweets or chocolate and crisps were consumed most frequently by the greatest number of young people (approximately six out of ten ate each of these foods on a daily basis). Almost half (48%) of all young people ate cakes or biscuits at least once a day and almost three out of ten (29%) ate chips or fried potatoes daily. The survey did not distinguish the type of chips consumed, either the size or whether fried or oven-baked. Ordinary or full-fat milk was drunk by about a quarter (27%) of the young people at least once a day compared with seven out of ten who drank skimmed or semi-skimmed milk

(70%). Indeed almost two-thirds (65%) of the young people rarely, if ever, drank full-fat milk (Tables 6c and 6d).

Table 6c   Frequency of eating 'more healthy' foods (%)

	At least once a day	At least once a week	Rarely/ never
Fruit	60	86	13
Raw vegetables or salad	36	71	29
Cooked vegetables	47	81	18
Skimmed or semi-skimmed milk	70	78	22
Low-fat yoghurt or fromage frais	28	58	41
Fish (including fish fingers)	12	56	44
Wholemeal or rye bread	26	46	53
Pasta or rice	23	74	25

Unweighted base: all respondents

Table 6d   Frequency of eating 'less healthy' foods (%)

	At least once a day	At least once a week	Rarely/ never
Coffee	21	31	68
Cola/soft drinks containing sugar	60	85	15
Sweets or chocolate	60	89	11
Peanuts	7	21	78
Crisps	61	86	14
Chips/fried potatoes	29	82	17
Hamburgers, hot dogs or sausages	15	60	40
Meat pies	9	39	61
Ordinary milk (full-fat)	27	34	65
Cakes or biscuits	48	82	17
White bread	77	91	8

Unweighted base: all respondents

Girls were more likely than boys to eat fruit, raw vegetables or salad and cooked vegetables on a daily basis. However, although it was consistently greater than the corresponding group of boys, the proportion of girls eating these 'more healthy' foods declined with age. Boys were generally more likely than girls to drink milk. This was shown both by the higher levels of boys drinking skimmed or semi-skimmed milk daily (73% of boys compared to 67% of girls) and by the higher proportion of boys drinking full-fat milk (30% of boys drank full-fat milk daily compared with 24% of girls). The proportion of boys drinking full-fat milk increased with school year such that one-third (33%) of Year 11 boys drank full-fat milk daily compared with 28% of Year 7 boys. There was very little difference across the years of boys drinking skimmed or semi-skimmed milk. For girls the proportion drinking full-fat milk every day declined with school year, with only one in five Year 11 girls drinking this type of milk. Boys were more likely than girls to eat all types of 'less healthy' foods, in particular chips, hamburgers, hot dogs and sausages, meat pies and cakes and biscuits. Over one-third (35%) of boys ate chips or fried potatoes every day compared to just over two out of ten girls (23%) (Tables 6e and 6f)).

Table 6e   Frequency of eating 'more healthy' foods, by sex and school year (%)

| | Total | School year | | | | |
		7	8	9	10	11
Those eating at least once a day						
Boys						
Fruit	56	62	59	57	51	52
Raw vegetables or salad	31	31	33	33	29	29
Cooked vegetables	43	41	42	44	43	43
Skimmed or semi-skimmed milk	73	71	73	75	71	73
Low-fat yoghurt or fromage frais	27	33	30	26	20	24
Fish (including fish fingers)	16	19	18	16	13	12
Wholemeal or rye bread	25	27	26	26	22	23
Pasta or rice	23	24	24	23	21	21
Base	*5063*	*1073*	*1011*	*1051*	*1009*	*917*
Girls						
Fruit	63	70	67	63	57	57
Raw vegetables or salad	41	45	44	42	36	37
Cooked vegetables	51	50	50	53	52	52
Skimmed or semi-skimmed milk	67	66	65	70	68	67
Low-fat yoghurt or fromage frais	28	37	34	26	24	22
Fish (including fish fingers)	9	13	11	9	7	5
Wholemeal or rye bread	29	27	26	29	27	28
Pasta or rice	23	25	24	24	22	22
Base	*5241*	*1105*	*1040*	*1042*	*1087*	*967*
Total						
Fruit	60	66	63	60	54	55
Raw vegetables or salad	36	38	39	37	33	33
Cooked vegetables	47	46	46	49	48	48
Skimmed or semi-skimmed milk	70	68	70	73	70	70
Low-fat yoghurt or fromage frais	28	35	32	26	22	22
Fish (including fish fingers)	12	16	14	12	10	8
Wholemeal or rye bread	26	27	26	28	25	25
Pasta or rice	23	25	24	24	21	21
Base	*10407*	*2141*	*2081*	*2105*	*2121*	*1905*

Unweighted base: all respondents; multi-coding possible

Table 6f   **Frequency of eating 'less healthy' foods, by sex and school year (%)**

		School year				
	Total	7	8	9	10	11
Those eating at least one a day						
Boys						
Coffee	23	17	18	23	26	32
Cola/soft drinks containing sugar	65	60	64	67	68	67
Sweets or chocolate	62	56	63	67	63	61
Peanuts	9	13	10	9	7	6
Crisps	63	62	67	63	62	61
Chips/fried potatoes	35	36	37	36	33	34
Hamburgers, hot dogs or sausages	20	24	22	19	17	19
Meat pies	12	13	13	13	10	11
Ordinary milk (full-fat)	30	28	30	29	29	33
Cakes or biscuits	55	54	57	56	54	54
Base	*5063*	*1073*	*1011*	*1051*	*1009*	*917*
Girls						
Coffee	19	14	16	16	23	26
Cola/soft drinks containing sugar	55	54	58	56	56	52
Sweets or chocolate	58	55	60	59	62	55
Peanuts	5	11	5	3	4	3
Crisps	59	60	61	62	59	51
Chips/fried potatoes	23	26	26	25	21	19
Hamburgers, hot dogs or sausages	10	13	12	9	8	8
Meat pies	6	8	7	5	5	4
Ordinary milk (full-fat)	24	27	25	21	24	20
Cakes or biscuits	42	47	46	42	41	35
Base	*5241*	*1105*	*1040*	*1042*	*1087*	*967*
Total						
Coffee	21	15	17	20	24	29
Cola/soft drinks containing sugar	60	57	61	62	62	60
Sweets or chocolate	60	55	62	63	63	58
Peanuts	7	11	8	6	5	4
Crisps	61	61	64	63	60	56
Chips/fried potatoes	29	31	32	30	27	27
Hamburgers, hot dogs or sausages	15	19	17	14	12	13
Meat pies	9	11	10	9	7	7
Ordinary milk (full-fat)	27	27	27	25	26	27
Cakes or biscuits	48	50	51	49	47	44
Base	*10407*	*2141*	*2081*	*2105*	*2121*	*1905*

Unweighted base: all respondents; multi-coding possible

6.2   DIETING

Two-thirds (67%) of the young people were happy with their weight at the time of the interview. One in ten (10%) of all young people were on a diet and approximately one in five (22%) thought that they needed to lose weight even though they were not on a diet. Girls were almost three times more likely than boys to be on a diet (14% of girls compared to 5% of boys), and amongst those not on a diet, girls were more likely to be worrying about their weight (27% of girls worried about their weight but were not on a diet compared to 17% of boys). The proportion of girls on a diet and those worrying about their weight increased with school year such that almost half the girls (47%) in Year 11 were unhappy with their weight and one in five (17%) was on a diet (Table 6g and Figure 15).

Table 6g   Dieting to lose weight, by sex and school year (%)

		School year				
	Total	7	8	9	10	11
Boys						
Yes, I am dieting to lose weight	5	6	5	5	4	3
No, but should lose weight	17	18	19	19	15	16
No, because my weight is fine	76	74	74	75	78	78
Not stated	2	2	2	1	2	2
Base	*5063*	*1073*	*1011*	*1051*	*1009*	*917*
Girls						
Yes, I am dieting to lose weight	14	9	13	13	19	17
No, but should lose weight	27	22	26	26	30	30
No, because my weight is fine	58	68	60	59	50	52
Not stated	1	1	1	1	1	1
Base	*5241*	*1105*	*1040*	*1042*	*1087*	*967*
Total						
Yes, I am dieting to lose weight	10	8	9	9	12	10
No, but should lose weight	22	20	22	23	23	24
No, because my weight is fine	67	71	67	67	64	65
Not stated	2	2	2	1	1	2
Base	*10407*	*2193*	*2063*	*2102*	*2102*	*1891*

Unweighted base: all respondents

Figure 15   **Respondents on a diet to lose weight**

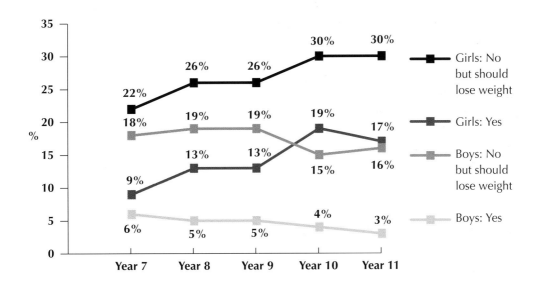

Base: all respondents (10407)

6.3   ATTITUDES TOWARDS DIET

The young people were presented with a series of statements designed to measure their attitudes towards food and healthy eating, and asked to indicate their level of agreement with each one.

Levels of agreement with the statements were generally low. A quarter (23%) of all young people thought that people of their age did not need to think about the foods they ate. Three out of ten (29%) said that they found healthy foods too boring. One-third (35%) of the young people said that they just ate the foods they liked without worrying whether they were healthy or not and the same proportion (32%) thought that they did not know enough about which foods were good for them. A slightly larger proportion (41%) agreed with the statements 'as long as you are reasonably active you can eat what you like' and 'experts never agree which foods are good for you' (Table 6h).

Table 6h   **Attitudes towards diet (%)**

	Agree strongly (100)	Agree slightly (66.6)	Disagree slightly (33.3)	Disagree strongly (0)	Neither/ not stated	Mean score
As long as you are reasonably active you can eat what you like	8	33	41	8	10	48.22
Experts never agree which foods are good for you	6	32	32	7	23	49.57
I just eat the food I like and I don't worry about whether it's healthy or not	11	25	39	20	6	42.79
I don't know enough about which foods are good for you	5	27	43	15	11	49.51
People of my age don't need to worry about the foods they eat	3	20	50	17	10	36.94
I find healthy foods too boring	7	22	44	21	6	38.77

Unweighted base: all respondents

Those young people who did not eat any of the 'more healthy' foods or those who ate a greater number of the 'less healthy' foods were more likely than others to hold less healthy attitudes towards diet. They were especially likely to agree with the statements: 'as long as you are reasonably active you can eat what you like' (54% of those who ate four or more less healthy foods agreed with this statement compared to 32% who ate none of the less healthy foods on a daily basis), 'I just eat the foods I like and I don't worry about whether they are healthy or not' (57% of those who ate four or more 'less healthy foods' agreed with this statement compared to 17% who ate none of the 'less healthy foods' on a daily basis), 'I find healthy foods too boring' (42% of those who ate four or more 'less healthy foods' agreed with this statement compared to 18% who ate none of the 'less healthy foods' on a daily basis), and 'I don't know enough about which foods are good for you' (39% of those who ate four or more 'less healthy' foods agreed with this statement compared to 25% who ate none of the 'less healthy' foods on a daily basis) (Table 6i).

Young people eating greater numbers of 'more healthy' foods were less likely to say that they just ate the food they liked without worrying about whether it was healthy or not (20% compared with 51% of those who ate none of the 'more healthy' foods on a daily basis) and less likely to say that they found healthy foods too boring (15% compared with 45% who ate none of the 'more healthy' foods on a daily basis). What is slightly more surprising perhaps is that one in five (22%) of those eating all four of the 'more healthy' foods still thought that they did not know enough about which foods were good for them (Table 6i).

Table 6i   **Attitudes towards food, by 'healthy' and 'unhealthy' eaters (%)**

	Main sample	'More healthy' foods eaten daily		'Less healthy' foods eaten daily	
Those agreeing		4	0	0	4
As long as you are reasonably active you can eat what you like	41	35	46	32	54
Experts never agree which foods are good for you	38	38	40	32	45
I just eat the food I like and I don't worry about whether it's healthy or not	35	20	51	17	57
I don't know enough about which foods are good for you	32	22	37	25	39
People of my age don't need to worry about the foods they eat	23	21	25	16	34
I find healthy foods too boring	29	15	45	18	42
Base	*10407*	*1012*	*2201*	*1767*	*1538*

Unweighted base: all respondents

Boys were more likely than girls to indicate a less healthy attitude towards food. Approximately one-third (35%) of all boys said that they found healthy foods too boring compared to just over one in five girls. This attitude was stronger amongst older pupils – 34% of Year 11 pupils agreed with this statement compared to 22% of Year 7 pupils. Older pupils were more likely to agree with all statements than younger pupils. The only exception was with the statement 'people of my age don't need to worry about the food they eat'. Younger pupils were more likely to agree with this particular viewpoint, girls in Year 7 being twice as likely to agree with this as those in Year 11 (28% of girls in Year 7 agreed compared to 13% of girls in Year 11) (Table 6j).

Table 6j   Attitudes towards food, by sex and school year (%)

		School year				
	Total	7	8	9	10	11
Those agreeing						
Boys						
As long as you are reasonably active you can eat what you like	46	40	42	50	49	48
Experts never agree which foods are good for you	40	37	40	39	40	45
I just eat the food I like and I don't worry about whether it's healthy or not	40	31	36	40	46	49
I don't know enough about which foods are good for you	33	30	34	34	32	33
People of my age don't need to worry about the foods they eat	24	25	25	27	21	24
I find healthy foods too boring	35	27	33	38	38	40
Base	*5063*	*1073*	*1011*	*1051*	*1009*	*917*
Girls						
As long as you are reasonably active you can eat what you like	36	32	38	36	38	36
Experts never agree which foods are good for you	35	33	33	35	40	36
I just eat the food I like and I don't worry about whether it's healthy or not	31	22	30	32	34	36
I don't know enough about which foods are good for you	31	25	28	33	35	32
People of my age don't need to worry about the foods they eat	22	28	28	20	17	13
I find healthy foods too boring	23	18	23	23	26	27
Base	*5241*	*1105*	*1040*	*1042*	*1087*	*967*

Table 6j   **Attitudes towards food, by sex and school year (%) (continued)**

		School year				
	Total	7	8	9	10	11
Total						
As long as you are reasonably active you can eat what you like	41	36	40	43	43	42
Experts never agree which foods are good for you	38	35	36	37	40	41
I just eat the food I like and I don't worry about whether it's healthy or not	35	27	33	37	40	42
I don't know enough about which foods are good for you	32	28	31	33	34	33
People of my age don't need to worry about the foods they eat	23	27	27	24	19	18
I find healthy foods too boring	29	22	28	30	32	34
Base	*10407*	*2193*	*2063*	*2102*	*2102*	*1891*

Unweighted base: all respondents; multi-coding possible

6.4 FREQUENCY OF EATING BREAKFAST BEFORE GOING TO SCHOOL

Approximately six out of ten young people (62%) ate breakfast every day before going to school, although almost one in five (18%) never (or hardly ever) had breakfast before school (Table 6k).

Boys were more likely than girls to eat breakfast every day (69% of boys compared to 56% of girls) and girls were almost twice as likely to say that they never or hardly ever had breakfast (23% of girls compared to 13% of boys). Younger pupils were more likely to eat breakfast daily than older pupils – 71% of those in Year 7 ate breakfast every day compared with 56% of those in Year 11) and more older girls than younger ones never or rarely ate breakfast (31% of girls in Year 11 rarely or never ate breakfast compared to 12% of girls in Year 7) (Table 6k and Figure 16).

Table: 6k **Frequency of eating breakfast before going to school, by sex and school year (%)**

		School year				
	Total	7	8	9	10	11
Boys						
Every day	69	72	71	69	67	63
3–4 days a week	11	11	10	10	11	11
1–2 days a week	7	6	7	7	7	7
Hardly ever	13	10	11	12	14	19
Not stated	1	2	1	*	1	1
Base	*5063*	*1073*	*1011*	*1051*	*1009*	*917*
Girls						
Every day	56	70	59	52	48	49
3–4 days a week	12	10	14	12	13	10
1–2 days a week	9	7	9	8	9	10
Hardly ever	23	12	19	27	29	31
Not stated	*	1	–	*	1	*
Base	*5241*	*1105*	*1040*	*1042*	*1087*	*967*
Total						
Every day	62	71	65	61	57	56
3–4 days a week	11	10	12	11	12	10
1–2 days a week	8	7	8	8	8	8
Hardly ever	18	11	15	19	22	25
Not stated	1	1	1	*	1	*
Base	*10407*	*2193*	*2063*	*2102*	*2102*	*1891*

Unweighted base; all respondents

Figure 16   Eating breakfast every day

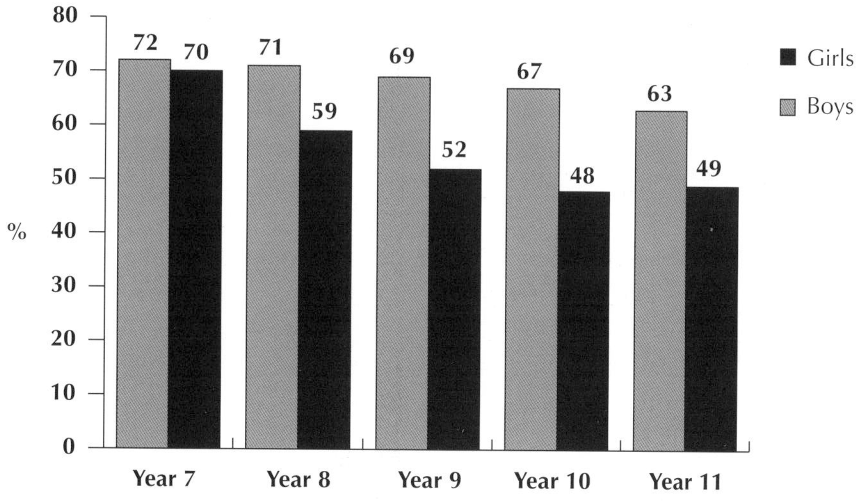

Base: all respondents (10407)

Young people who considered themselves 'very healthy' were more likely than those describing themselves as only 'quite' or 'not very' healthy to eat breakfast every day (73% of those describing themselves as 'very healthy' compared with 59% of those describing themselves as only 'quite' or 'not very' healthy). Correspondingly those never having breakfast were more likely to describe themselves as only 'quite' or 'not very' healthy (24% of those who ate breakfast every day compared with 12% of those who hardly ever or never ate breakfast).

Those on diets, and also those who thought they needed to be on diets, were more likely than others never to eat breakfast before going to school. Less than half (48%) of the young people who were on a diet ate breakfast every day compared to over two-thirds (68%) of those happy with their weight (Table 6l).

Young people who ate a greater number of 'more healthy' foods were most likely to eat breakfast every day. Indeed as many as seven out of ten (70%) who ate at least four 'more healthy' foods daily ate breakfast every day. In contrast, less than six out of ten (57%) of those young people who ate at least four 'less healthy' foods daily had breakfast before going to school (Table 6l).

Table 6l **Frequency of eating breakfast before going to school, by reported foods eaten and dieting behaviour** (%)

	Unweighted base	Having breakfast every day	Never having breakfast
Reported health			
'Very healthy'	2159	73	11
'Quite/not very healthy'	8179	59	20
'More healthy' foods eaten daily			
4	1012	70	14
0	2201	55	23
'Less healthy' foods eaten daily			
0	1767	62	17
4	1538	57	22
On a diet			
Yes	1006	48	30
No – but need to lose weight	2318	52	26
No – no need	6928	68	14

Unweighted base: all respondents

6.5   FREQUENCY OF EATING SNACKS BETWEEN MEALS

Young people were asked how many times they had eaten snacks between meals – 'things like chocolate, crisps, cakes, biscuits and peanuts' on the day before they were interviewed. Seven out of ten (71%) of them had eaten at least two snacks on the previous day and almost four out of ten (38%) had eaten at least three. In all school years, girls were more likely than boys to have eaten snacks 'once only or not at all' on the previous day – a third of all girls had either not had a snack on the previous day or had eaten only one snack (32%) compared to just under a quarter of all boys (23%) – and following from this, were less likely to eat snacks three times or more (18% of boys compared with 21% of girls). The proportion of girls who had not eaten a snack on the previous day or who had had only one snack increased overall with school year, from three out of ten (30%) in Year 7 to four out of ten (40%) in Year 11. The proportion of girls who had eaten three or more snacks declined with age so that by Year 11 there was the greatest difference between the proportions of boys and girls who had eaten several snacks (27% of girls compared to 45% of boys) (Table 6m and Figure 17).

Table 6m   **Frequency of eating a snack yesterday outside main meals, by sex and school year (%)**

	Total	School year				
		7	8	9	10	11
Boys						
None/once only	23	26	22	25	20	23
Twice	31	32	30	31	31	32
At least three times	45	40	48	44	48	45
Not stated	1	2	1	1	1	1
Base	*5063*	*1073*	*1011*	*1051*	*1009*	*917*
Girls						
None/once only	33	30	34	30	31	40
Twice	36	37	32	39	37	33
At least three times	31	32	34	30	31	27
Not stated	*	1	*	1	*	–
Base	*5241*	*1105*	*1040*	*1042*	*1087*	*967*
Total						
None/once only	28	28	28	27	25	32
Twice	33	34	31	35	35	32
At least three times	38	36	40	37	39	36
Not stated	1	1	1	1	1	1
Base	*10407*	*2193*	*2063*	*2102*	*2102*	*1891*

Unweighted base: all respondents

Figure 17   **Eating at least three snacks a day**

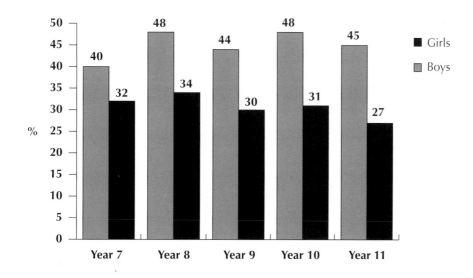

Base: all respondents (10407)

As would be expected, the more of the 'less healthy' foods young people said they ate on a daily basis, the more snacks they had eaten on the day before being interviewed. Young people who were concerned about their weight ate fewer snacks of this type than those who thought their weight was acceptable. Over half (51%) of those on diets had not eaten a snack or had had only one snack on the previous day and only one in five (18%) had eaten three or more snacks (Table 6n).

Table 6n **Frequency of eating a snack, by foods eaten and dieting behaviour (%)**

	Unweighted base	Having no or only one snack yesterday	Having three or more snacks yesterday
'More healthy' foods eaten daily			
4	1012	38	26
0	2201	23	44
'Less healthy' foods eaten daily			
0	1767	54	13
4	1538	11	63
On a diet			
Yes	1006	51	18
No – but need to lose weight	2318	30	31
No – no need	6928	24	43

Unweighted base: all respondents

6.6   DENTAL HEALTH

Young people were asked how often they brushed their teeth. Seven in ten young people (70%) brushed their teeth more than once a day, and almost all of them (96%) did so at least once a day. Girls were more likely than boys to brush more than once a day (80% of girls compared with 60% of boys), and older girls were more likely to do so than younger girls (85% of girls in Year 11 brushed their teeth more than once every day compared with 75% of those in Year 7) (Table 6o).

Young people who described themselves as 'very healthy' were more likely than those who perceived themselves as 'quite' or 'not very' healthy to clean their teeth more than once a day (76% compared with 69%).

Table 60   **Frequency of brushing teeth, by sex and school year (%)**

| | Total | School year | | | | |
		7	8	9	10	11
Boys						
More than once a day	60	60	58	59	61	64
Once a day	33	32	35	35	34	31
At least once a week but not daily	4	4	4	4	3	3
Less than once a week	1	2	2	1	*	1
Not stated	1	1	1	*	1	1
Base	*5063*	*1073*	*1011*	*1051*	*1009*	*917*
Girls						
More than once a day	80	75	77	81	82	85
Once a day	18	22	20	17	17	14
At least once a week but not daily	1	2	2	1	1	*
Less than once a week	*	*	1	*	*	*
Not stated	*	1	*	*	*	*
Base	*5241*	*1105*	*1040*	*1042*	*1087*	*967*
Total						
More than once a day	70	67	68	70	72	75
Once a day	26	27	27	26	25	22
At least once a week but not daily	2	3	3	3	2	2
Less than once a week	1	1	1	*	*	1
Not stated	1	1	*	*	*	*
Base	*10407*	*2193*	*2063*	*2102*	*2102*	*1891*

Unweighted base: all respondents

6.7   COMPARISON WITH 1995 WAVE

When comparing the results of the 1995 and the 1997 waves of the study, some encouraging trends can be observed in the attitudes of young people towards food. In the second wave young people were more likely to show a healthy attitude towards food. The number of young people who thought that people of their own age did not have to worry about the food they ate had fallen by almost a third. The proportion agreeing with the statement 'as long as you are reasonably active you can eat what you like' had declined by almost a quarter (23%) (Table 6p).

Table 6p   **Attitudes towards food, by sex and school year –
comparison with 1995 wave (%)[†]**

Those agreeing	Total	Year 7			Year 9			Year 11		
		Boys	Girls	Total	Boys	Girls	Total	Boys	Girls	Total
As long as you are reasonably active you can eat what you like	40 (53)	40 (52)	32 (46)	36 (49)	50 (56)	36 (49)	43 (53)	48 (60)	36 (49)	42 (55)
Experts never agree about which foods are good for you	37 (40)	37 (40)	33 (34)	35 (37)	39 (38)	35 (36)	37 (37)	45 (48)	36 (44)	41 (46)
I just eat the foods I like and I don't worry about whether they are healthy or not	35 (38)	31 (32)	22 (28)	27 (30)	40 (43)	32 (32)	37 (38)	49 (52)	36 (38)	42 (46)
I don't know enough about which foods are good for you	31 (36)	30 (32)	25 (34)	28 (33)	34 (39)	33 (37)	33 (38)	33 (38)	32 (39)	33 (38)
People of my age don't need to worry about the food they eat	23 (33)	25 (39)	28 (40)	27 (40)	27 (32)	20 (30)	24 (32)	24 (31)	13 (25)	18 (28)
I find healthy foods too boring	29 (35)	27 (33)	18 (27)	22 (31)	38 (42)	23 (32)	30 (37)	40 (41)	27 (32)	34 (37)
Base 1997 (Base: 1995)	*6186 (6406)*	*1073 (1162)*	*1105 (1072)*	*2193 (2258*	*1051 (1233)*	*1042 (1049)*	*2102 (2288)*	*917 (1001)*	*967 (855)*	*1891 (1860)*

[†]1995 figures are shown in brackets

The percentage of young people on a diet had declined by a quarter since the first wave of the study in 1995. The greatest reduction (30%) can be seen amongst girls in Years 7 and 9 and a decline approaching similar proportions occurred among boys in Years 9 and 11. However, the proportion of Year 7 girls who thought that they needed to lose weight had increased from 18% to 22% and the proportion of Year 11 boys sharing this view had increased from 13% to 16% (Table 6q).

Table 6q   **Dieting behaviour, by sex and school year – comparison with 1995 wave (%)[†]**

	Total	Year 7			Year 9			Year 11		
		Boys	Girls	Total	Boys	Girls	Total	Boys	Girls	Total
Yes, on a diet to lose weight	9	6	9	8	5	13	9	3	17	10
	(12)	(7)	(13)	(10)	(7)	(20)	(13)	(4)	(23)	(13)
No, but should lose weight	22	18	22	20	19	26	23	16	30	24
	(20)	(16)	(18)	(17)	(19)	(26)	(22)	(13)	(27)	(20)
No, because my weight is fine	68	74	68	71	75	59	67	78	52	65
	(68)	(76)	(68)	(72)	(73)	(54)	(64)	(82)	(50)	(67)
Base: 1997	*6186*	*1073*	*1105*	*2193*	*1051*	*1042*	*2102*	*917*	*967*	*1891*
(Base: 1995)	*(6406)*	*(1162)*	*(1072)*	*(2258)*	*(1233)*	*(1049)*	*(2288)*	*(1001)*	*(855)*	*(1860)*

[†]1995 figures shown in brackets

The frequency of eating snacks such as crisps, biscuits, chocolate, cakes and peanuts has shown an overall increase. The proportion who had eaten a snack at least three times on the previous day increased by a third between 1995 and 1997 (from 28% to 37%). Amongst boys and girls in each age group there had been at least a 20% increase in those who ate snacks of this type at least three times in the day before interview and in Year 9 the proportion of girls who ate snacks, such as chocolate, crisps, cake and peanuts, at least three times in the day before interview increased from 21% to 30% (Table 6r).

Table 6r   **Frequency of eating snacks yesterday apart from main meals, by sex and school year – comparison with 1995 wave (%)[†]**

	Total	Year 7			Year 9			Year 11		
		Boys	Girls	Total	Boys	Girls	Total	Boys	Girls	Total
None/once only	29	26	30	28	25	30	27	23	40	32
	(37)	(40)	(38)	(40)	(32)	(40)	(36)	(27)	(47)	(36)
Twice	34	32	37	24	31	39	35	32	33	32
	(34)	(29)	(34)	31	(33)	(38)	(35)	(36)	(33)	(35)
At least three times	37	40	32	36	44	30	37	45	27	36
	(28)	(30)	(26)	(28)	(35)	(21)	(29)	(37)	(20)	(29)
Base 1997	*6186*	*1073*	*1105*	*2193*	*1051*	*1042*	*2102*	*917*	*967*	*1891*
(Base 1995)	*(6406)*	*(1162)*	*(1072)*	*(2258)*	*(1233)*	*(1049)*	*(2288)*	*(1001)*	*(855)*	*(1860)*

[†]1995 figures shown in brackets

REFERENCES

1   Department of Health (1998) *Our healthier nation: a contract for health.* London: Stationery Office.

2   Health Education Authority (1995) *Diet and health in school age children: nutrition briefing paper.* London: HEA.

3   Health Education Authority (1998) *Young and active? Young people and health-enhancing physical activity: evidence and implications.* London: HEA.

4   Department of Health (1989) *The diets of British schoolchildren.* London: HMSO.

7 Exercise and recreational activity

Key findings

- The majority of young people (58%) had two PE/games lessons a week although 22% had less than this. (Section 7.1)

- There was quite a large drop in the number of PE lessons per week that young people took part in when they went into Year 10, and by Year 11 the majority had only one lesson a week. (Section 7.1)

- Boys were much more likely than girls to say they exercised every day in their free time (29% compared with 15%). (Section 7.1)

- Boys were more likely than girls to do two or more hours' physical activity outside school per week. This was especially true for older boys (43% of boys in Year 7 compared with 60% of those in Year 11). A greater proportion of girls than boys did no exercise out of school hours in a typical week (8% compared with 5% of boys). (Section 7.2)

- Young people who said that they were very healthy were much more likely to say that they exercised every day than those who said they were not very healthy. (Section 7.2)

- Half (51%) of the young people said they did not walk for at least half an hour a day while a third said they did so every day. (Section 7.3)

- Boys were much more likely than girls to cycle every day (18% of boys compared to 3% of girls). (Section 7.3)

- Boys were more likely than girls to cycle for half an hour every day (14% compared with 2%). Those in Years 9 and 10 were most likely to cycle for half an hour every day. (Section 7.4)

- Outside school, boys tended to focus on ball games (79%) and running around/kicking a ball about (68%) whilst the most popular activities for girls were swimming (52%), ball games (47%) and dancing (46%). (Section 7.5)

- Those young people who said they were very healthy were much more likely than those who said they were quite healthy or not very healthy to do 11 or more activity sessions of at least half an hour per week (49% of the very healthy did 11 or more compared with 32% of the less healthy group). (Section 7.6)

- Nearly three-quarters (72%) of young people watched television for more than two hours a day. Boys were far more likely than girls to play computer games and amongst those who did so, the boys spent a lot more time than the girls playing them. (Section 7.7)

- Those who said they were very healthy tended to watch slightly less television than other young people. In particular, whilst three-quarters (73%) of those who said they were quite or not very healthy watched television for two or more hours a day, only two-thirds (65%) of those who said they were very healthy watched this much television. (Section 7.7)

- There was a small increase in the proportion of all young people playing computer games from 1995. The increase occurred across all years and for both boys and girls but was most marked for girls. (Section 7.8)

Physical activity was identified by the nutrition task force as important in relation to weight control and obesity.[1] In September 1993 a national task force for physical activity was set up, with the specific remit to develop a national strategy for promoting physical activity. In April 1994 the HEA held an international symposium that came to a consensus about recommended levels of physical activity for adults.[2] These were adopted in the US Surgeon General's report of 1995. The symposium recommended that young people (under 16) should be recognised as a priority group for the delivery of health promotion messages.

In 1996 the HEA hosted an international symposium which looked specifically at the physical activity needs of young people.[3] This symposium recognised the importance of instilling the foundation skills for engaging in lifetime physical activity at an early age. It also stressed the importance of an early understanding of the benefits of physical activity. These benefits include improved psychological well-being, enhanced self-esteem, an enhanced moral and social development and a small but significant benefit of increased physical activity on reducing body fat, when combined with appropriate dietary modification. The symposium recommended that young people should take part in activity of at least moderate intensity for at least 30 minutes per day.[4] Moderate intensity activity is defined as activity usually equivalent to brisk walking, which might be expected to leave the participant feeling warm and slightly out of breath. Vigorous intensity activity is usually equivalent to at least slow jogging which might be expected to leave the participant feeling out of breath and sweaty.

The symposium also reported that there is little research into the physiological benefit to young people of regular physical activity. More research was recommended to establish physical activity baseline measures for future assessments.[5] The current HBSC will provide some information on current levels of activity.

This chapter looks at the amount of time young people spent playing sports or games in school. Young people were also asked to assess their own level of fitness. The survey looked for the first time at the frequency and duration of young people's participation in walking and cycling activities, both to and from school and for leisure purposes. A number of sports and activities were listed and respondents indicated those they took part in outside school hours and how long they spent on these activities. The second part of the chapter discusses how much time young people spent watching television or videos, or playing computer games. This is examined for two reasons. Firstly, time devoted to these essentially passive activities is not available for the physical activity important to health, and secondly, those who spend a lot of time watching television tend to develop poor nutrition habits.[6]

7.1 EXERCISE AT SCHOOL

The majority of young people (58%) had two PE or games lessons a week, although 22% had less than this. The number of lessons was similar for girls and boys and across all those years that had yet to embark on their GCSE courses (Years 7, 8 and 9). However, there was quite a large drop in the number of PE or games lessons per week that young people took part in when they went into Year 10, and by Year 11 half (49%) had only one games lesson a week. This decline in the number of PE or games lessons for those in their GCSE years was more dramatic amongst girls than boys so that by Year 11 55% of girls had one PE or games lesson per week or less compared with 46% of boys. Ninety per cent of PE or games lessons across all years were for at least half an hour and a quarter were for an hour or more (Tables 7a and 7b).

Table 7a   **Number of PE or games lessons per week, by sex and school year (%)**

	Total	School year				
		7	8	9	10	11
Boys						
None	1	*	1	1	1	2
1 lesson a week	19	4	5	9	36	44
2 lessons a week	7	66	71	70	37	36
3 lessons a week	13	18	14	13	9	8
4 lessons a week	6	5	4	4	10	6
5 lessons a week	2	1	1	1	5	2
Not stated	3	5	3	3	2	2
Base	*5241*	*1073*	*1011*	*1051*	*1009*	*917*
Girls						
None	1	*	*	1	2	3
1 lesson a week	23	7	7	9	41	53
2 lessons a week	59	66	74	77	45	31
3 lessons a week	10	17	13	8	5	6
4 lessons a week	4	6	4	3	4	4
5 lessons a week	2	2	1	1	3	1
Not stated	1	2	2	1	1	1
Base	*5241*	*1105*	*1040*	*1042*	*1087*	*967*
Total						
None	1	*	1	1	1	2
1 lesson a week	21	6	6	9	38	49
2 lessons a week	58	66	73	73	41	33
3 lessons a week	11	18	13	11	7	7
4 lessons a week	5	5	4	3	7	5
5 lessons a week	2	2	1	1	4	2
Not stated	2	3	3	2	1	2
Base	*10407*	*2193*	*2063*	*2102*	*2102*	*1891*

Unweighted base: all respondents

Table 7b   Number of PE or games lessons per week, by duration (%)

	Number of lessons				
	1	2	3	4	5 or more
Less than 15 minutes	1	1	1	2	1
At least 15 minutes but less than 30 minutes	7	8	12	11	12
At least 30 minutes but less than an hour	66	63	65	59	59
1 hour or more	25	27	22	28	27
At least 30 minutes	92	90	87	87	87
Not stated	*	*	*	1	–
Base	*2250*	*5930*	*1171*	*512*	*193*

Unweighted base: all who have at least one PE or games lesson per week

Those who said they were very healthy were more likely than those who said they were only quite healthy or not very healthy to have three or more PE or games lessons per week (23% compared with 17%). Those who said they liked school were more likely than those who did not like it to have two or more PE or games lessons a week (78% of those who liked school had two or more games lessons a week compared to 71% of those who disliked school) (Table 7c).

Table 7c   Number of PE or games lessons per week, by self-assessment of health (%)

	Health		Attitude to school	
	Very healthy	Not very/ quite healthy	Like school	Dislike school
None	*	1	1	1
1 lesson a week	15	22	19	26
2 lessons a week	58	58	60	53
3 lessons a week	14	10	11	11
4 lessons a week	6	5	5	5
5 lessons a week	2	1	2	2
Not stated	3	2	2	2
Base	*2159*	*8179*	*7472*	*2767*

Unweighted base: all respondents

7.2   OUTSIDE SCHOOL HOURS

The young people were also asked on how many occasions they did vigorous intensity activity in their free time, that is activity that left them out of breath and sweaty. Boys were much more likely than girls to say they exercised every day in their free time (29% compared with 15%). They also showed much more consistent patterns of exercise across the school years – approximately three out of ten boys in every year, except Year 11, said they did vigorous intensity activity every day and although there was a fall in the proportion of boys doing vigorous intensity activity every day in Year 11 (24%), there was a corresponding rise in the proportion of boys taking part in activity of vigorous intensity between two and six times a week (55% of boys in Year 11 said they did vigorous intensity activity between two and six times a week compared to 47% in Year 10). Older girls were less likely to take part in out-of-school activity of vigorous intensity between two and seven times a week than younger ones (71% of girls in Year 7 compared with 50% of Year 11 girls) (Table 7d and Figure 18).

Table 7d   **Occasions of physical activity undertaken outside school hours, by sex and school year (%)**

	Total	School year				
		7	8	9	10	11
Boys						
Every day	29	30	31	30	32	24
4–6 times a week	25	24	25	25	23	26
2–3 times a week	25	23	25	25	24	29
Once a week	12	13	11	13	13	13
Once a month	2	2	2	2	2	3
Less than once a month	2	2	2	2	3	2
Never	3	5	3	2	3	2
Not stated	1	1	1	*	1	1
Base	*5063*	*1073*	*1011*	*1051*	*1009*	*917*
Girls						
Every day	15	21	18	15	12	10
4–6 times a week	16	22	20	17	13	10
2–3 times a week	30	28	31	31	29	29
Once a week	23	18	20	23	27	28
Once a month	5	3	4	6	7	8
Less than once a month	5	4	3	4	6	7
Never	5	4	4	4	5	6
Not stated	*	1	*	*	*	1
Base	*5241*	*1105*	*1040*	*1042*	*1087*	*967*
Total						
Every day	22	25	24	22	22	17
4–6 times a week	21	23	22	21	18	18
2–3 times a week	27	25	28	28	26	29
Once a week	18	15	16	18	21	21
Once a month	4	2	3	4	5	5
Less than once a month	4	3	2	3	4	5
Never	4	4	4	3	4	4
Not stated	1	1	1	*	*	1
Base	*10407*	*2193*	*2063*	*2102*	*2102*	*1891*

Unweighted base: all respondents

Figure 18   Frequency of getting out of breath and sweaty playing games or sport in free time

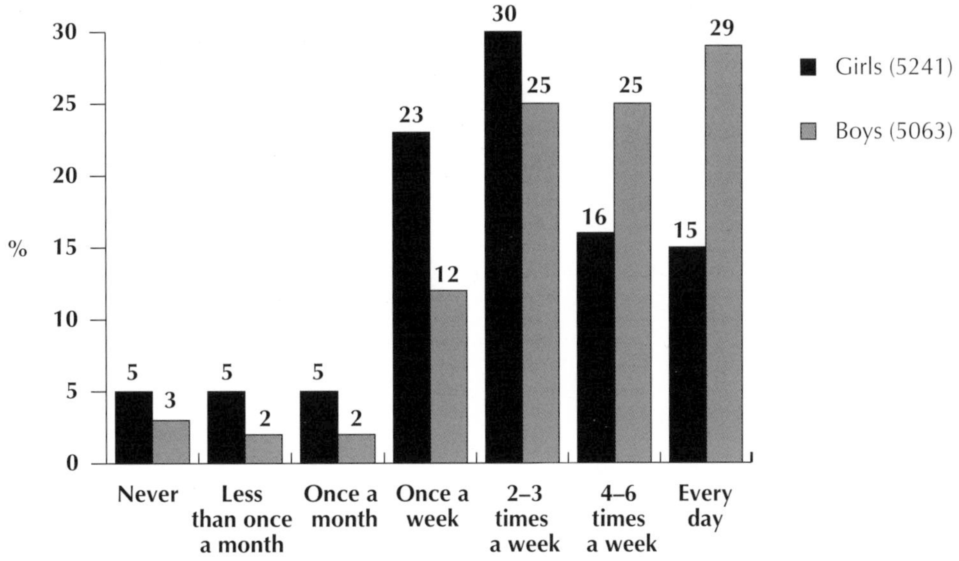

Base: all respondents (10407)

The young people were then asked for how many hours they did vigorous intensity activity outside school hours each week. Again boys did a greater amount than girls. They were more likely to do two or more hours of vigorous intensity activity, particularly as they got older (43% of those in Year 7 compared with 60% of those in Year 11) whilst a greater proportion of girls did no vigorous intensity activity out of school hours (8% compared with 5% for boys) (Table 7e).

Young people who said that they were very healthy were much more likely to take part in activity of vigorous intensity every day than those that said they were not very healthy (41% compared to 10% who said they were not very healthy). Conversely those who said they were not very healthy were more likely than those who said they were very healthy or quite healthy to do no vigorous activity outside school (13% compared to 3% saying they were very healthy) (Table 7f).

Table 7e **Duration of physical activity undertaken outside school hours, by sex and school year (%)**

| | | School year | | | | |
	Total	7	8	9	10	11
Boys						
None	5	6	5	5	5	4
About half an hour	17	22	19	16	13	13
About 1 hour	23	25	24	23	20	22
About 2–3 hours	26	24	27	25	29	28
About 4–6 hours	15	11	14	18	17	19
7 hours or more	12	9	9	13	15	13
Not stated	2	4	2	1	1	2
Base	*5241*	*1073*	*1011*	*1051*	*1009*	*917*
Girls						
None	8	6	8	7	10	11
About half an hour	25	30	26	23	24	22
About 1 hour	26	25	26	28	25	26
About 2–3 hours	24	21	23	26	23	25
About 4–6 hours	10	10	9	10	10	10
7 hours or more	5	6	7	5	5	5
Not stated	2	2	2	1	1	1
Base	*5241*	*1105*	*1040*	*1042*	*1087*	*967*
Total						
None	7	6	6	6	8	7
About half an hour	21	26	22	19	19	18
About 1 hour	25	25	25	25	23	24
About 2–3 hours	25	22	25	26	26	27
About 4–6 hours	13	10	11	14	13	14
7 hours or more	9	7	8	9	10	9
Not stated	2	3	2	1	1	1
Base	*10407*	*2193*	*2063*	*2102*	*2102*	*1891*

Unweighted base: all respondents

Table 7f **Exercise outside school hours and self-assessment of health (%)**

	Very healthy	Quite healthy	Not very healthy
Every day	41	18	10
4–6 times a week	26	20	8
2–3 times a week	19	30	21
Once a week	9	20	28
Once a month	1	4	8
Less than once a month	1	4	12
Never	3	3	13
Not stated	1	1	1
Base	*2159*	*7561*	*618*

Unweighted base: all respondents

7.3 WALKING

Most young people took a walk lasting for at least ten minutes on one or more days per week and there was very little difference between the number of days on which girls and boys walked. However, older pupils were more likely to walk for ten minutes every day (54% of those in Year 11 compared to 47% of those in Year 7) (Table 7g).

Table 7g **Number of days per week on which respondent walked for more than ten minutes, by sex and school year (%)**

		School year				
	Total	7	8	9	10	11
Boys						
None	2	2	3	1	2	2
1 day a week	4	6	4	4	4	3
2 days a week	5	7	6	6	5	3
3 days a week	6	6	6	6	6	5
4 days a week	5	5	7	6	6	4
5 days a week	12	14	14	11	11	11
6 days a week	13	12	12	15	12	14
7 days a week	51	46	48	50	54	56
Not stated	1	2	1	*	1	1
Base	*5063*	*1073*	*1011*	*1051*	*1009*	*917*
Girls						
None	2	1	2	1	2	2
1 day a week	4	4	3	5	4	3
2 days a week	5	6	6	6	4	3
3 days a week	6	7	6	5	6	6
4 days a week	5	6	6	5	5	6
5 days a week	12	13	14	13	11	11
6 days a week	14	12	12	15	15	17
7 days a week	51	48	50	50	53	53
Not stated	1	1	1	1	*	*
Base	*5241*	*1105*	*1040*	*1042*	*1087*	*967*
Total						
None	2	2	2	1	2	2
1 day a week	4	5	4	4	4	3
2 days a week	5	7	6	6	4	3
3 days a week	6	7	6	6	6	5
4 days a week	5	5	6	6	5	5
5 days a week	12	14	14	12	11	11
6 days a week	14	12	12	15	14	15
7 days a week	51	47	49	50	54	54
Not stated	1	1	1	1	*	1
Base	*10407*	*2193*	*2063*	*2102*	*2102*	*1891*

Unweighted base: all respondents

Table 7h   **Number of days per week on which respondent walked for more than half an hour, by sex and school year (%)**

		School year				
	Total	7	8	9	10	11
Boys						
None	51	55	53	50	48	49
1 day a week	1	2	1	*	1	1
2 days a week	2	2	2	2	2	1
3 days a week	2	2	3	2	2	2
4 days a week	2	2	3	2	2	1
5 days a week	4	5	4	4	5	4
6 days a week	6	6	5	7	5	6
7 days a week	32	26	29	32	36	37
Base	*5241*	*1073*	*1011*	*1051*	*1009*	*917*
Girls						
None	52	56	56	51	47	49
1 day a week	1	1	1	2	1	1
2 days a week	2	2	2	2	2	1
3 days a week	2	2	2	2	2	2
4 days a week	2	2	2	1	1	2
5 days a week	4	4	4	5	4	3
6 days a week	7	5	6	7	7	8
7 days a week	31	27	28	31	36	34
Base	*5241*	*1105*	*1040*	*1042*	*1087*	*967*
Total						
None	51	55	55	51	47	49
1 day a week	1	2	1	1	1	1
2 days a week	2	2	2	2	2	1
3 days a week	2	2	2	2	2	2
4 days a week	2	2	2	2	2	2
5 days a week	4	5	4	4	4	4
6 days a week	6	6	6	7	6	7
7 days a week	32	27	28	32	36	35
Base	*10407*	*2193*	*2063*	*2102*	*2102*	*1891*

Unweighted base: all respondents

The young people were asked for how long they walked on each day that they did any walking, and from that it was calculated on how many days they walked for at least half an hour This calculation shows a clear polarisation between those who never walked for half an hour or more (51%) and those who did so every day (32%). Older pupils were more likely than younger ones to walk for half an hour or more per day (35% of those in Year 11 compared to 27% of those in Year 7). About a third of those living in urban areas (37% of those living in a city or large town and 33% of those living in a town) walked for half an hour or more per day compared to about a quarter of those living in more rural areas (26% of those living in a village and 21% of those living in the countryside). Those who went to independent or voluntary-aided schools were also less likely to walk for at least half an hour a day – 18% of those attending independent schools walked for this long every day compared to 31% in grant-maintained schools and 33% in local-authority schools (Table 7h).

7.4   CYCLING

Boys were much more likely than girls to cycle every day (18% of boys compared to 3% of girls). The proportion of boys cycling every day, increased with age, up to Year 10. However, fewer Year 11 than Year 10 boys cycled every day (16% compared to 21% of those in Year 10). Cycling activity also varied by school attended. Two-fifths (42%) of those attending independent schools did not cycle at all compared with a third of those in local-authority-maintained schools (33%) and a similar proportion of those in grant-maintained schools (34%) (Tables 7i and 7j).

Table 7i **Number of days per week on which respondent cycled for more than ten minutes, by sex and school year (%)**

		School year				
	Total	7	8	9	10	11
Boys						
None	22	18	16	20	24	35
1 day a week	13	14	13	12	11	13
2 days a week	12	14	14	13	10	9
3 days a week	11	12	13	12	10	8
4 days a week	8	8	11	7	7	5
5 days a week	9	10	10	8	8	6
6 days a week	6	6	6	7	6	4
7 days a week	18	16	17	19	21	16
Not stated	2	3	1	1	2	3
Base	*5241*	*1073*	*1011*	*1051*	*1009*	*917*
Girls						
None	44	23	31	44	58	68
1 day a week	20	22	23	22	16	16
2 days a week	12	17	16	13	9	5
3 days a week	8	13	10	7	5	3
4 days a week	4	7	6	5	3	1
5 days a week	4	7	5	2	2	1
6 days a week	2	4	2	1	1	*
7 days a week	3	5	4	3	2	2
Not stated	3	2	2	2	3	4
Base	*5241*	*1105*	*1040*	*1042*	*1087*	*967*
Total						
None	33	20	24	31	42	52
1 day a week	16	18	18	17	14	15
2 days a week	12	16	15	13	10	7
3 days a week	9	13	12	9	7	5
4 days a week	6	8	8	6	5	3
5 days a week	6	8	8	5	5	4
6 days a week	4	5	4	4	4	2
7 days a week	10	10	11	11	11	9
Not stated	2	2	1	2	3	3
Base	*10407*	*2193*	*2063*	*2102*	*2102*	*1891*

Unweighted base: all respondents

Table 7j   **Number of days per week on which respondent cycled for more than ten minutes, by type of school (%)**

	Total	Type of school		
		Independent	Grant-maintained	Local-authority
None	33	42	34	33
1 day a week	16	21	16	16
2 days a week	12	13	12	12
3 days a week	9	9	9	9
4 days a week	6	5	6	6
5 days a week	6	3	6	6
6 days a week	4	2	4	4
7 days a week	10	4	11	11
Not stated	2	1	2	2
Base	*10407*	*641*	*1758*	*8008*

Unweighted base: all respondents

Boys were much more likely to cycle for half an hour every day than girls (14% compared with 2%). On this measure, cycling activity again peaked in Years 9 and 10 (Table 7k).

Table 7k   **Number of days per week on which respondent cycled for more than half an hour, by sex and school year (%)**

		School year				
	Total	7	8	9	10	11
None	59	55	55	56	59	70
1 day a week	4	4	4	4	4	4
2 days a week	5	7	6	6	4	3
3 days a week	5	7	7	6	3	3
4 days a week	4	4	7	5	4	2
5 days a week	5	6	5	4	5	3
6 days a week	4	5	4	5	4	3
7 days a week	14	12	13	15	16	12
Base	*5063*	*1073*	*1011*	*1051*	*1009*	*917*
Girls						
None	80	71	74	80	85	91
1 day a week	6	6	6	6	5	5
2 days a week	5	7	6	5	4	1
3 days a week	3	4	4	3	2	1
4 days a week	2	3	3	2	1	1
5 days a week	2	3	3	1	1	1
6 days a week	1	2	1	1	*	*
7 days a week	2	3	3	2	2	1
Base	*5241*	*1105*	*1040*	*1042*	*1087*	*967*
Total						
None	69	63	65	68	73	81
1 day a week	5	5	5	5	4	4
2 days a week	5	7	6	6	4	2
3 days a week	4	6	5	4	3	2
4 days a week	3	4	5	3	3	1
5 days a week	3	5	4	3	3	2
6 days a week	3	3	3	3	2	1
7 days a week	8	8	8	9	9	6
Base	*10407*	*2193*	*2063*	*2102*	*2102*	*1891*

Unweighted base: all respondents

7.5   ACTIVITIES NOT IN SCHOOL LESSONS

Although the young people had already been asked about how often they participated in vigorous intensity activities (that is, those which made them out of breath or sweaty) outside school hours, further questions were asked. These were about moderate intensity activities, that is those that left them feeling warm and slightly out of breath, that they took part in outside school hours. They were also asked about how often and how long they spent on average on these activities, and from these questions the number of half-hour sessions they spent altogether on these moderate intensity activities was calculated (Table 7l).

Table 71 **Types of physical activity undertaken outside school hours, by sex and school year (%)**

	Total	School year				
		7	8	9	10	11
Boys						
Swimming	42	47	47	45	34	36
Football, tennis, basketball, hockey or other ball games	79	80	80	82	77	76
Athletics, gymnastics, boxing, karate and judo	21	23	21	21	19	19
Aerobics, keep fit, jogging, running	39	43	43	39	35	35
Running about outdoors/ kicking a ball about	68	69	71	70	67	64
Roller skating, rollerblading, skateboarding or ice-skating	34	45	42	37	26	20
Dancing (disco, rave, ballet, at home or at clubs)	16	14	14	17	15	20
Any other activities that make you out of breath or warmer than usual	39	35	37	42	41	41
None	2	2	1	2	3	4
Base	*5063*	*1073*	*1011*	*1051*	*1009*	*917*
Girls						
Swimming	52	61	57	55	45	42
Football, tennis, basketball, hockey or other ball games	47	59	56	49	37	32
Athletics, gymnastics, boxing, karate and judo	16	23	18	18	11	8
Aerobics, keep fit, jogging, running	41	46	42	40	35	40
Running about outdoors/ kicking a ball about	39	52	49	39	29	23
Roller skating, rollerblading, skateboarding or ice-skating	34	49	40	36	24	19
Dancing (disco, rave, ballet, at home or at clubs)	46	42	45	48	45	50
Any other activities that make you out of breath or warmer than usual	42	39	42	43	44	42
None	4	2	2	3	5	6
Base	*5241*	*1105*	*1040*	*1042*	*1087*	*967*

Table 7l   **Types of physical activity undertaken outside school hours, by sex and school year (%) (continued)**

| | Total | School year | | | | |
		7	8	9	10	11
Total						
Swimming	47	54	52	50	40	39
Football, tennis, basketball, hockey or other ball games	63	69	68	66	57	54
Athletics, gymnastics, boxing, karate and judo	18	23	19	20	15	13
Aerobics, keep fit, jogging, running	40	45	42	39	35	38
Running about outdoors/ kicking a ball about	53	61	60	55	47	43
Roller skating, rollerblading, skateboarding or ice-skating	34	47	41	37	25	19
Dancing (disco, rave, ballet, at home or at clubs)	31	28	29	32	30	35
Any other activities that make you out of breath or warmer than usual	41	37	39	42	43	42
None	3	2	2	3	4	5
Not stated	1	2	1	1	1	1
Base	*10407*	*2193*	*2063*	*2102*	*2102*	*1891*

Unweighted base: all respondents

The activities of at least moderate intensity varied in popularity between the sexes. Boys tended to focus on ball games (79%) and running around/kicking a ball about (68%), whilst the most popular activities for girls were swimming (52%), ball games (47%) and dancing (46%). Older respondents, both boys and girls, were less likely to take part in most of the activities listed. However, there were two exceptions – older boys and girls were more likely to take part in dancing (35% of all Year 11 pupils said they went dancing compared to 28% of those in Year 7) and girls in Year 11 were as likely as those in Year 8 to take part in aerobics or keep fit (40% of girls in each of these years) (Table 7l).

Boys were more likely than girls to take part in activities of at least moderate intensity outside school on a daily basis (17% of boys compared to 8% of girls). Young people in Years 7 and 8 were more likely than those in the higher years to take part in activities of at least moderate intensity outside school hours every day (14% of those in Year 7 took part in one or more of these activities every day compared to 10% of those in Year 11), although boys in Year 11 were less likely than those in Year 7 to do none of these activities (19% compared to 24% of boys in Year 7). There was little change by year in the proportion of girls doing none of these activities (Table 7m).

Table 7m **Number of days per week on which respondent took part in other non-school activities for more than half an hour, by sex and school year (%)**

		School year				
	Total	7	8	9	10	11
Boys						
None	22	24	24	23	19	19
1 day a week	5	6	5	4	4	7
2 days a week	9	9	9	8	10	9
3 days a week	12	11	10	11	13	14
4 days a week	11	10	9	12	11	15
5 days a week	14	13	13	14	15	13
6 days a week	10	10	10	12	10	8
7 days a week	17	17	20	16	18	14
Base	*4881*	*1034*	*983*	*1016*	*972*	*874*
Girls						
None	30	31	28	29	32	32
1 day a week	12	10	12	12	15	15
2 days a week	13	12	11	13	14	17
3 days a week	13	11	13	14	12	14
4 days a week	10	10	11	11	9	7
5 days a week	8	9	11	8	7	6
6 days a week	5	6	5	6	5	3
7 days a week	8	11	10	9	6	5
Base	*4998*	*1068*	*1005*	*1004*	*1015*	*906*
Total						
None	26	27	26	26	26	25
1 day a week	9	8	8	8	9	11
2 days a week	11	11	10	10	12	13
3 days a week	12	11	12	13	13	14
4 days a week	11	10	10	11	10	11
5 days a week	11	11	12	11	11	9
6 days a week	8	8	7	9	7	6
7 days a week	13	14	15	12	12	10
Base	*9971*	*2117*	*2000*	*2029*	*1993*	*1783*

Unweighted base: all respondents

7.6 PHYSICAL RECREATION AND SELF-ASSESSMENT OF HEALTH

In order to get a measure of how much physical activity young people did in total, a calculation was made of the number of half-hour (or longer) sessions of at least moderate intensity young people did in a week. This was calculated by summing the number of days per week that young people did at least half an hour of walking, cycling, other non-school physical activities or PE at school. It was then possible to assess whether the amount of activity of at least moderate intensity was related to the young people's self-assessment of their health.

Those young people who said they were 'very healthy' were much more likely than those who said they were 'quite healthy' or 'not very healthy' to do 11 or more sessions of at least moderate intensity and lasting at least half an hour (49% of the 'very healthy' did eleven or more compared with 32% of the 'less healthy' group). Correspondingly, those who said they were quite healthy or not very healthy were more likely than those who were 'very healthy' to do five or fewer activity sessions of at least moderate intensity per week (35% compared with 21%) (Table 7n and Figure 19).

Figure 19   Number of half-hour activity sessions per week, by self-reported health

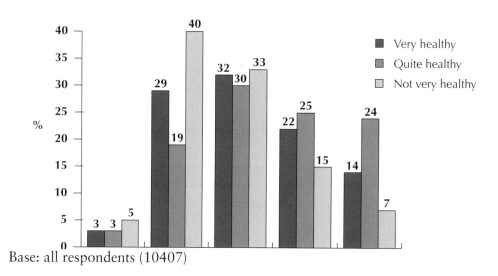

Base: all respondents (10407)

Table 7n   Total number of half-hour activity sessions, by self-assessment of health (%)

		Assessment of health	
	Total	Very healthy	Quite/not very healthy
None	3	3	3
1–5	29	19	32
6–10	32	30	33
11–15	22	25	21
16+	14	24	11
Base	*10407*	*2159*	*8179*

Unweighted base: all respondents

7.7   NON-PHYSICAL RECREATION

Just 1% of the entire sample said they did not watch television at all on an average day and only 1 in 20 watched for less than half an hour a day. Nearly three-quarters (71%) of young people watched television for more than two hours a day. Boys and girls were similar in terms of television consumption and there was little difference between those in Years 9, 10 and 11 – although those in Years 7 and 8 watched slightly less on average than their elders (38% of those in Year 7 watched less than two hours of television a day compared to 24% of those in Year 11) (Table 7o).

Table 7o   Hours per day spent watching television, by sex and school year (%)

		School year				
	Total	7	8	9	10	11
Boys						
Not at all	1	1	1	1	1	*
Less than half an hour	5	8	5	3	3	3
Half an hour to an hour	22	27	22	21	20	20
2 to 3 hours	43	37	41	45	46	46
4 hours	13	9	13	13	13	14
More than 4 hours	16	15	18	16	16	15
Not stated	1	2	1	1	1	*
Base	*5063*	*1073*	*1011*	*1051*	*1009*	*917*
Girls						
Not at all	1	2	*	1	1	1
Less than half an hour	5	7	6	4	4	3
Half an hour to an hour	22	30	24	19	18	20
2 to 3 hours	44	40	42	46	46	48
4 hours	12	7	11	15	14	15
More than 4 hours	15	12	17	16	16	12
Not stated	1	1	1	*	1	*
Base	*5241*	*1105*	*1040*	*1042*	*1087*	*967*
Total						
Not at all	1	1	1	1	1	1
Less than half an hour	5	8	5	4	3	3
Half an hour to an hour	22	28	23	20	19	20
2 to 3 hours	44	39	41	45	46	47
4 hours	12	8	12	14	14	15
More than 4 hours	15	14	17	16	16	14
Not stated	1	2	1	1	1	*
Base	*10407*	*2193*	*2063*	*2102*	*2102*	*1891*

Unweighted base: all respondents

Those who said they were very healthy tended to watch slightly less television than other young people. In particular, whilst three-quarters (73%) of those who said they were 'quite' or 'not very healthy' watched television for two or more hours a day, two thirds (65%) of those who said they were 'very healthy' watched this much television (Table 7p and Figure 20).

Table 7p   Hours per day spent watching television, by self-assessed health (%)

	Assessment of health	
	Very healthy	Quite/not very healthy
Not at all	1	1
Less than half an hour	8	4
Half an hour to an hour	24	22
2 to 3 hours	40	45
4 hours	11	13
More than 4 hours	15	16
Not stated	1	1
Base	*2159*	*8179*

Unweighted base: all respondents

Figure 20   Hours of television watched per day, by self-reported health

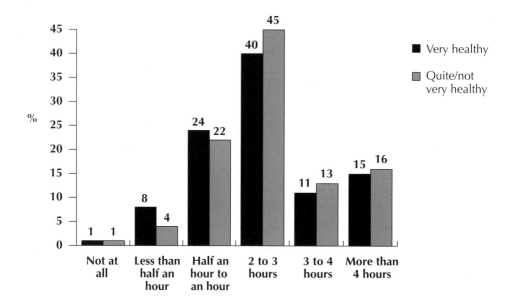

Base: all respondents (10407)

Nearly three-quarters (73%) of young people said they played computer games in an average week. Boys were far more likely to play these games than girls, and amongst those who did play computer games, the boys spent a lot more time on average than girls did playing them (Table 7q).

The older boys were almost as likely to play computer games, and to play them for as long, as the younger boys. However, there was a marked decrease in the amount of playing among girls in Year 9 and especially in Year 11 when compared to Year 7 (31% of girls in Year 7 did not play computer games compared to 38% in Year 9 and 57% in Year 11) (Table 7q).

Table 7q   **Hours per week spent playing computer games, by sex and school year (%)**

		School year				
	Total	7	8	9	10	11
Boys						
Not at all	12	11	8	12	12	18
Less than one hour	21	24	22	19	18	22
1–3 hours	33	37	37	31	30	29
4–6 hours	17	14	16	19	19	16
7–9 hours	7	6	6	9	9	7
10 hours or more	9	6	11	8	11	8
Not stated	1	1	1	1	1	1
Base	*5063*	*1073*	*1011*	*1051*	*1009*	*917*
Girls						
Not at all	41	31	33	38	45	57
Less than one hour	34	38	35	37	33	28
1–3 hours	19	23	24	19	15	12
4–6 hours	4	3	4	4	4	2
7–9 hours	1	1	1	1	1	*
10 hours or more	1	2	1	1	1	*
Not stated	1	1	1	*	*	–
Base	*5241*	*1105*	*1040*	*1042*	*1087*	*967*
Total						
Not at all	27	21	21	25	30	38
Less than one hour	28	31	29	28	26	25
1–3 hours	26	30	30	25	22	20
4–6 hours	10	9	10	12	11	9
7–9 hours	4	4	4	5	5	4
10 hours or more	5	4	6	5	6	4
Not stated	1	1	1	1	1	*
Base	*10407*	*2193*	*2063*	*2102*	*2102*	*1891*

Unweighted base: all respondents

7.8   COMPARISON WITH 1995 WAVE

The questions on physical recreation were not strictly comparable between this wave and the last wave, making it impossible to draw any real conclusions. However, the questions on non-physical recreation were comparable and it is possible to see a small increase in the proportion of young people playing computer games. The increase occurred across all years and for both girls and boys but is most marked for girls (Table 7r).

Table 7r   **Hours per week spent playing computer games, by sex and school year (%)†**

	Total	School year		
		7	9	11
Boys				
Not at all	13 (21)	11 (20)	12 (17)	18 (25)
Less than one hour	22 (27)	24 (29)	19 (25)	22 (27)
1–3 hours	33 (30)	37 (30)	31 (32)	29 (28)
4–6 hours	16 (12)	14 (11)	19 (13)	16 (12)
7–9 hours	7 (4)	6 (3)	9 (5)	7 (4)
10 hours or more	7 (6)	6 (6)	8 (8)	8 (4)
Not stated	1 (*)	1 (*)	1 (*)	1 (–)
Base 1997	*3041*	*1073*	*1051*	*917*
(Base 1995)	*(3641)*	*(1162)*	*(1233)*	*(1001)*
Girls				
Not at all	42 (52)	31 (41)	38 (47)	57 (67)
Less than one hour	34 (30)	38 (34)	37 (35)	28 (23)
1–3 hours	18 (13)	23 (18)	19 (13)	12 (8)
4–6 hours	3 (3)	3 (4)	4 (3)	2 (2)
7–9 hours	1 (1)	1 (1)	1 (1)	* (*)
10 hours or more	1 (1)	2 (1)	1 (1)	* (*)
Not stated	1(*)	1 (1)	* (*)	– (*)
Base 1997	*3114*	*1105*	*1042*	*967*
(Base 1995)	*(2976)*	*(1072)*	*(1049)*	*(855)*
Total				
Not at all	28 (35)	21 (29)	25 (30)	38 (45)
Less than one hour	28 (29)	31 (31)	28 (29)	25 (25)
1–3 hours	25 (22)	30 (25)	25 (23)	20 (19)
4–6 hours	10 (8)	9 (8)	12 (8)	9 (7)
7–9 hours	4 (3)	4 (3)	5 (3)	4 (2)
10 hours or more	4(4)	4 (4)	5 (4)	4 (2)
Not stated	1 (*)	1 (1)	1 (1)	* (1)
Base 1997	*6186*	*2193*	*2102*	*1891*
(Base 1995)	*(6406)*	*(2258)*	*(2288)*	*(2135)*

Unweighted base: all respondents
†1995 figures shown in brackets

REFERENCES

1   Health Education Authority (1995) *Diet and health in school-age children*. London: HEA.

2   Killoran, A. *et al.* (eds) (1994) *Moving on - international perspectives on promoting physical activity*. London: HEA.

3   Health Education Authority (1998) *Young and active? A policy framework on young people and health-enhancing physical activity*. London: HEA.

4   Biddle, S., Sallis, J. and Cavill, N. (eds) (1998) *Young and active? Young people and health-enhancing physical activity: evidence and implications*. London: HEA.

5   King, A. and *et al.* (1996) *The health of youth: a cross-national survey*. Copenhagen: WHO Regional Office for Europe.

6   Felts, M. *et al.* (1992) Adolescents' perceptions of relative weight and self-reported weight loss activity. *Journal of School Health*, **62**(8), 372–6.

8 Smoking

Key findings

- Almost half of the sample (45%) had smoked at least one cigarette. Girls were more likely to have tried smoking than boys – 48% of girls compared to 41% of boys. (Section 8.1)

- The proportion of young people who said they had tried a cigarette increased sharply with age: in Year 7, one in five (18%) had smoked a cigarette, whereas by Year 11, 65% of pupils had smoked a cigarette. (Section 8.1)

- Those who disliked school were more likely to have tried a cigarette than those who liked it (64% compared with 38%). (Section 8.1)

- Amongst those who had smoked, the average age for young people to smoke their first cigarette was 12, although a quarter of all those who had ever tried a cigarette had smoked it before they were 11years old. (Section 8.1)

- One in five young people in the sample (19%) were current smokers. (Section 8.2)

- 22% of girls were currently smoking compared with 16% of boys, and girls were more likely to smoke every day (11% compared with 9%). (Section 8.2)

- The incidence of smoking increased with age, from just 4% in Year 7 to 36% in Year 11. (Section 8.2)

- Boys were slightly more likely to be very heavy smokers, smoking over 40 cigarettes a week (24% of male smokers compared to 16% of female smokers smoked this number). (Section 8.2)

- Three in five (61%) of all those currently smoking said they would like to give up. (Section 8.3)

- The desire to give up rose with the frequency of smoking: 49% of those who smoked less than once a week wanted to give up, rising to 67% of those who smoked every day. (Section 8.3)

- Two-thirds (66%) of current smokers had tried to give up. (Section 8.3)

- 82% of those who wanted to give up smoking had tried to do so and 46% of those who did not currently want to give up smoking had tried to do so in the past. (Section 8.3)

- Around a third of young people agreed that 'smokers tend to be more rebellious than people who don't smoke' (37%), 'smoking can calm you down' (34%), and 'sometimes it is difficult to say no when people offer you a cigarette' (34%). Less than one in ten agreed with the statements 'smokers have more fun than people who don't smoke' (5%), 'smoking makes you look more grown up' (8%), 'smoking can help you make friends' (9%), and 'smokers are more likely to have girlfriends or boyfriends than people who don't smoke' (9%). (Section 8.4)

- In every year group the proportion of boys who had never smoked decreased between 1995 and 1997, whereas for the girls the proportion who had never smoked either increased or remained static. (Section 8.5)

It is estimated that smoking is the biggest preventable cause of early death in England.[1] It has been calculated that for every 10,000 young smokers, 25% of them will die because of smoking-related illness. The government has prepared a comprehensive strategy to reduce smoking to support *Our Healthier Nation*.[2] This was published in December 1998.[3]

This chapter examines smoking prevalence and attitudes towards smoking. It covers such topics as age and circumstances of first experimentation, current smoking prevalence, contact with other smokers and beliefs about the effects of smoking. Previous surveys have shown that experimentation with cigarettes starts at an early age.[4] Early experimentation does not point irrevocably towards smoking in later life, but is a powerful predictor. Although a number of surveys have looked at smoking prevalence among young people,[5,6] this survey allows comparisons across a number of health behaviours.

Despite a decrease in the prevalence of cigarette smoking amongst adults, the same cannot be said for smoking amongst teenagers. Government strategy over the past few years has recognised this and is continuing to take measures that have a particular focus on young people.[7]

8.1 EXPERIENCE OF SMOKING

Almost half of the sample (45%) had smoked at least one cigarette. Girls were more likely to have tried smoking than boys – 48% of girls compared to 41% of boys (Table 8a).

The proportion of young people who said they had tried a cigarette increased sharply with age: in Year 7, one in five (18%) had smoked a cigarette. At this age boys were more likely to have tried smoking than girls. However, older girls were more likely to have experimented with smoking than older boys. In Year 9, 49% had smoked at least one cigarette (52% of girls and 45% of boys), whereas by Year 11, 65% of pupils had smoked a cigarette (70% of girls and 59% of boys) (Table 8a and Figure 21).

Table 8a   **Experience of smoking, by sex and school year (%)**

| | Total | School year | | | | |
		7	8	9	10	11
Girls						
Ever smoked at least one cigarette	48	16	36	52	65	70
Base	*5241*	*1105*	*1040*	*1042*	*1087*	*967*
Boys						
Ever smoked at least one cigarette	41	20	32	45	52	59
Base	*5063*	*1073*	*1011*	*1051*	*1009*	*917*
Total						
Ever smoked at least one cigarette	45	18	34	49	59	65
Base	*10407*	*2193*	*2063*	*2102*	*2102*	*1891*

Unweighted base: all respondents

Figure 21   **Experience of smoking**

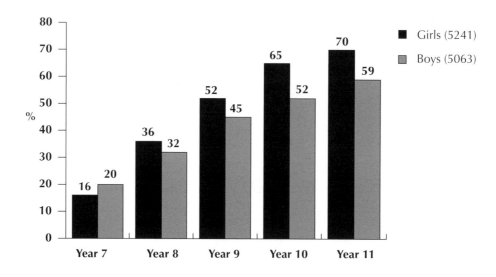

Base: all respondents (10407)

Those who disliked school were more likely to have tried a cigarette than those who liked it (64% compared with 38%).

Amongst those who had smoked the average age for young people to smoke their first cigarette was 12, although a quarter of all those who had ever tried a cigarette had smoked it before they were 12 years old (Table 8b).

Table 8b   **Current smoking habits, by age first smoked a cigarette (%)**

| | Total | Age first smoked | |
		11 or younger	12 or older
Boys			
I only ever tried smoking once	30	26	33
I used to smoke sometimes, but I never smoke cigarettes now	27	26	28
I sometimes smoke cigarettes now, but not as many as one a week	11	10	12
I smoke at least one cigarette a week, but not as many as one a day	10	11	10
I smoke every day	22	26	17
Not stated	1	*	1
Base	*4620*	*2124*	*2193*

Unweighted base: all who ever smoked

Respondents who had their first cigarette when they were younger than 12 years old were slightly more likely to go on to be smoking every day at the time of interview than respondents who were older when they first experimented with smoking (Table 8b).

8.2   CURRENT SMOKING HABITS

One in five young people (19%) in the sample were current smokers (defined as those who smoke every day, those who smoke at least once a week but not every day and those who smoke sometimes but not as many as one a week); 22% of girls were currently smoking compared with 16% of boys, and girls were also more likely to smoke every day (11% compared with 9%). The incidence of smoking increased with school year, from just 4% in Year 7 to 36% in Year 11, as did the likelihood of young people smoking every day. This rise in the proportion of current smokers as pupils got older was even more marked amongst the girls – from just 3% in Year 7 to 41% in Year 11 (compared with 31% of Year 11 boys). There was also a rise with increasing age in the proportion saying they used to smoke but had given up (Table 8c).

The number of cigarettes current smokers smoked in a week was similar for boys and girls, although boys were slightly more likely to smoke over forty a week (24% of male smokers compared to 16% of female smokers). One in eight (13%) smoked one cigarette a week on average, and a further one in five smoked between two and five cigarettes a week. A third of all smokers (34%) smoked over 20 cigarettes a week. The number of cigarettes smoked rose sharply with the young person's age. Only one in ten current smokers in Year 7 (11%) smoked over 20 cigarettes a week compared to nearly half (47%) of current smokers in Year 11 (Table 8d).

Table 8c   Current smoking behaviour, by sex and school year (%)

| | Total | School year | | | | |
		7	8	9	10	11
Boys						
Never smoked	53	73	61	49	43	35
Only smoked once or twice	19	15	19	22	19	18
Used to smoke, now given up	11	4	9	13	14	15
Current smoker	16	5	9	14	24	31
– smoke sometimes but not every week	4	2	3	4	5	6
– smoke sometimes but not every day	4	2	3	3	6	4
– smoke every day	9	1	3	7	13	21
Not stated	2	3	3	2	1	1
Base	*5063*	*1073*	*1011*	*1051*	*1009*	*917*
Girls						
Never smoked	49	81	60	45	32	27
Only smoked once or twice	15	11	17	16	16	15
Used to smoke, now given up	13	4	11	16	16	17
Current smoker	22	3	12	21	37	41
– smoke sometimes but not every week	6	1	5	7	8	7
– smoke sometimes but not every day	6	1	4	7	8	9
– smoke every day	11	1	3	8	20	24
Not stated	1	1	1	1	*	*
Base	*5241*	*1105*	*1040*	*1042*	*1087*	*967*
Total						
Never smoked	51	77	60	47	37	31
Only smoked once or twice	17	13	18	19	17	17
Used to smoke, now given up	12	4	10	15	15	16
Current smoker	19	4	11	18	30	36
– smoke sometimes but not every week	5	2	4	5	7	6
– smoke sometimes but not every day	5	1	4	5	7	7
– smoke every day	10	1	3	8	17	23
Not stated	1	2	2	1	1	1
Base	*10407*	*2193*	*2063*	*2102*	*2102*	*1891*

Unweighted base: all respondents

Table 8d **Number of cigarettes smoked per week, by sex and school year (%)**

| | Total | School year | | | | |
		7	8	9	10	11
Boys						
1 or less	11	31	12	15	9	7
2–5	19	27	44	14	16	14
6–10	13	16	11	17	16	8
11–15	3	4	1	5	4	3
16–20	9	2	7	12	10	9
21–30	7	4	3	7	9	7
31–40	7	2	5	8	6	9
41–60	12	4	3	8	16	16
61+	11	2	2	7	8	21
Not stated	8	9	12	7	7	7
Base	*806*	*55*	*92*	*148*	*235*	*276*
Girls						
1 or less	14	41	26	21	10	8
2–5	20	17	36	26	17	15
6–10	14	13	12	16	15	12
11–15	6	3	4	5	8	5
16–20	8	–	9	6	8	10
21–30	10	7	1	7	13	11
31–40	5	–	4	3	4	9
41–60	8	3	2	5	8	11
61+	8	–	2	4	9	13
Not stated	7	17	5	8	7	6
Base	*1148*	*30*	*124*	*219*	*391*	*384*
Total						
1 or less	13	35	20	18	10	7
2–5	20	24	40	21	16	14
6–10	14	15	11	17	16	10
11–15	5	4	3	5	6	4
16–20	9	1	8	8	9	10
21–30	9	5	2	7	12	9
31–40	6	1	5	5	5	9
41–60	10	3	2	6	11	13
61+	9	1	2	5	9	16
Not stated	7	12	8	8	7	6
Base	*1979*	*86*	*217*	*370*	*631*	*663*

Unweighted base: all who currently smoke cigarettes

8.3   GIVING UP

Young people who smoked were also asked whether they would like to give up smoking. Three in five (61%) of all those currently smoking said they would like to give up. The proportion wanting to give up was higher for girls (63%) than boys (58%), and increased from 51% in Year 7 to 64% in Year 11 (69% in Year 11 girls). The high correlation between age and wanting to give up can be seen in Table 8e.

Table 8e   **Whether would like to give up smoking, by sex and school year (%)**

	Total	School year				
		7	8	9	10	11
Boys						
Would like to give up	58	53	50	57	61	58
Have tried to give up	61	50	58	61	68	58
Base	806	55	92	148	235	276
Girls						
Would like to give up	63	50	51	57	64	69
Have tried to give up	69	57	63	64	70	74
Base	1148	30	124	219	391	384
Total						
Would like to give up	61	51	51	57	63	64
Have tried to give up	66	52	60	63	69	67
Base	1979	86	217	370	631	663

Unweighted base: current smokers; multi-coding possible

The desire to give up rose with increased frequency of smoking: 49% of those who smoked less than once a week wanted to give up, compared to 67% of those who smoked every day.

Smokers were then asked if they had ever tried to give up. Two-thirds (66%) had already tried, a slightly larger group than those who said they would like to give up. Again levels were higher among girls (69%) than boys (61%) and the proportion rose with age from 52% in Year 7 to 67% in Year 11. As with the desire to give up, the more frequently young people smoked, the more likely they were to have tried to give up – 44% of those who did not smoke every week had tried, compared with 78% of those who smoked every day.

Further analysis of those two questions shows that 82% of those who wanted to give up had already tried to do so at some time. However, 46% of those who did not currently want to give up smoking had still tried to do so at some point in the past.

8.4   ATTITUDES TO SMOKING

All young people, whether smokers or non-smokers, were presented with a group of statements about smoking and asked whether they agreed or disagreed with each individual statement.

The highest levels of agreement were with the statements, 'smokers, tend to be more rebellious than people who don't smoke' (37%), 'smoking can calm you down' (34%), and 'sometimes it is difficult to say no when people offer you a cigarette' (34%). Very few young people agreed with the statements, 'smokers have more fun than people who don't smoke' (5%), 'smoking makes you look more grown up' (8%), 'smoking can help you make friends' (9%) and 'smokers are more likely to have girlfriends or boyfriends than people who don't smoke' (9%) – all of which investigated whether or not smoking made young people more socially acceptable in the eyes of their peers (Table 8f and Figure 22).

Table 8f   Beliefs about smoking, by smoking behaviour (%)

	Total	Current smoker	Lapsed smoker	Never smoked
Those agreeing that				
Smoking makes you look more grown up	8	14	10	5
Smoking can help to calm you down	34	79	38	15
Smoking helps to give you confidence	11	28	12	5
Smoking can put you in a better mood	19	54	18	7
Smoking can help you to stay slim	12	22	12	7
Smoking can help you to make friends more easily	9	15	12	5
Smokers have more fun than people who don't smoke	5	10	5	3
Smokers are more likely to have boyfriends or girlfriends than people who don't smoke	9	10	10	7
Smokers are more boring than people who don't smoke	27	9	26	34
Smokers tend to be more rebellious than people who don't smoke	37	33	38	38
Sometimes it is difficult to say no when people offer you cigarettes	34	62	37	22
Base	*10407*	*1979*	*2983*	*5316*

Unweighted base: all respondents

Figure 22   **Beliefs about smoking**

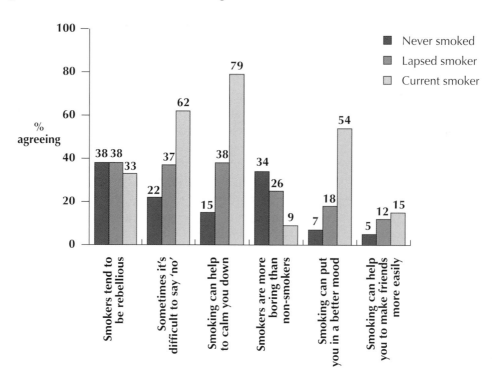

Base: all respondents (10407)

It is not surprising that levels of agreement with the statements were very strongly correlated with whether or not the young person smoked. Smokers were much more likely than non-smokers to agree with the positive statements about smoking, in particular 'smoking helps calm you down' (79% of current smokers agreed compared to 38% of lapsed smokers and 15% of those who have never smoked) and 'smoking can help put you in a better mood' (54% of current smokers agreed compared to 18% of lapsed smokers and 7% of those who had never smoked). Smokers were also much more likely to agree that 'sometimes it is difficult to say no when people offer you a cigarette, (62% compared to 37% of lapsed smokers and 22% of those who have never smoked) (Table 8f).

Attitudes were less well correlated with age than they were with smoking behaviour. Agreement with positive statements about smoking tended to be more common amongst the older age groups but it should be remembered that these were the people who were most likely to smoke and the two might be interlinked. It is worth noting that there were similar levels of agreement with the statement, 'sometimes it is difficult to say no when people offer you a cigarette' across all years despite the fact that there was a strong correlation between this statement and smoking behaviour (Table 8g).

Table 8g   Beliefs about smoking, by sex and school year (%)

		School year				
Those agreeing that	Total	7	8	9	10	11
Boys						
Smoking makes you look more grown up	9	8	9	10	9	9
Smoking can help to calm you down	33	18	27	33	41	48
Smoking helps to give you confidence	11	6	9	12	13	15
Smoking can put you in a better mood	20	11	16	17	24	32
Smoking can help you to stay slim	10	7	7	10	15	14
Smoking can help you to make friends more easily	11	6	9	12	12	14
Smokers have more fun than people who don't smoke	6	6	6	7	6	4
Smokers are more likely to have boyfriends or girlfriends than people who don't smoke	10	11	11	11	8	8
Smokers are more boring than people who don't smoke	32	44	40	33	25	16
Smokers tend to be more rebellious than people who don't smoke	39	34	38	42	42	41
Sometimes it is difficult to say no when people offer you cigarettes	32	32	33	34	32	30
Base	*5063*	*1073*	*1011*	*1051*	*1009*	*917*

Table 8g   **Beliefs about smoking, by sex and school year (%) (continued)**

		School year				
Those agreeing that	Total	7	8	9	10	11
Girls						
Smoking makes you look more grown up	8	7	9	10	7	6
Smoking can help to calm you down	36	13	24	37	51	55
Smoking helps to give you confidence	11	5	9	12	17	14
Smoking can put you in a better mood	19	8	13	20	27	28
Smoking can help you to stay slim	13	6	10	12	17	20
Smoking can help you to make friends more easily	8	5	7	10	9	6
Smokers have more fun than people who don't smoke	4	4	5	5	4	2
Smokers are more likely to have boyfriends or girlfriends than people who don't smoke	7	9	10	7	7	3
Smokers are more boring than people who don't smoke	22	38	29	19	13	11
Smokers tend to be more rebellious than people who don't smoke	34	33	29	38	37	33
Sometimes it is difficult to say no when people offer you cigarettes	36	26	37	38	42	35
Base	*5241*	*1105*	*1040*	*1042*	*1087*	*967*

Table 8g   **Beliefs about smoking, by sex and school year (%) (continued)**

		School year				
Those agreeing that	Total	7	8	9	10	11
Total						
Smoking makes you look more grown up	8	8	9	10	8	7
Smoking can help to calm you down	34	15	25	35	46	51
Smoking helps to give you confidence	11	6	9	12	15	14
Smoking can put you in a better mood	19	9	14	19	26	30
Smoking can help you to stay slim	12	6	9	11	16	17
Smoking can help you to make friends more easily	9	6	8	11	11	10
Smokers have more fun than people who don't smoke	5	5	6	6	5	3
Smokers are more likely to have boyfriends or girlfriends than people who don't smoke	9	10	11	9	7	5
Smokers are more boring than people who don't smoke	27	41	34	26	19	14
Smokers tend to be more rebellious than people who don't smoke	37	34	33	40	40	37
Sometimes it is difficult to say no when people offer you cigarettes	34	29	35	36	37	33
Base	*10407*	*2193*	*2063*	*2102*	*2102*	*1891*

Unweighted base: all respondents

8.5 COMPARISON WITH 1995 WAVE

Although many of the questions on smoking changed between the 1995 wave and the 1997 wave, it is possible to see some small changes in smoking behaviour. In every year the proportion of boys who had smoked increased between 1995 and 1997, whereas the proportion of girls who had ever smoked either decreased or remained static. Although some of this change might be accounted for by a fall in the proportion of 'not stateds' and a small increase in those who had smoked in the past, in Year 11 it is mainly accounted for by an increase in boys smoking every day from 15% in 1995 to 21% in 1997. Between 1995 and 1997 there was no change in the proportion of girls smoking every day (Table 8h).

Table 8h   **Current smoking behaviour, by sex and school year –
comparison with 1995(%)[†]**

	Total	School year		
		7	9	11
Boys				
Never smoked	53	73	49	35
	(56)	(77)	(54)	(39)
Only smoked once or twice	19	15	22	18
	(19)	(13)	(22)	(21)
Used to smoke, now given up	11	4	13	15
	(7)	(2)	(9)	(9)
Current smoker	16	5	14	31
	(15)	(5)	(13)	(30)
– smoke sometimes but not every week	4	2	4	6
	(4)	(2)	(3)	(8)
– smoke sometimes but not every day	4	2	3	4
	(4)	(1)	(4)	(7)
– smoke every day	9	1	7	21
	(7)	(1)	(6)	(15)
Not stated	2	3	2	1
	(3)	(5)	(2)	(1)
Base 1997	*3041*	*1073*	*1051*	*917*
(Base 1995)	*(3396)*	*(1162)*	*(1233)*	*(1001)*
Girls				
Never smoked	52	81	45	27
	(49)	(77)	(45)	(28)
Only smoked once or twice	14	11	16	15
	(17)	(11)	(20)	(21)
Used to smoke, now given up	12	4	16	17
	(9)	(4)	(11)	(11)
Current smoker	21	3	21	41
	(22)	(3)	(22)	(40)
– smoke sometimes but not every week	5	1	7	7
	(6)	(2)	(8)	(8)
– smoke sometimes but not every day	5	1	7	9
	(5)	(1)	(6)	(8)
– smoke every day	11	1	8	24
	(11)	(1)	(8)	(24)
Not stated	1	1	1	*
	(2)	(4)	(2)	(1)
Base 1997	*3114*	*1105*	*1042*	*967*
(Base 1995)	*(2976)*	*(1072)*	*(1049)*	*(855)*

Table 8h **Current smoking behaviour, by sex and school year – comparison with 1995(%)[†] (continued)**

	Total	School year 7	School year 9	School year 11
Total				
Never smoked	52	77	47	31
	(53)	(77)	(50)	(34)
Only smoked once	16	13	19	17
or twice	(18)	(12)	(21)	(21)
Used to smoke,	11	4	15	16
now given up	(8)	(3)	(10)	(10)
Current smoker	18	4	18	36
	(19)	(4)	(18)	(34)
– smoke sometimes	4	2	5	6
but not every week	(5)	(2)	(6)	(8)
– smoke sometimes	5	1	5	7
but not every day	(5)	(1)	(5)	(7)
– smoke every day	10	1	8	23
	(9)	(1)	(7)	(19)
Not stated	1	2	1	1
	(3)	(5)	(2)	(1)
Base 1997	*6186*	*2193*	*2102*	*1891*
(Base 1995)	*(6406)*	*(2258)*	*(2288)*	*(2135)*

Unweighted base: all respondents
[†]1995 figures shown in brackets

REFERENCES

1   Callum, C. (1998) *The UK smoking epidemic: deaths in 1995*. London: HEA.

2   Department of Health (1998) *Our healthier nation: a contract for health*. London: Stationery Office.

3   Department of Health (1998) Smoking kills: a White Paper on tobacco. London: Stationery Office.

4   Turtle, J., Jones, A. and Hickman M. (1997) *Young people and health: the health behaviour of school-aged children*. London: HEA.

5   Diamond, A. and Goddard, E. (1995) *Smoking among secondary school children in England 1994*. London: Stationery Office.

6   Jarvis, L., *et al.* (1997) *Teenage smoking attitudes*. London: Stationery Office.

7   Department of Health (1992) *Health of the nation: a strategy for health in England*. London: HMSO.

9 Alcohol

Key findings

- The majority of young people said they had tasted an alcoholic drink. (Section 9.1)

- The proportion saying they had done so increased with school year, from 77% of those in Year 7 to 93% of Year 9 to virtually all (96%) of those in Year 11. In all years, there was no real difference between the proportion of boys and girls who had tasted alcohol. (Section 9.1)

- One in five (19%) of the sample said they did not currently drink alcohol at all. (Section 9.2)

- 15% of young people drank a moderate amount of alcohol and 7% drank more than a moderate amount. (Section 9.2)

- The amount young people drank increased with school year. (Section 9.2)

- One in twenty (5%) of those in Year 7 said they drank more than a little alcohol, compared to one in six (17%) of those in Year 9 and almost half of those in Year 11. (15% of those in Year 11 said they drank quite heavily.) (Section 9.2)

- Just 3% of current smokers and only 9% of lapsed smokers did not drink compared with 31% of those who never smoked. (Section 9.2)

- Alcoholic soft drinks were most popular with school-aged young people: 18% of those drinking alcohol said they drank this type of drink at least once a week. Next in popularity was cider (14% of drinkers drank cider at least once a week), normal strength lager (12%) and spirits/liqueurs/cocktails (12%). (Section 9.3)

- Consumption of all types of drink except wine increased sharply with the school year of the young person, which corresponds to the higher and heavier levels of drinking among the older respondents. (Section 9.3)

- Just over one in five (22%) had been really drunk once and nearly two-fifths (39%) up to three times. A further 9% had been really drunk between four and ten times and one in ten drinkers had been really drunk more than 10 times. One in five (20%) of Year 11 drinkers had been drunk more than 10 times. (Section 9.4)

- Two-thirds of the sample agreed that they liked soft drinks more than alcoholic drinks (66% agreed) and the same proportion said that young people didn't know enough about the dangers of drinking (66%). (Section 9.5)

- Just over half (54%) said that drinking was only dangerous if you became addicted to it. (Section 9.5)

> • One in ten young people (12%) agreed with the statement 'I sometimes feel pressurised into having an alcoholic drink by my friends even if I don't want one'. (Section 9.5)
>
> • On the whole young people were less likely in the 1997 wave than in 1995 to agree with the positive statements about alcohol. (Section 9.6)

In December 1995 the government published a review of the scientific and medical evidence on the health effects of drinking alcohol.[1] The report set benchmarks for sensible drinking for adults that differ from previous recommended levels, because they are based on a daily rather than a weekly intake. A new strategy on alcohol is currently being planned. It will set out a practical framework for a responsible approach to drinking.[2] Research has shown that the social pressures to drink clearly increase in the teenage years, as parental influences decline.[3] The effects of peer-group pressure and the parallel need for peer-group standing or esteem appear to be very strong influences upon adolescent drinking.[4] Several recent studies of adolescent drinking in England have reported that drinking experience begins between the ages of 8 and 12 years, with the majority of 12- to 14-year-olds having some experience of drinking.[5, 6]

The White Paper on drugs published by the government argues that whilst the proportion of 11 to 15-year-olds who drink at all has remained static, those who do drink are drinking more.[7] However, these data must be kept in proportion and there are few examples of teenage alcoholics. Adolescence is, nonetheless, the stage of life at which drinking patterns are established, and health education aims to encourage sensible drinking patterns at this time.[3] The majority of young people use alcohol sensibly during adolescence and continue these drinking patterns into adult life without any harm. Therefore we should not overestimate the problems of youthful drinking. However, there is a need to monitor young people's behaviour and beliefs about the use of alcohol.

As with adults, accurately measuring how much young people drink is subject to possible bias in self-reporting. However, this study does not aim to measure alcohol consumption in units, but rather to find out the frequency with which young people consume alcoholic drinks, and their attitudes towards alcohol and its use. In this chapter, therefore, we look at young people's experience of alcoholic drinks; whether they have ever tried them, how often they currently drink, what they drink and with whom, whether they have ever been drunk and whether their friends drink alcohol. Young people's attitudes towards alcohol were also measured. This survey took place after the introduction of the new alcoholic colas, lemonades and fruit cocktails so has been able to include these in the questionnaire.

9.1 EXPERIENCE OF ALCOHOL

The majority of young people said they had tasted an alcoholic drink. Understandably the proportion saying they had done so increased with school year, from 77% in Year 7 to 93% of Year 9 to virtually all (96%) of those in Year 11. In all years, there was no real difference between the proportion of boys and that of girls who had tasted alcohol (Table 9a and Figure 23).

Table 9a   **Experience of alcohol, by sex and school year (%)**

	Total	School year				
		7	8	9	10	11
Ever tasted an alcoholic drink						
Boys						
Yes	89	78	86	93	92	95
No	10	20	13	6	7	4
Not stated	1	2	1	1	1	1
Base	*5063*	*1073*	*1011*	*1051*	*1009*	*917*
Girls						
Yes	89	76	84	93	96	96
No	11	24	15	7	4	4
Not stated	*	*	1	*	*	*
Base	*5241*	*1105*	*1040*	*1042*	*1087*	*967*
Total						
Yes	89	77	85	93	94	96
No	10	22	14	6	5	4
Not stated	1	1	1	*	1	1
Base	*10407*	*2193*	*2063*	*2102*	*2102*	*1891*

Unweighted base: all respondents

Figure 23   **Experience of tasting an alcoholic drink**

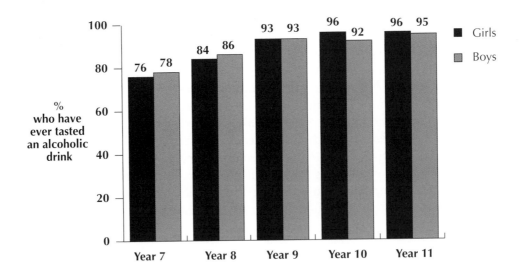

Base: all respondents (10407)

9.2   CURRENT DRINKING HABITS

When asked to describe their current drinking habits, one in five (19%) of the sample said they did not drink alcohol at all (18% of boys and 20% of girls) – 52% of this group had never tasted an alcoholic drink. Fifty-nine per cent of the sample said either that they hardly drank alcohol at all or that they drank a little alcohol. Fifteen per cent drank a moderate amount of alcohol and 7% drank more than a moderate amount. Amount of drinking increased significantly with school year (Table 9b).

Table 9b   **Experience of alcohol, by sex and school year (%)**

		School year				
	Total	7	8	9	10	11
Boys						
I do not drink alcohol at all	18	31	22	13	14	7
I hardly drink alcohol at all	30	36	36	37	20	17
I drink a little alcohol	28	23	27	31	32	27
I drink a moderate amount of alcohol	15	4	9	13	21	31
I drink quite a lot of alcohol	6	2	2	4	8	13
I drink heavily	2	1	2	1	3	5
Not stated	2	2	2	1	2	1
Base	*5063*	*1073*	*1011*	*1051*	*1009*	*917*
Girls						
I do not drink alcohol at all	20	36	28	18	9	7
I hardly drink alcohol at all	32	44	39	35	26	19
I drink a little alcohol	26	16	23	30	33	30
I drink a moderate amount of alcohol	15	2	6	13	24	30
I drink quite a lot of alcohol	5	*	2	3	8	12
I drink heavily	1	*	*	*	1	2
Not stated	1	1	1	1	*	*
Base	*5241*	*1105*	*1040*	*1042*	*1087*	*967*
Total						
I do not drink alcohol at all	19	34	25	16	12	7
I hardly drink alcohol at all	31	40	37	36	23	18
I drink a little alcohol	27	20	25	30	32	28
I drink a moderate amount of alcohol	15	3	8	13	23	31
I drink quite a lot of alcohol	5	1	2	3	8	12
I drink heavily	1	1	1	1	2	3
Not stated	1	2	2	1	1	1
Base	*10407*	*2193*	*2063*	*2102*	*2102*	*1891*

Unweighted base: all respondents

Three-quarters (74%) of Year 7 pupils said they either did not drink alcohol or they hardly drank it at all, compared to just over half of those in Year 9 (51%) and a quarter (25%) of those in Year 11. Similarly, only one in twenty (5%) of those in Year 7 said they drank more than a little alcohol, compared to one in six (17%) of those in Year 9 and almost half (46%) of Year 11 (15% of those in Year 11 said they drank quite heavily) (Table 9b).

Young people who disliked school were more likely to drink alcohol (10% not drinking alcohol compared with 22% of those who liked school). In addition fewer of this group described their drinking as very light – 23% of those with negative attitudes to school said they drank hardly at all compared with 34% of those who liked school. Fourteen per cent of those who disliked school either drank a lot of alcohol or drank heavily compared with 4% of those who liked school.

Just 3% of current smokers and only 9% of lapsed smokers did not drink compared with 31% of those who had never smoked. Current smokers were also more likely to drink more than a moderate amount ('quite a lot' or 'heavily') – 23% of current smokers compared with 5% of lapsed smokers and 2% of those who had never smoked.

9.3 FREQUENCY OF DRINKING DIFFERENT ALCOHOLIC DRINKS

Alcoholic 'soft' drinks were the most popular with school-aged young people: 18% of those drinking alcohol said they drank this type of drink at least once a week. Next in popularity was cider (14% of drinkers drank cider at least once a week), normal-strength lager (12%) and spirits/liqueurs/cocktails (12%) (Tables 9c and 9d).

Table 9c   Frequency of drinking beer and lager (%)

	Type of alcohol			
Frequency of drinking	High/extra-strength lager	Normal-strength lager	High/extra-strength beer	Normal-strength beer
Every day	1	1	1	1
Every week	6	11	4	8
Every month	8	14	8	13
Less than once a month	20	29	18	28
Never	60	41	64	45
Not stated	4	3	5	4

Unweighted base: all who drank alcohol; don't know/not stated answers not shown

Table 9d   Frequency of drinking other alcoholic drinks (%)

Frequency of drinking	Type of alcohol				
	Spirits/ liqueurs/ cocktails	Sherry/ martini	Wine	Cider	Alcoholic 'soft' drinks
Every day	3	1	1	2	4
Every week	9	4	8	12	14
Every month	14	8	16	15	19
Less than once a month	30	20	39	26	29
Never	41	64	32	41	32
Not stated	3	4	3	4	3

Unweighted base: all who drank alcohol; don't know/not stated answers not shown

On average boys drank more beer and lager than girls. Conversely girls were slightly more likely to drink spirits and wine. Girls and boys were equally likely to drink cider and alcoholic soft drinks. For each of the types of alcohol given in the questionnaire, Table 9e shows the proportion of drinkers who drank that type at least once a week (Table 9e and Figure 24).

Figure 24   Alcoholic drinks consumed at least once a week

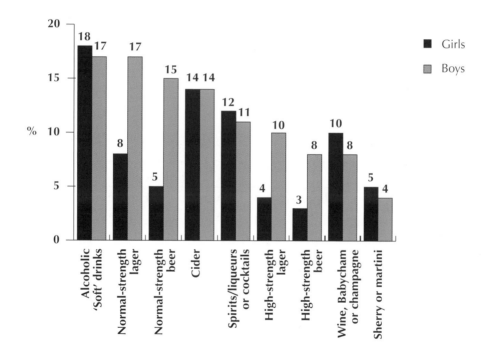

Base: all who ever drink alcohol (8286)

Consumption of all types of drink except wine increased sharply with the school year of the young person, which corresponds to the higher and heavier levels of drinking among the older respondents. The frequency of drinking wine and sherry or martini increased only slightly with school year (Table 9e).

Table 9e **Types of alcoholic drink consumed weekly, by sex and school year (%)**

	Total	School year				
		7	8	9	10	11
Boys						
High/extra-strength lager	10	6	6	8	13	18
Normal-strength lager	17	7	10	11	22	35
High/extra-strength beer	8	4	4	6	10	14
Normal-strength beer	15	9	10	11	18	24
Spirits/liqueurs or cocktails	11	11	10	8	11	14
Sherry or martini	4	4	5	3	4	5
Wine, Babycham or champagne	8	6	8	8	9	10
Cider	14	9	10	13	19	19
Alcoholic 'soft' drinks	17	16	14	18	20	19
Base	*4065*	*714*	*764*	*893*	*848*	*845*
Girls						
High/extra-strength lager	4	2	3	3	5	8
Normal-strength lager	8	2	5	5	8	15
High/extra-strength beer	3	1	2	2	3	4
Normal-strength beer	5	3	3	4	5	7
Spirits/liqueurs or cocktails	12	8	10	7	12	22
Sherry or martini	5	1	3	3	5	9
Wine, Babycham or champagne	10	6	9	9	11	14
Cider	14	4	8	12	22	17
Alcoholic 'soft' drinks	18	8	13	15	24	26
Base	*4141*	*689*	*731*	*846*	*983*	*892*
Total						
High/extra-strength lager	7	4	4	5	9	13
Normal-strength lager	12	5	7	8	14	25
High/extra-strength beer	5	3	3	4	6	9
Normal-strength beer	10	6	7	7	11	16
Spirits/liqueurs or cocktails	12	10	10	8	12	19
Sherry or martini	4	3	4	3	5	7
Wine, Babycham or champagne	9	6	8	8	10	12
Cider	14	7	9	12	21	18
Alcoholic 'soft' drinks	18	12	14	16	22	23
Base	*8256*	*1413*	*1505*	*1746*	*1837*	*1742*

Unweighted base: all who ever drink alcohol

9.4 GETTING DRUNK

Nearly half (43%) of those who currently drank alcohol had never, in their own estimation, had so much to drink that they were really drunk. The proportion who had never been drunk decreased with school year, from 69% of Year 7 drinkers, to 44% of Year 9 drinkers, to 21% of drinkers in Year 11. There were no real differences by sex (Table 9f).

Just over one in five (22%) had been really drunk once and nearly two-fifths (39%) up to three times. A further 9% had been really drunk between four and ten times and one in ten drinkers (9%) had been really drunk more than ten times. This rose to one in five (20%) of Year 11 drinkers. In general, perhaps not surprisingly, the older the drinker the more often they had been really drunk (Table 9f).

Table 9f   Experience of having been really drunk, by sex and school year (%)

	Total	School year 7	8	9	10	11
Those who drink at least once a week						
Boys						
No, never	41	62	52	45	28	20
Yes, once	21	22	23	26	20	15
Yes, 2–3 times	17	9	15	16	23	22
Yes, 4–10 times	9	2	4	7	12	18
Yes, more than 10 times	11	3	4	6	16	23
Not stated	1	3	1	1	1	1
Base	*4065*	*714*	*764*	*893*	*848*	*845*
Girls						
No, never	45	77	58	43	34	22
Yes, once	22	17	23	29	20	21
Yes, 2–3 times	16	4	11	17	22	23
Yes, 4–10 times	9	*	5	6	11	18
Yes, more than 10 times	8	*	2	4	12	16
Not stated	1	1	1	2	*	*
Base	*4141*	*689*	*731*	*846*	*983*	*892*
Total						
No, never	43	69	55	44	32	21
Yes, once	22	20	23	27	20	18
Yes, 2–3 times	17	6	13	16	22	23
Yes, 4–10 times	9	1	4	7	12	18
Yes, more than 10 times	9	2	3	5	14	20
Not stated	1	2	1	1	1	1
Base	*8286*	*1413*	*1505*	*1746*	*1837*	*1742*

Unweighted base: all who ever drink alcohol

9.5   ATTITUDES TOWARDS ALCOHOL

All the young people were presented with a series of statements about alcohol and drinking and were asked whether they agreed or disagreed with each one.

Two-thirds of the sample agreed that they liked soft drinks more than alcoholic drinks (66%) and the same proportion said that young people didn't know enough about the dangers of drinking (66%). However, three in five believed drinking was only dangerous if you became addicted to it (54%) and over half (52%) said they enjoyed the taste of alcoholic drinks. The lowest levels of agreement were with the statements 'I sometimes feel pressurised into having an alcoholic drink by my friends even if I don't want one' (12%) and 'there is no point in drinking if you don't get drunk' (16%) (Table 9g).

Table 9g   **Attitudes to statements about alcohol, by sex and school year (%)**

	Total	School year				
		7	8	9	10	11
Those agreeing that						
Boys						
Life is more fun when you have a drink	27	15	19	24	35	45
Drinking is only dangerous if you get addicted to it	59	63	63	63	53	51
I feel more confident when I have a drink	22	10	12	18	30	42
Young people don't know enough about the dangers of drinking	63	69	70	67	62	48
I enjoy the taste of alcoholic drinks	54	32	45	56	66	73
I like soft drinks more than alcoholic drinks	66	75	74	67	63	50
I sometimes worry about the amount I drink	23	24	26	22	22	18
I sometimes feel pressurised into having an alcoholic drink by my friends even if I don't want one	13	13	12	14	13	12
There is no point in drinking if you don't get drunk	20	20	17	19	21	22
Base	*5063*	*1073*	*1011*	*1051*	*1009*	*917*

Table 9g **Attitudes to statements about alcohol, by sex and school year (%) (continued)**

	Total	School year				
		7	8	9	10	11
Those agreeing that						
Girls						
Life is more fun when you have a drink	19	6	12	17	29	33
Drinking is only dangerous if you get addicted to it	50	56	54	50	47	40
I feel more confident when I have a drink	26	5	10	22	40	53
Young people don't know enough about the dangers of drinking	68	78	74	67	61	58
I enjoy the taste of alcoholic drinks	50	23	39	53	67	73
I like soft drinks more than alcoholic drinks	66	83	75	68	54	48
I sometimes worry about the amount I drink	18	18	17	16	18	19
I sometimes feel pressurised into having an alcoholic drink by my friends even if I don't want one	10	8	10	12	11	11
There is no point in drinking if you don't get drunk	13	14	12	13	14	14
Base	*5241*	*1105*	*1040*	*1042*	*1087*	*967*

Table 9g   **Attitudes to statements about alcohol, by sex and school year (%) (continued)**

	Total	School year				
		7	8	9	10	11
Those agreeing that						
Total						
Life is more fun when you have a drink	23	11	15	21	32	39
Drinking is only dangerous if you get addicted to it	54	59	59	56	50	45
I feel more confident when I have a drink	24	8	11	20	35	48
Young people don't know enough about the dangers of drinking	66	73	72	67	62	53
I enjoy the taste of alcoholic drinks	52	27	42	54	66	73
I like soft drinks more than alcoholic drinks	66	79	75	68	58	49
I sometimes worry about the amount I drink	20	21	21	19	20	19
I sometimes feel pressurised into having an alcoholic drink by my friends even if I don't want one	12	11	11	13	12	11
There is no point in drinking if you don't get drunk	16	17	15	16	17	18
Base	*10407*	*2193*	*2063*	*2102*	*2102*	*1891*

Unweighted base: all respondents

Since there was a high correlation between school year and drinking habits, it is not surprising that much the same pattern is seen between school year of the young person and tendency to give a positive answer about drinking. Interestingly the statement 'drinking is only dangerous if you get addicted to it' elicited higher agreement from younger than older pupils: 59% of those in Year 7 thought drinking was only dangerous if you became addicted to it compared with 56% of Year 9 and 45% of Year 11. Also younger pupils tended to be more worried about the amount they drank than older pupils: 21% of Year 7 sometimes worried about the amount they drank, compared to 19% of Year 9 and 19% of Year 11. As respondents got older they were more likely to disagree that there is no point drinking if you don't get drunk (66% of Year 7 disagreed with this statement compared to 73% of Year 9 and 74% of Year 11). Those who drank heavily were much more likely to agree with this statement than those who did not drink at all (51% compared with 14% respectively) (Table 9g and Figure 25).

Figure 25   Attitudes to alcohol and drinking

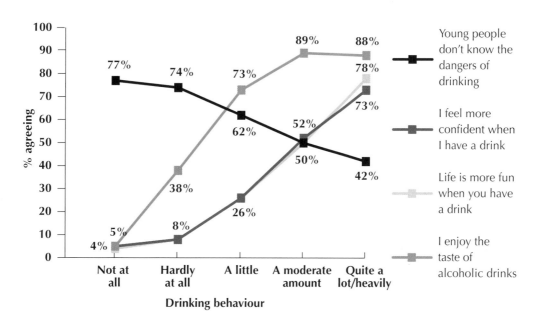

Base: all respondents (10407)

There were not many differences between boys and girls in agreement to these statements. The most noticeable difference was that 59% of boys thought drinking was only dangerous if you became addicted to it, compared with 50% of girls. Boys were also more likely to agree that life is more fun when you've had a drink (27% compared with 19% of girls) and that there is no point in drinking if you don't get drunk (20% compared with 13% of girls) (Table 9g).

As already noted, on almost all the statements, the more the respondent drank, the more likely they were to be more favourable to statements related to drinking alcohol – most notably for the statements: 'I enjoy the taste of alcoholic drinks' (4% of those who did not drink at all agreed with this statement, rising sharply to 89% of those who drank a moderate amount and 88% of those who drank a lot or drank heavily); 'Life is more fun when you have a drink' (5% of those who did not drink at all agreed with this compared to 78% of those who drank quite a lot or drank heavily) and 'I feel more confident when I have a drink (4% of those who did not drink at all compared with 70% of those who drank quite a lot or drank heavily). The exceptions to this general trend were 'drinking is only dangerous if you become addicted to it' and 'I sometimes feel pressurised into having an alcoholic drink by my friends even if I don't want one'. For these statements, levels of agreement were fairly similar whatever the drinking behaviour. Table 9h shows these results in full.

Table 9h   **Beliefs about drinking, by drinking behaviour (%)**

Those agreeing that	Total	Not at all	Hardly at all	A little	Moderate amount	Quite a lot/ heavily
Life is more fun when you have a drink	23	5	8	26	50	78
Drinking is only dangerous if you get addicted to it	54	50	52	59	55	55
I feel more confident when I have a drink	24	4	9	27	54	70
Young people don't know enough about the dangers of drinking	66	77	74	62	52	42
I enjoy the taste of alcoholic drinks	52	4	38	73	89	88
I like soft drinks more than alcoholic drinks	66	85	83	61	36	23
I sometimes worry about the amount I drink	20	13	18	22	25	31
I sometimes feel pressurised into having an alcoholic drink by my friends even if I don't want one	12	9	13	13	10	12
There is no point in drinking if you don't get drunk	16	14	12	15	21	40

Unweighted base: all respondents

9.6   COMPARISON WITH 1995 WAVE

The main difference between the two waves was the emergence of alcoholic 'soft' drinks as the alcoholic drink of choice of most young people. Alcoholic 'soft' drinks were not asked about in the previous wave as they had only just come on to the market at that point. It is of considerable note therefore that within two years they have become the most popular drink amongst this age group.

Other changes concerned attitudes to alcohol. On the whole, young people were less likely in the 1997 wave to agree with positive statements about alcohol (Table 9i).

Table 9i   **Attitudes to statements about alcohol, by school year and sex-comparison with 1995 wave (%)**[†]

| | Total | School year | | |
		7	9	11
Those agreeing that				
Life is more fun when you have a drink	23 (27)	11 (13)	21 (25)	39 (43)
Drinking is only dangerous if you get addicted to it	54 (59)	59 (66)	56 (63)	45 (49)
I feel more confident when I have a drink	24 (28)	8 (8)	20 (22)	48 (54)
Young people don't know enough about the dangers of drinking	65 (74)	73 (80)	67 (75)	53 (67)
I enjoy the taste of alcoholic drinks	51 (54)	27 (31)	54 (55)	73 (74)
I like soft drinks more than alcoholic drinks	66 (74)	79 (85)	68 (77)	49 (61)
I sometimes worry about the amount I drink	20 (26)	21 (30)	19 (27)	19 (22)
I sometimes feel pressurised into having an alcoholic drink by my friends even if I don't want one	12 (13)	11 (13)	13 (14)	11 (13)
Base 1997	*6186*	*2193*	*2102*	*1891*
(Base 1995)	*(6406)*	*(2258)*	*(2288)*	*(1860)*

Unweighted base: all respondents
[†]1995 figures shown in brackets

REFERENCES

1   Department of Health (1995) *Sensible drinking – the report of an inter-departmental working group*. London: HMSO.

2   Department of Health (1998) *Our healthier nation: a contract for health*. London: Stationery Office.

3   Ritson, B. (1992) *Alcohol and young people (learning to cope)*. A conference held by the Addictions Forum in association with the Portman Group and the alcohol research group, University of Edinburgh, 7 October 1992. Royal College of Physicians, London (unpublished).

4   King, A. *et al.* (1996) *The health of youth: a cross-national survey*. Copenhagen: WHO Regional Office for Europe.

5   Health Education Authority (1992) *Tomorrow's young adults*. London: HEA.

6   Turtle, J., Jones, A. and Hickman, M. (1997) *Young people and health: the health behaviour of school-aged children*. London, HEA.

7   *Tackling drugs to build a better Britain: the government's 10-year strategy for tackling drug misuse*. (1998) London: Stationery Office.

10 Drugs

Key findings

- 30% of pupils in Years 10 and 11 had tried cannabis and 17% had tried it on three or more occasions. (Section 10.1)

- The next highest levels of experimentation were for glues or solvents to inhale (11%) and gas/aerosols/butane/lighter fuel to inhale (11%). There was also a high level of experimentation with amphetamines (10%) and with magic mushrooms (6%). (Section 10.1)

- Levels of drug use were fairly similar for boys and girls. However, where there were differences in the use of particular drugs, boys were found to be slightly heavier users. (Section 10.1)

- Most of those in Years 10 and 11 who had taken drugs had first tried them when they were 13 (26%) or 14 (32%). (Section 10.2)

- For all drugs except cannabis, less than 30% of those in Years 10 and 11 who had ever used the stated drug had used it in the past four weeks and the majority of those who had used it in the past month had used it once or twice. By contrast, over half (55%) of those who had ever used cannabis had done so within the last four weeks and nearly a quarter (23%) had done so three or more times. (Section 10.3)

In 1995 the government introduced a three-year strategy to tackle drug misuse.[1] The strategy focused on three main areas: crime, young people and public health, with a particular emphasis on reducing the acceptability and availability of drugs to young people.

Strategy objectives for young people were to:

- discourage young people from taking drugs;

- ensure that schools offered effective programmes of drug education, giving pupils the facts, warning them of the risks, and helping them to develop the skills and attitudes to resist drug misuse;

- raise awareness amongst school staff, governors and parents of the issues associated with drug misuse and young people;

- develop effective national and local public education strategies focusing particularly on young people;

- ensure that young people at risk of drug misuse or who experiment with or become dependent on drugs, have access to a range of advice, counselling, treatment, rehabilitation and after-care services.

Since the fieldwork for this report the government has published its drugs strategy for the next ten years.[2] This argues that drug misuse amongst school children is increasing and that they are taking drugs at a younger age. The report states that multiple drug use is also increasing, especially amongst the young. It recommends that young people need to be prepared early so that they understand the risk to themselves of taking illegal substances. Effective drug education in school is seen as one important way to do this.

This chapter discusses older pupils' experiences of, and beliefs and attitudes about, the use of illegal drugs. Before presenting any results from the survey on these issues, there are a few points that require explanation. The first is that questions on drug awareness and use were only asked of young people in Years 10 and 11, which is therefore the base for most of the tables in this chapter. One point of interest concerns the fictitious drug 'nadropax'. This was included in the answer lists for the survey (as for other surveys in Britain covering drug use) in an attempt to determine whether young people were exaggerating their knowledge or usage of drugs. Two per cent of young people in Years 10 and 11 said they had tried the fictitious drug, and these were excluded from further analyses.

10.1 EXPERIENCE OF EVER TRYING DRUGS

Those in Years 10 and 11 were asked about their experience of and attitude towards non-prescribed drugs. They were asked whether they had ever used any of a number of drugs listed. This list included nadropax, a dummy drug which was used in order to try and make sure that there was no overstating of the drugs tried. By far the most commonly tried drug was cannabis, which 30% had tried and 17% had tried on three or more occasions. Levels of experimentation with this drug were higher amongst Year 11 students, with 36% having ever used the drug and 22% having tried it on three or more occasions. Although there was little difference between Year 10 girls and boys, boys in Year 11 were more likely to have tried cannabis on three or more occasions than were girls. Of those who had tried any drugs, 82% had tried cannabis (Tables 10a and 10b).

Levels of experimentation for crack (3%), heroin (3%) and cocaine (4%) seemed quite high for a survey of young people. This can be accounted for, in part, by some overstating by the young people. This overstating can be seen by 1% of the young people saying they had tried nadropax, the dummy drug. However, even in the nadropax-excluded sample the percentages remained quite high (2% had tried crack, 2% had tried heroin and 3% had tried cocaine) (Tables 10a and 10b and Figure 26).

Table 10a   **Experience of ever trying different drugs (%)**

	Total	Nadropax excluded
Those who had tried at all		
Cannabis	30	30
Glue or solvents	11	11
Gas to inhale	12	11
Amphetamines	11	10
Acid	7	6
Magic mushrooms	7	6
Amyl nitrite	6	5
Ecstasy	4	3
Cocaine	4	3
Tranquillisers	4	3
Crack	3	2
Anabolic steroids	3	2
Methadone	2	1
Heroin	3	2
Nadropax	1	N/A
Something else	1	1
Base	*4025*	*363*

Unweighted base: all in Years 10 and 11

Table 10b   Experience of ever trying different drugs, by sex and school year (nadropax excluded) (%)

	Total	Year 10		Year 11	
		Boys	Girls	Boys	Girls
Those who have tried at all					
Cannabis	30	24	25	37	33
Glue or solvents	11	8	12	11	11
Gas to inhale	11	9	13	12	10
Amyl nitrite	5	4	4	7	8
Amphetamines	10	8	7	14	12
Acid	6	5	5	9	7
Magic mushrooms	6	6	5	9	5
Ecstasy	3	3	2	5	4
Cocaine	3	3	3	4	4
Tranquillisers	3	1	4	4	3
Crack	2	1	2	2	2
Anabolic steroids	2	1	2	2	1
Heroin	2	2	2	2	1
Methadone	1	1	*	1	1
Something else	1	1	*	1	*
Base	*3932*	*987*	*1081*	*890*	*961*

Unweighted base: all in Years 10 and 11

Figure 26   Experience of trying drugs

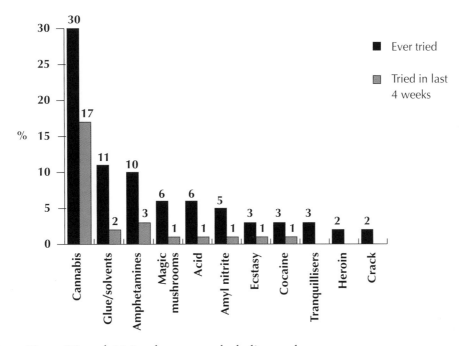

Base: Years 10 and 11 'nadropax-excluded' sample

The next highest levels of experimentation were for glue or solvents to inhale (11%) and gas/aerosols/butane/lighter fuel to inhale (11%). Amphetamines also had a similar level of experimentation (10%) as did magic mushrooms and acid (6% each) and amyl nitrite (5%) (Table 10b).

Levels of drug use were much the same for boys and girls. Where there were differences, in general levels of trying these drugs were slightly higher among boys than girls. The differences between the proportion of girls and boys trying drugs was often accounted for by a higher proportion of boys saying they tried the drug 'three or more times' rather than just trying once (Table 10b).

There were also some differences between Year 10 and Year 11 pupils, with those in Year 11 generally being more likely to have tried the drugs listed. In the discussion that follows all young people who have tried at least one drug will be referred to as experimenters (Table 10b).

10.2 AGE OF TAKING FIRST DRUG

Pupils in Years 10 and 11 who had tried one or more of the drugs listed were asked about the first drug they had taken and how old they had been when they first took it. The overwhelming majority said that the first drug they had taken was cannabis (66%) (Table 10c).

Table 10c   Drug first tried (%)

	Total	Nadropax excluded
First drug tried		
Cannabis	66	67
Amyl nitrite	3	3
Glue or solvents	3	3
Gas to inhale	2	2
Amphetamines	3	4
Acid	2	2
Magic mushrooms	1	1
Ecstasy	1	1
Cocaine	1	*
Tranquillisers	1	1
Crack	*	*
Anabolic steroids	*	*
Methadone	*	*
Heroin	*	–
Something else	1	1
Not stated	17	16
Base	*1472*	*1415*

Unweighted base: all in Years 10 and 11 who have ever tried drugs

Although a small percentage of young people had taken their first drug when they were as young as 10, most of those who had taken drugs had first tried them when they were 13 (26%) or 14 (32%) (Table 10d).

Table 10d   Age first tried drugs (%)

	Total	Sex	
		Boys	Girls
10	2	2	2
11	3	4	3
12	10	11	8
13	26	20	30
14	32	31	33
15	13	16	11
16	1	1	1
Not stated	13	16	11
Base	*1451*	*917*	*967*

Unweighted base: all in Years 10 or 11 who have ever tried drugs (nadropax excluded)

10.3   RECENT DRUG-TAKING BEHAVIOUR

Young people who had taken a particular drug were asked whether they had taken that drug in the last four weeks. For all drugs except cannabis, less than 30% of those who had ever used the drug had used it in the past four weeks and the majority of those who had, had used it once or twice in that time. This suggests that for most of the time, young people who had experimented with these drugs did not go on to use them regularly. However, a substantial minority had used them in the past four weeks, in this report defined as current users. It should be remembered that for some of these drugs the bases were very small, but the similar pattern across drug types does appear to be conclusive (Tables 10e and 10f).

Cannabis has a different pattern of usage to the other drugs included in the survey. Over half (54%) of those who had ever used the drug had done so within the last four weeks and nearly a quarter had done so three or more times. For the other drugs that young people had ever tried, a relatively small proportion had used them in the last four weeks. Six per cent of those who had ever used heroin, had used it three times or more in the past four weeks. Although this may, initially seem quite a high proportion, it should be remembered that this is 6% of those who have ever used heroin and indeed represents only four people in the nadropax-excluded sample (Tables 10e and 10f).

Table 10e **Whether taken drugs in the last four weeks (nadropax excluded) as a percentage of all who have taken that drug**

	Base	Not in the last 4 weeks	Once or twice	Three times or more	Not stated
Cannabis	(1158)	37	32	23	8
Amyl nitrite	(215)	67	16	7	10
Glue or solvents	(417)	60	16	6	18
Gas to inhale	(438)	57	18	9	15
Amphetamines	(398)	58	21	6	15
Acid	(250)	65	12	7	16
Magic mushrooms	(230)	64	16	4	16
Ecstasy	(125)	55	23	4	18
Cocaine	(123)	54	13	7	26
Tranquillisers	(111)	65	11	3	22
Crack	(67)	62	11	4	22
Anabolic steroids	(65)	49	11	1	38
Heroin	(63)	58	9	6	27
Methadone	(37)	35	19	6	41
Something else	(33)	27	9	9	55

Unweighted base: all in Years 10 and 11 who have ever tried drugs

Table 10f **Whether taken drugs in the last four weeks (nadropax excluded), by sex as a percentage of all who have taken that drug**

	Boys			Girls		
	Not in the last four weeks	Once or twice	Three times or more	Not in the last four weeks	Once or twice	Three times or more
Cannabis	33	31	27	42	32	18
Amyl nitrite	68	18	5	66	14	9
Glue or solvents	58	17	5	63	14	7
Gas to inhale	58	17	9	57	19	9
Amphetamines	54	22	5	62	20	6
Acid	62	13	10	68	11	5
Magic mushrooms	62	15	4	66	17	4
Ecstasy	45	31	3	68	12	3
Cocaine	49	11	11	59	15	3
Tranquillisers	64	17	–	65	7	5
Crack	60	15	9	23	3	–
Anabolic steroids	53	8	–	45	14	3
Heroin	53	11	11	65	7	–
Methadone	34	16	12	36	21	–

Unweighted base: all in Years 10 and 11 who have ever tried drugs

10.4 PERCEPTIONS OF DRUGS AND HEALTH

At least half the young people considered each type of drug listed to be very harmful if taken on a regular basis, with the exceptions of magic mushrooms (44% thought them very harmful), amphetamines (44%), amyl nitrite (43%), tranquillisers (42%) and cannabis (34%). Alcohol was thought to be very harmful by 12% and caffeine by 15%. Heroin, ecstasy and cocaine were thought very harmful by more than two thirds of the sample (Table 10g and Figure 27).

Figure 27   Whether consider drugs harmful if taken on a regular basis

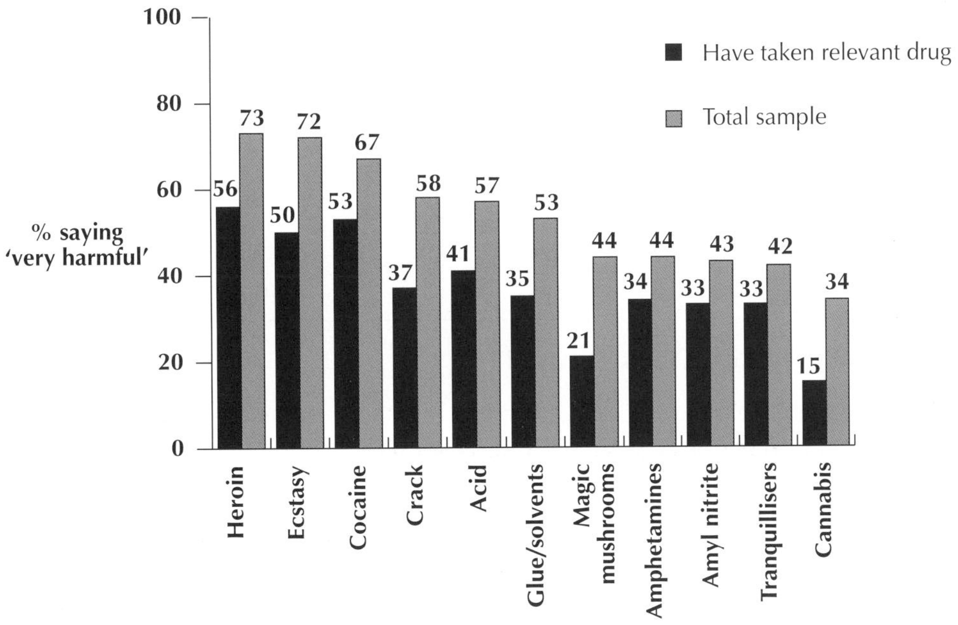

Base: all Years 10 and 11

As might be expected, if a young person had taken the drug in question, they were less likely to believe that it was dangerous. This result should be treated with some caution as the bases are very small and so differences may not be significant. However, the general pattern points towards young people who have tried a drug being less likely to think it is harmful than those that have not tried the drug. For almost all of the drugs, a higher proportion of girls than boys considered them 'very harmful' if taken on a regular basis (Table 10g).

Table 10g   **Perceptions of how harmful drugs are, by sex and whether ever used that drug (%)**

	Total	Have taken relevant drug	Sex	
			Boys	Girls
Those saying 'very harmful'				
Heroin	73	56	69	77
Ecstasy	72	50	67	78
Cocaine	67	53	64	69
Crack	58	37	57	59
Glue-sniffing	53	35	52	54
Acid	57	41	55	58
Tranquillisers	42	33	41	42
Magic mushrooms	44	21	41	46
Amphetamines	44	34	42	46
Cigarettes	22	NA	23	21
Amyl nitrite	43	33	44	43
Cannabis	34	15	31	38
Alcohol	12	NA	12	12
Caffeine	15	NA	16	14
Caffeine	*3993*		*1926*	*2054*

Unweighted base: all in Years 10 and 11

10.5 ATTITUDES TO DRUG TAKING

Finally, the young people were asked whether they agreed with a series of statements about taking drugs. The statements were largely about the positive effects of drugs and about their patterns of usage. Tables 10h and 10i show the proportions of young people agreeing ('agree strongly' or 'agree slightly') with each statement.

Less than one in five young people agreed with the statements 'drugs are not as harmful as people say they are' (16% agreeing at all, with 47% disagreeing strongly) and 'taking drugs is OK if it makes you feel good' (18% agreeing and 45% disagreeing strongly) (Table 10h).

There were higher levels of agreement for 'taking drugs is exciting' (23%) and 'it's OK to use soft drugs like cannabis but I'd never touch hard drugs like heroin' (34%), but here again the proportion of people disagreeing strongly matched or exceeded the proportion agreeing. Nearly half the sample agreed with the statement 'People take drugs to relax' (46%) (Table 10h and Figure 28).

Table 10h   Agreement with statements about drugs, by sex (%)

		Sex	
	Total	Boys	Girls
Those agreeing			
Taking drugs is exciting	23	25	22
Taking drugs is OK if it makes you feel good	18	19	16
Most young people will try drugs at some time	61	56	65
People take drugs to relax	46	44	48
It's OK to use soft drugs like cannabis but I'd never touch hard drugs like heroin	34	35	33
Drugs are not as harmful as they say they are	16	19	14
Base	*3993*	*1926*	*2054*

Unweighted base: all in Years 10 and 11

Figure 28   Attitudes to drug use

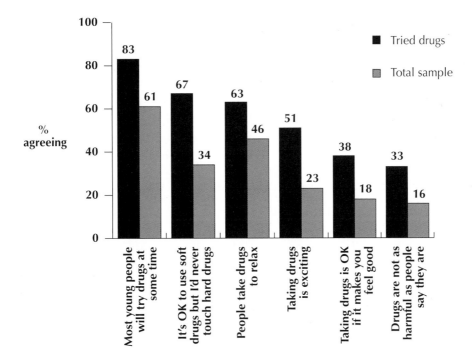

Base: all Years 10 and 11

Boys were slightly more likely than girls to agree with the statements 'taking drugs is exciting' (25% compared with 22% of girls), 'taking drugs is OK if it makes you feel good' (19% compared with 16% of girls), 'it's OK to use soft drugs like cannabis but I wouldn't touch hard drugs like heroin' (35% compared with 33% of girls) and 'drugs are not as harmful as they say they are' (19% compared with 14% of girls). As boys were marginally more likely to have taken drugs than girls, these results may be related to those given in Table 10i.

Young people who had tried drugs and were current smokers were more likely to agree with each of the statements. As will be discussed in Chapter 13, there is a strong correlation between smokers and those who have experimented with drugs and this might go some way towards accounting for the similar patterns of agreement (Table 10i).

Table 10i   **Attitudes to drug taking, by whether tried drugs and smoking status (%)**

	Tried drugs		Smoking status		
	Yes	No	Current	Lapsed	Never
Those agreeing:					
Taking drugs is exciting	50	8	42	21	8
Taking drugs is OK if it makes you feel good	38	6	35	13	6
Most young people will try drugs at some time	83	51	74	62	47
People take drugs to relax	63	38	57	44	36
It's OK to use soft drugs like cannabis but I'd never touch hard drugs like heroin	67	16	57	32	14
Drugs are not as harmful as they say they are	33	7	30	13	6
Base	*1472*	*1095*	*1924*	*1302*	*1373*

Unweighted base: all in Years 10 and 11

More than four out of five (83%) of those who had experimented with drugs agreed with the statement 'most young people will try drugs at some point' compared with just over half (51%) of those who had not experimented. The most dramatic differences of opinion between those who had experimented with drugs and those who had never tried drugs were over the statements 'it's OK to use soft drugs like cannabis but I'd never touch hard drugs like heroin' (67% of those who had experimented with drugs agreed with this compared to only 16% of those who had never tried drugs) and 'taking drugs is exciting' (50% compared with 8%). The former of the two probably reflects that the fact that over 80% of those who had experimented with drugs had tried cannabis (Table 10i).

For all the statements, those who had not tried any drugs were much more likely to say they could not answer than those who had. However, this was particularly pronounced for the statements 'taking drugs is exciting' and 'people take drugs to relax'. In each of these cases, nearly a quarter of all those who had never tried drugs said they did not know whether or not they agreed with the statement.

10.6 COMPARISON WITH 1995 WAVE

Since some similar questions about patterns of drug use were asked in the 1995 wave of Health Behaviour in School-aged Children, it is possible to analyse some of the trends that have occurred since then. For the purpose of comparability, only the Year 11 part of the 1997 questionnaire is used.

The proportion of young people using any of the drugs listed has remained broadly similar, although there appears to have been a small increase in those who had tried amphetamines and cocaine and a similar decline in those experimenting with acid and amyl nitrite (Table 10j).

Table 10j   Experience of trying drugs – comparison with 1995 wave (%)

	Year 11 1997 total (nadropax excluded)	1995 total (semeron excluded)
Those who had tried at all		
Cannabis	35	35
Glue or solvents	11	11
Gas to inhale	11	(included in glue or solvents)
Amphetamines	13	11
Acid	8	11
Amyl nitrite	7	10
Magic mushrooms	7	6
Ecstasy	4	4
Cocaine	4	2
Tranquillisers	4	3
Crack	2	1
Heroin	2	1
Anabolic steroids	2	N/A
Methadone	1	N/A
Something else	1	1
Base	*1858*	*1552*

Unweighted base: all in Year 11

One of the biggest changes between the two waves of this survey has been in young people's perceptions of how harmful drugs are. This is shown in Table 10k. Young people were less likely to say that a particular substance was harmful in 1997 than in 1995.

Table 10k   Perceptions of how harmful drugs are – comparison with 1995 wave

	1997 wave	1995 wave
Those saying 'very harmful'		
Heroin	78	82
Ecstasy	73	70
Cocaine	71	75
Crack	63	66
Glue-sniffing	58	69
Acid	58	59
Tranquillisers	43	46
Magic mushrooms	44	44
Amphetamines	46	48
Cigarettes	24	28
Amyl nitrite	45	55
Cannabis	33	32
Alcohol	12	12
Caffeine	15	15
Base	*1891*	*2135*

Unweighted base: all in Year 11

REFERENCES

1   *Tackling drugs together: a strategy for England 1995–1998.* (1995). London: HMSO.

2   *Tackling drugs to build a better Britain: the government's 10-year strategy for tackling drug misuse.* (1998). London: Stationery Office.

11 Injuries

Key findings

- Just under two in five young people (38%) had received an injury requiring treatment from a doctor or nurse in the past 12 months. (Section 11.1)

- Boys were more injury-prone than girls and the difference between the sexes increased as the young people got older. (Section 11.1)

- There was a higher incidence of injuries amongst young people who had been bullied (43%) and who had bullied others (46%). (Section 11.1)

- Young people who said they were 'very healthy' showed a higher incidence of injury (41%) than average, as did those who took part in 16 or more half-hour activity sessions per week (47%). (Section 11.1)

- Injuries most commonly occurred at home (24%) or at a non-school sporting facility (23%). (Section 11.1)

- Most injuries occurred when the young person was engaged in a hobby or leisure activity (43%) or playing sport (31%). (Section 11.2)

- Nearly half (48%) of the injuries did not result in any of the types of medical treatment about which the young people were asked. However, one in five of the injuries resulted in a cast being put on and only a slightly smaller proportion (16%) required stitches. (Section 11.5)

- One in ten of the injuries described by the young people occurred because someone meant to harm them; 12% of injuries to boys and 7% of those to girls occurred because someone meant to hurt them. (Section 11.6)

- Two-thirds of young people (65%) always wore a seat belt and a further one in six (14%) often wore a seat belt. (Section 11.8)

- Only one in ten of the young people always wore a helmet when they cycled and half never or rarely did so. Boys were more likely to say they rarely or never wore a helmet (58% of boys compared with 42% of girls). (Section 11.8)

Injuries are the greatest health problem facing school children in the western world.[1] The majority of deaths from injury throughout the world are among children and young people, with childhood accidents accounting for 27% of deaths among children under 15 years of age. Injuries represent the leading cause of death in the human life span.[2] Non-fatal injuries account for a large proportion of hospital stays and school days lost, as well as an unacceptable amount of life-time disability.[3] *The Health of the Nation*[4] specifically identified injury targets; these were:

- to reduce the death rate for accidents among children aged under 15 years by at least 33% by the year 2005;

- to reduce the death rates among young people aged 15–24 years by at least 25% by the year 2005.

This survey was carried out before the introduction of the government's Green Paper, *Our Healthier Nation* and therefore planned within the framework of earlier government strategy. However, the recent government Green Paper on health identified four priority areas for targets in their new health strategy and one of these was a reduction in the number of accidents. These targets build on those in *The Health of the Nation*. They aim to reduce the rate of accidents requiring medical attention by 20% by 2010 from the 1996 baseline.[5] A number of environmental recommendations in the paper were relevant for school children, including safer routes to school, making playgrounds safe and providing child pedestrian and cycle training. The Green Paper also recommended that whole-school approaches to health and safety should be undertaken.

Young people were asked whether they had had any serious injuries in the last 12 months. Those who had were asked in depth about their most serious recent injury and whether it required professional medical attention or time off school.

11.1 INJURIES REQUIRING TREATMENT FROM A DOCTOR OR NURSE

Just under two in five young people had received an injury requiring treatment from a doctor or nurse in the past twelve months: 20% had just one injury; 9% received two injuries and a further 9% suffered three or more injuries in that time. As shown in Table 11a, boys were more injury-prone than girls and the difference between the sexes increased as the young people got older. Year 9 pupils of both sexes were the age group most likely to receive an injury (45% for boys and 37% for girls); by Year 11 the proportion of girls who had received at least one injury had fallen to 28% whereas the figure for Year 11 boys was nearly the same as Year 9 boys at 44% (Table 11a and Figure 29).

Table 11a **Number of injuries requiring treatment from a doctor or nurse, by sex and school year (%)**

		School year				
	Total	7	8	9	10	11
Boys						
None	49	46	49	45	52	53
1	20	19	19	21	20	21
2	10	9	10	11	11	11
3	6	4	5	7	5	7
4 or more	6	6	6	6	6	5
Not stated	9	16	11	10	6	3
Base	*5063*	*1073*	*1011*	*1051*	*1009*	*917*
Girls						
None	61	54	58	58	63	71
1	20	21	19	22	20	16
2	7	7	7	9	8	6
3	3	3	3	4	3	3
4 or more	3	4	4	2	4	2
Not stated	6	11	9	5	3	2
Base	*5241*	*1105*	*1040*	*1042*	*1087*	*967*
Total						
None	55	50	54	51	58	62
1	20	20	19	22	20	19
2	9	8	8	10	9	8
3	4	4	4	6	4	5
4 or more	5	5	5	4	5	4
Not stated	8	13	10	7	4	2
Base	*10407*	*2193*	*2063*	*2102*	*2102*	*1891*

Unweighted base: all respondents

Figure 29 **Injuries requiring treatment by a doctor or a nurse in the past 12 months**

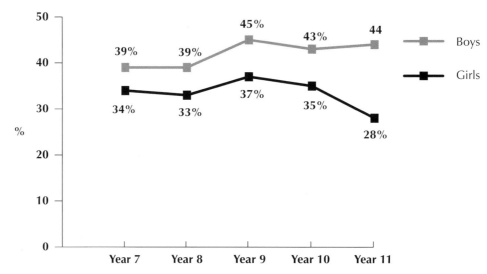

Base: all respondents (10407)

An above-average incidence of injuries was evident amongst young people who had been bullied (43%) and who had bullied others (46%). There were also higher rates of injury among those with a negative attitude to school (41%) and those who intended leaving full-time education and going into work, training or being unemployed at age 16 (45%). There is a suggested link between injuries and sports participation: those who claimed to be 'very healthy' had a higher incidence of injury (41%) than the average as did those who did 16 or more half-hour physical activities per week (47%) (Table 11b).

Table 11b **Number of injuries requiring treatment by a doctor or nurse, in the last 12 months, by psycho-social factors (%)**

| | Attitude to school | | Bullying | |
	Like school	Dislike school	Been bullied	Bullied others
None	56	52	52	49
1	20	20	22	22
2	9	9	10	12
3	4	6	5	6
4 or more	4	6	6	6
Not stated	7	7	5	6
Base	*7472*	*2767*	*5087*	*2906*

Unweighted base: all respondents

Young people who had been injured in the past 12 months were asked where they were when their most serious injury occurred. The most common places for injuries to occur were at home (24%) or at a non-school sporting facility (23%). In addition, one in five injuries described by the young people occurred at school, and a slightly smaller percentage (17%) occurred in the street (Table 11c).

Table 11c   Site of most serious injury, by sex and school year (%)

	Total	School year 7	8	9	10	11
Boys						
At home (yours or someone else's)	19	24	22	19	15	16
At school (including school grounds)	19	21	18	19	18	18
At a sports facility or field	29	22	25	28	35	35
In the street/road	18	16	19	18	19	18
In some other place	5	3	5	4	7	8
On holiday	1	1	1	2	1	*
In park/other public recreation area	3	5	3	4	2	1
Not stated	6	8	7	6	4	4
Base	*2144*	*415*	*399*	*485*	*433*	*411*
Girls						
At home (yours or someone else's)	30	38	35	24	27	27
At school (including school grounds)	22	20	20	25	26	18
At a sports facility or field	15	11	13	15	18	21
In the street/road	17	16	16	17	17	16
In some other place	8	4	7	7	7	15
On holiday	1	1	2	3	1	*
In park/other public recreation area	4	6	4	5	1	1
Not stated	4	5	4	4	3	1
Base	*1761*	*379*	*352*	*388*	*375*	*267*
Total						
At home (yours or someone else's)	24	31	28	21	21	20
At school (including school grounds)	20	21	19	22	22	18
At a sports facility or field	23	17	19	22	27	30
In the street/road	17	16	18	17	18	18
In some other place	6	3	6	5	7	11
On holiday	1	1	1	2	1	*
In park/other public recreation area	3	5	4	5	1	1
Not stated	5	7	6	5	3	3
Base	*3942*	*798*	*753*	*877*	*809*	*680*

Unweighted base: all respondents with an injury

Boys were more likely than girls to have been injured at a sports facility (29% compared with 15%). Girls were considerably more likely than boys to have been injured at home (30% compared with 19% of boys) and slightly more likely than boys to have been injured at school (22% compared with 19%). School year also appears to be a factor in where injuries occurred, with younger respondents tending to receive more injuries while at home, and older respondents at a sports facility (31% of pupils in Year 7 received their injury at home – compared to 20% of Year 11 pupils who were injured, whereas 30% of injuries occurring to Year 11 pupils occurred at a sports facility – compared to 17% of Year 7 injuries) (Table 11c).

Injuries incurred by ABC1 pupils were more likely than injuries to C2DE pupils to be sustained at a sports facility (27% compared with 20% of C2DE injuries). Conversely injuries to C2DE pupils were more likely to happen in the street or at home than those to ABC1 pupils (20% of injuries sustained by C2DE pupils occurred in the street compared to 15% of those sustained by ABC1 pupils and 25% of injuries to C2DE pupils occurred at home compared to 21% of those to ABC1 pupils). Those who reported being very healthy were also more likely to receive their injuries at a sports facility as were those who participated in 16 or more half-hour physical activity sessions (31% and 28% respectively compared to 23% of all injuries).

11.2 ACTIVITY AT TIME OF RECEIVING AN INJURY

Most injuries occurred when the young person was engaged in a hobby or leisure activity (43%) or playing sport (31%). Boys were equally likely to have received their injuries whilst involved in sports (38%) or another leisure activity (37%) whereas when girls had an accident it was more than twice as likely to have happened during a non-sporting leisure activity than a sporting one (49% compared with 22%). The difference in patterns of accidents is probably related to the greater participation in sporting activities by boys (Table 11d).

Table 11d   **What respondents were doing when most serious injury occurred, by sex and school year** (%)

		School year				
	Total	7	8	9	10	11
Boys						
Sports	38	32	35	38	41	46
Hobby/leisure activity	37	39	39	39	40	30
Paid work	1	*	*	*	1	1
At school	3	5	4	3	2	1
Working around the house	2	2	2	1	2	2
Sleeping, resting, eating washing or other vital activity	5	5	6	4	3	7
Other specified activity	3	3	1	3	4	3
Not stated	6	7	7	6	4	4
Base	*2144*	*415*	*399*	*485*	*433*	*411*
Girls						
Sports	22	16	19	29	22	21
Hobby/leisure activity	49	52	50	45	46	54
Paid work	1	–	–	–	1	4
At school	6	6	7	6	6	4
Working around the house	4	3	3	4	5	3
Sleeping, resting, eating washing or other vital activity	9	13	13	8	7	4
Other specified activity	3	2	1	3	5	4
Not stated	3	3	2	4	4	3
Base	*1761*	*379*	*352*	*388*	*375*	*267*
Total						
Sports	31	24	28	34	32	36
Hobby/leisure activity	43	45	44	41	42	40
Paid work	1	*	*	*	1	2
At school	4	6	5	4	4	2
Working around the house	3	2	2	3	4	3
Sleeping, resting, eating washing or other vital activity	7	9	9	6	5	6
Other specified activity	3	2	1	3	4	3
Insuffcient information	5	7	5	4	4	4
Not stated	5	5	5	5	4	4
Base	*3942*	*798*	*753*	*877*	*809*	*680*

Unweighted base: all respondents who were injured

11.3 PART OF THE BODY INJURED

Most injuries occurred to limbs (34% to legs and feet and 31% to arms and hands) and one in five injuries (18%) occurred to the young person's head. Sports injuries were more likely than injuries sustained doing other activities to occur to pupils' limbs and abdomen. The location of injuries did not vary much with school year or sex (Table 11e).

Table 11e   Part of the body injured (%)

Head	18
Neck	2
Thorax	2
Abdomen	5
Leg	17
Ankle, foot	17
Arm, shoulder	14
Wrist, hand	17
Unspecified location	5
Not stated	7

Unweighted base: all who had an injury

11.4 TYPE OF INJURY

About one in three (32%) of the injuries young people had cited as their most serious resulted in broken or dislocated bones, and just over a quarter (26%) in strained muscles. Other relatively frequent consequences of injury were cuts or puncture wounds, bruising and head or neck injuries (Table 11f). Injuries that occurred whilst the respondent was engaged in sports or leisure activities were more likely than injuries occurring during other activities to result in broken or dislocated bones (37% and 35% respectively). Similarly, strains and sprains were more likely to occur during sport (33%) or if pupils injured themselves while at school (31%). Those sustaining an injury while working around the house were more likely than average to receive cuts, puncture wounds or stab wounds (42% of those injured whilst working around the house received this type of injury compared with 19% of all those injured) (Table 11g).

Table 11f   Results of most serious injury (%)

Bone was broken, dislocated or out of joint	32
Sprain, strain or pulled muscle	26
Cuts, puncture or stab wounds	19
Bruises, black and blue marks or internal bleeding	19
Concussion or other head or neck injury, knocked out, whiplash	11
Burns	3
Other result	7
Not stated	6

Unweighted base: all who had an injury (3942)

Table 11g   **Main result of most serious injury, by activity at time of accident (%)**

| | | | | | | While sleeping eating, washing | |
| | | Hobby/ leisure activity (not sport) | Doing paid work | At school | Working around the house | or other vital activity | Other specified activity |
	Sport						
Broken bone	37	35	15	24	19	25	31
Sprain or strain	33	23	19	31	12	18	23
Cuts/punctures/ stab wounds	10	24	29	18	42	22	36
Bruises	16	23	27	17	12	20	33
Concussion	8	13	11	12	2	14	17
Burns	1	3	7	5	14	6	3
Other	7	6	4	8	6	11	8
Not stated	4	4	4	4	4	3	3
Base	*1206*	*1687*	*27*	*170*	*110*	*267*	*112*

Unweighted base: all who had an injury

11.5 SEVERITY OF INJURY

The young people were asked if they had received any of a number of types of medical treatment that are associated with the most serious types of injuries. Nearly half (48%) of the injuries did not result in any of the types of medical treatment listed. However, one in five (20%) resulted in a cast being put on and only a slightly smaller proportion (16%) required stitches. Only one in ten injuries resulted in an overnight stay in hospital and an even smaller proportion (7%) needed an operation (Table 11h).

Table 11h   **Severity of injury**

Cast put on	20
Stitches	16
Crutches or a wheelchair	11
Operation	7
Overnight stay in hospital	10
None of the above	48
Not stated	5

Unweighted base: all who had an injury (3942)

Given the small bases for some of the activities, it is difficult to see any significant difference in the severity of the injury that might be caused while involved in different activities. However, it does appear that sports injuries were somewhat less likely to require stitches than injuries that occurred while young people were engaged in other pursuits (Table 11i).

Table 11i   Severity of injury, by activity at time of accident (%)

				Activity at time of accident			
	Sport	Hobby/ leisure activity (not sport)	Doing paid work	At school	Working around the house	While sleeping, eating, washing or other vital activity	Other specified activity
Cast put on	21	23	8	18	10	15	17
Stitches	9	20	19	10	25	18	20
Crutches or a wheelchair	13	11	7	10	6	8	7
Operation	8	11	14	7	4	15	11
Overnight stay in hospital	6	7	7	3	8	7	10
None of the above	55	45	63	60	52	53	57
Not stated	2	2	–	1	3	1	3
Base	*1206*	*1687*	*27*	*170*	*110*	*267*	*112*

Unweighted base: all those who had an accident

Another way of assessing the severity of an injury is by looking at the number of days on which the young person missed school or their other usual activities. About half (53%) of the injuries resulted in the loss of at least one day.

11.6   INTENDED HARM

One in ten (10%) of the injuries described by the young people occurred because someone meant to harm them. Injuries to boys (12%) were more likely than those to girls (7%) to have occurred because some one meant to hurt them. Similarly injuries occurring to older pupils were more likely than those to younger pupils to have been as a result of this (Table 11j).

Table 11j   **Whether injury was a result of someone intending to harm young person, by sex and school year (%)**

| | Total | School year | | | | |
		7	8	9	10	11
Boys						
Yes	12	11	11	11	14	14
No	81	79	78	82	82	82
Not stated	7	10	10	7	4	4
Base	*2144*	*415*	*399*	*485*	*433*	*411*
Girls						
Yes	7	7	4	4	9	9
No	89	88	91	90	88	90
Not stated	4	5	5	5	3	1
Base	*1761*	*379*	*352*	*388*	*375*	*267*
Total						
Yes	10	9	8	8	12	12
No	84	83	84	86	85	85
Not stated	6	8	8	6	3	3
Base	*3942*	*798*	*753*	*877*	*809*	*680*

Unweighted base: all respondents

11.7 INJURIES NOT TREATED BY A DOCTOR OR NURSE

The young people were also asked on how many occasions they had had to miss a full day of school or other usual activity in the past 12 months as a result of an injury for which they were not treated by a doctor or nurse. Two in five young people (39%) said they had sustained an injury which required no treatment but resulted in their absence from school or another activity in the past year. For 5% of all pupils this had happened at least four times. Boys were slightly more prone to these injuries than girls. No real differences were apparent between the year groups (Table 11k).

Table 11k   **Number of injuries not requiring treatment from a doctor or nurse, by sex and school year (%)**

	Total	School year				
		7	8	9	10	11
Boys						
None	47	47	44	45	51	51
1	20	18	22	21	19	21
2	10	9	11	10	12	11
3	5	4	5	6	5	7
4 or more	6	5	6	6	7	7
Not stated	11	17	13	12	6	5
Base	*5063*	*1073*	*1011*	*1051*	*1009*	*917*
Girls						
None	57	57	57	55	57	62
1	19	18	17	21	20	20
2	9	7	9	9	12	7
3	3	3	3	5	4	4
4 or more	5	4	5	5	5	5
Not stated	6	12	9	5	3	2
Base	*5241*	*1105*	*1040*	*1042*	*1087*	*967*
Total						
None	52	52	51	50	54	56
1	20	18	19	21	20	21
2	10	8	10	10	12	9
3	4	4	4	5	4	5
4 or more	5	4	6	5	6	6
Not stated	8	15	11	8	4	3
Base	*10407*	*2193*	*2063*	*2102*	*2102*	*1891*

Unweighted base: all respondents

11.8   ACCIDENT PREVENTION

Two-thirds of young people (65%) always wore a seat belt and a further one in six (14%) often wore a seat belt when travelling in a car. However, 5% rarely or never wore such a safety device. There was little difference between girls and boys in the likelihood of wearing a seat belt but older respondents were less likely to do so than younger ones (70% of Year 7 pupils always wore a seat belt compared to 62% of Year 11 pupils) (Table 11l).

Table 11l   Frequency of using a seat belt in the car, by sex and school year (%)

	Total	School year 7	8	9	10	11
Boys						
Usually there is no seat belt where I sit	3	3	3	3	2	3
Always	62	65	62	62	61	59
Often	14	10	12	16	15	15
Sometimes	9	6	9	9	10	11
Rarely or never	6	4	4	5	8	10
I never travel by car	1	1	2	1	1	*
Not stated	5	10	7	6	2	2
Base	*5063*	*1073*	*1011*	*1051*	*1009*	*917*
Girls						
Usually there is no seat belt where I sit	2	2	3	2	2	2
Always	67	75	68	66	63	64
Often	15	11	13	17	18	17
Sometimes	8	4	7	8	11	11
Rarely or never	4	1	4	4	4	6
I never travel by car	1	1	1	1	1	*
Not stated	3	5	4	2	1	*
Base	*5241*	*1105*	*1040*	*1042*	*1087*	*967*
Total						
Usually there is no seat belt where I sit	2	3	3	2	2	2
Always	65	70	65	64	62	62
Often	14	10	12	16	17	16
Sometimes	9	5	8	8	11	11
Rarely or never	5	3	4	5	6	8
I never travel by car	1	1	1	1	1	*
Not stated	4	7	6	4	1	1
Base	*10407*	*2193*	*2063*	*2102*	*2102*	*1891*

Unweighted base: all respondents

The young people were also asked whether or not they wore a helmet when they cycled. Only one in ten (10%) always wore a helmet and half (50%) rarely or never did. Boys were more likely to rarely or never wear a helmet (58% of boys compared with 42% of girls). Older boys were more likely than younger ones to rarely or never wear a helmet (45% of boys in Year 7 rarely or never did compared to 64% of boys in Year 11). Girls in Year 9 were the least likely to wear a helmet (50% said they rarely or never wore one) whilst similar proportions of those in Years 7 and 11 did not wear a helmet (35% of girls in Year 7 and 37% of girls in Year 11 did not wear a helmet when cycling) (Table 11m).

Table 11m **Frequency of wearing a helmet when cycling, by sex and school year** (%)

| | | School year | | | | |
	Total	7	8	9	10	11
Boys						
Always	10	16	10	9	7	5
Often	7	11	8	7	5	4
Sometimes	8	10	11	8	6	6
Rarely or never	58	45	55	60	67	64
I do not ride bicycles	12	8	9	10	13	18
Not stated	6	10	8	6	3	2
Base	*5063*	*1073*	*1011*	*1051*	*1009*	*917*
Girls						
Always	10	22	13	7	4	4
Often	8	13	11	7	4	4
Sometimes	9	15	10	9	8	4
Rarely or never	42	35	44	50	43	37
I do not ride bicycles	28	10	17	25	40	50
Not stated	3	5	5	2	1	1
Base	*5241*	*1105*	*1040*	*1042*	*1087*	*967*
Total						
Always	10	19	11	8	6	4
Often	7	12	9	7	4	4
Sometimes	9	13	11	9	7	5
Rarely or never	50	40	50	55	55	50
I do not ride bicycles	20	9	13	17	27	35
Not stated	4	7	6	4	2	2
Base	*10407*	*2193*	*2063*	*2102*	*2102*	*1891*

Unweighted base: all respondents

11.9 COMPARISON WITH 1995 WAVE

Changes to the questionnaire between the 1995 and 1997 waves make a detailed comparison impossible, but it would appear that a similar proportion in 1997 to that in 1995 sustained injuries requiring treatment from a doctor or nurse.

REFERENCES

1   Committee on Trauma Research, Commission on Life Sciences, National Research Council and the Institute of Medicine (1985) *Injury in America*. Washington DC: National Academy Press.

2   Barss P., *et al.* (1991) *Injuries to adults in developing countries: epidemiology and policy.* Washington DC: The World Bank.

3   Harel, Y. (1988) 'Family psychosocial contributors to childhood injuries'. *Microfilm International* (vol. 49 (12), No. 8907049), Ann Arbour, MI.

4   Department of Health (1992) *Health of the nation: a strategy for health in England*. London: HMSO.

5   Department of Health (1998) *Our healthier nation: a contract for health*. London: The Stationery Office.

12 Sexual health

Key findings

- The topics which the most young people thought the school had not given them enough information on were lesbianism (44%) and homosexuality (42%). A third of all young people thought they had not received enough information on abortion or HIV/AIDS. (Section 12.2)

- Young people found sexual topics much easier to discuss with friends of their own age and sex, and girls tended to find discussing these topics with their friends easier than boys did. (Section 12.3)

- Almost as many young people (41%) found their mothers difficult to talk to about sexual topics as found them easy (42%), and only one in five (18%) found their fathers easy to talk to. Girls were much more likely than boys to find their mothers easy to talk to (51% compared to 31% of boys) and although boys found it easier to talk to their fathers than did girls, both sexes were more likely to find it easier to talk to their mothers. (Section 12.3)

- One in five thought their doctors were or would be easy to talk to about sexual matters. (Section 12.3)

- Two-thirds of young people in Years 10 and 11 said they got most of their information about sexual matters from school and a similar proportion (61%) said they got it from their friends. (Section 12.3)

- Nearly all young people had heard of HIV and AIDS but levels of knowledge about other sexually transmitted infections were much lower. (Section 12.4)

- Most young people (84%) thought that using a condom would protect them against sexually transmitted infections although somewhat fewer young people (69%) thought that not having sex would have the same effect. (Section 12.4)

- Nearly all of the young people asked had heard of the condom (94%), contraceptive pill (90%) and the female condom (89%). There were varying degrees of knowledge about other methods of contraception but generally girls were better informed than boys. (Section 12.5)

- Girls were more likely than boys to agree that if they wanted to have sex they would stop if they did not have a condom (72% compared with 56% of boys) and that a woman who carries a condom is sensible (79% compared with 73% of boys). (Section 12.6)

- Approximately half of all young people would feel embarrassed buying condoms in the shops. Girls were more likely than boys to say they would feel embarrassed (52% compared to 45% of boys). (Section 12.6)

Since September 1994, sex education has been mandatory in all maintained secondary schools and discretionary in primary schools. It must include teaching about HIV/AIDS and sexually transmitted diseases. In all schools, parents have a right to withdraw their child from sex education.[1]

The government Green Paper, *Our Healthier Nation*, highlighted sexual health, especially of teenage girls. It argued that teenage pregnancy has a number of adverse health effects, including the following. It harms the health of girls, their career chances and the health of their babies. Teenage girls who look after their young babies find that their education suffers and their ability to get a job is diminished. Poor living standards can result, which can lead to longer-term health problems. It also argues that a safe and responsible approach to sex is an important part of a healthy life and prevents the spread of sexually transmitted infections, including HIV.[2]

The survey asked pupils in Years 10 and 11 questions on their knowledge of sexual health issues and their attitudes towards condoms. Pupils were also asked where they obtained most of their information about sexual health issues.

12.1 SUBJECTS COVERED AT SCHOOL

All young people in Years 10 and 11 were asked if they had had lessons in school on a range of sexual topics. The results are reported in Table 12a. It should be noted that responses to this question were dependent upon pupils' ability to recall the lessons being asked about, and patterns of recall may vary with school year and sex and when the topics were covered.

Nearly all young people in Years 10 and 11 had had classes on 'How our bodies develop' (91%), sexual relationships (85%), contraception and birth control (84%) and pregnancy and having a baby (83%). By contrast, less than two in five had had lessons on homosexuality (37%) or lesbianism (35%). As would be expected, those in Year 11 were more likely than those in Year 10 to have had classes on all these topics, although the difference between the two years was most marked for abortion, how to use a condom and sexually transmitted infections other than HIV/AIDS (Table 12a and Figure 30).

Table 12a **Subjects covered at school, by sex and school year (%)**

		Year 10		Year 11	
	Total	Boys	Girls	Boys	Girls
Those who had had classes on					
Sexual relationships	85	82	84	86	88
Sexual feelings and emotions	73	72	73	75	73
How our bodies develop	91	85	92	91	94
Pregnancy and having a baby	83	74	85	84	87
Contraception or birth control	84	71	84	87	92
How to use a condom	68	58	62	77	76
Abortion	60	48	52	73	68
HIV/AIDS	76	69	70	83	83
Other sexually transmitted infections	73	63	67	80	82
Homosexuality	37	34	32	44	39
Lesbianism	35	32	30	42	35
Base	*3993*	*1009*	*1087*	*917*	*987*

Unweighted base: all in Years 10 and 11

Figure 30 **Topics discussed at school**

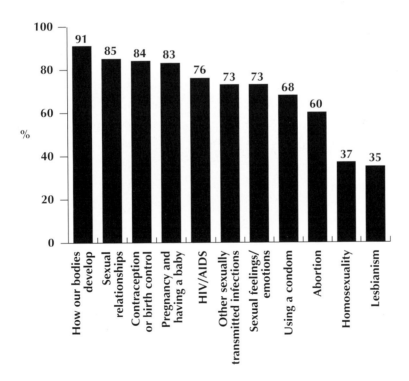

Base: all Years 10 and 11 (3993)

181

Girls were more likely than boys to recall having received lessons on most of the topics, particularly on contraception and birth control. Boys in both years were more likely than girls to recall having had lessons on homosexuality (39% compared with 35%) and lesbianism (37% and 33%). Also, although girls in Year 10 were more likely than boys to recall having received lessons on abortion (52% compared with 48%) by Year 11 this pattern had been reversed and 73% of boys compared to only 68% of girls recalled having received lessons on this topic (Table 12a).

12.2 SUBJECTS IN DEMAND

The young people were then asked if they felt that they had not been given enough information about any of the topics. A fifth (21%) of all those in Years 10 and 11 thought they had enough information on all the topics listed. The topics which the most young people thought the school had not given them enough information about were lesbianism (44%) and homosexuality (42%). In addition, a third of all these young people felt they had not received enough information on abortion or HIV/AIDS. Those in Year 10 were more likely than those in Year 11 to think that they had not received enough information on any particular topic (Table 12b).

Table 12b   **Topics young people thought they had not received enough information about, by sex and school year (%)**

		Year 10		Year 11	
	Total	Boys	Girls	Boys	Girls
Those who thought they had not had enough information on					
Sexual relationships	23	23	24	21	25
Sexual feelings and emotions	23	20	25	19	29
How our bodies develop	9	11	7	10	8
Pregnancy and having a baby	19	14	24	11	24
Contraception or birth control	19	17	25	13	20
How to use a condom	26	25	33	19	27
Abortion	33	25	46	21	41
HIV/AIDS	32	219	41	24	32
Other sexually transmitted infections	28	25	35	20	30
Homosexuality	42	34	51	30	51
Lesbianism	44	38	52	33	52
None	21	23	14	30	17
Base	*3993*	*1009*	*1087*	*917*	*987*

Unweighted base: all in Years 10 and 11; multi-coding possible

Boys were more likely than girls to think they had not received enough information on 'how our bodies develop' (10% compared with 7% of girls). On every other topic girls were more likely to feel they had not received enough information. This was particularly the case for information on abortion (43% of girls felt they had received insufficient information compared with 23% of boys) and homosexuality (51% of girls compared with 32% of boys) (Table 12b).

12.3 EASE OF DISCUSSING TOPICS TO DO WITH SEX

Those in Years 10 and 11 were also asked how easy they found it to talk to a range of people about sex-related subjects. Table 12c shows the proportion of young people who found it easy to discuss sexual matters with each of these people. Young people found it much easier to discuss sexual topics with friends of their own age than with anyone else on the list (71% said they found it easy to discuss such topics with their friends). Girls tended to find discussing these topics with their friends easier than boys did. A substantial proportion of young people also found it easy to discuss sexual topics with older friends (51%) and their boyfriends or girlfriends (46%) (Table 12c).

Opinion was divided about parents – almost as many young people found mothers easy to talk to about sexual topics as found them difficult (42% found them easy and 41% found them difficult) and only one in five (18%) found their fathers easy to talk to. Girls were much more likely than boys to find their mothers easy to talk to (51% compared with 31% of boys) and although boys found it easier to talk to their fathers than did girls, both sexes were more likely to find it easy to talk to their mothers (Table 12c).

Table 12c   **Ease of discussing topics to do with sex with different people, by sex and school year (%)**

	Total	Year 10		Year 11	
		Boys	Girls	Boys	Girls
Those who found it easy to discuss sex with					
Mother/stepmother	42	31	52	32	50
Father/stepfather	18	23	12	25	13
Older brother or sister	25	21	26	26	29
Teacher	12	11	12	11	14
Boyfriend or girlfriend	46	41	43	49	52
Friends of my age	71	55	81	64	85
Older friends	51	38	58	46	62
Doctor or GP	20	17	18	20	23
Family planning clinic	18	9	20	15	30
Base	*3993*	*1009*	*1087*	*917*	*987*

Unweighted base: all in Years 10 and 11; multi-coding possible

Health professionals – such as doctors or staff at family planning clinics – were seen as more approachable than fathers (18%) although for both GPs and staff at family planning clinics, a substantial proportion either did not know how easy they would be to talk to or had no contact with them. One in five (20%) thought their doctors were or would be easy to talk to about sexual matters but two in five thought they were or would be difficult to talk to. A similar proportion (18%) thought it would be easy to talk to people at the family planning clinic; only 22% thought they would be difficult to talk to (Table 12c and Figure 31).

Figure 31   Source of most information about sexual matters

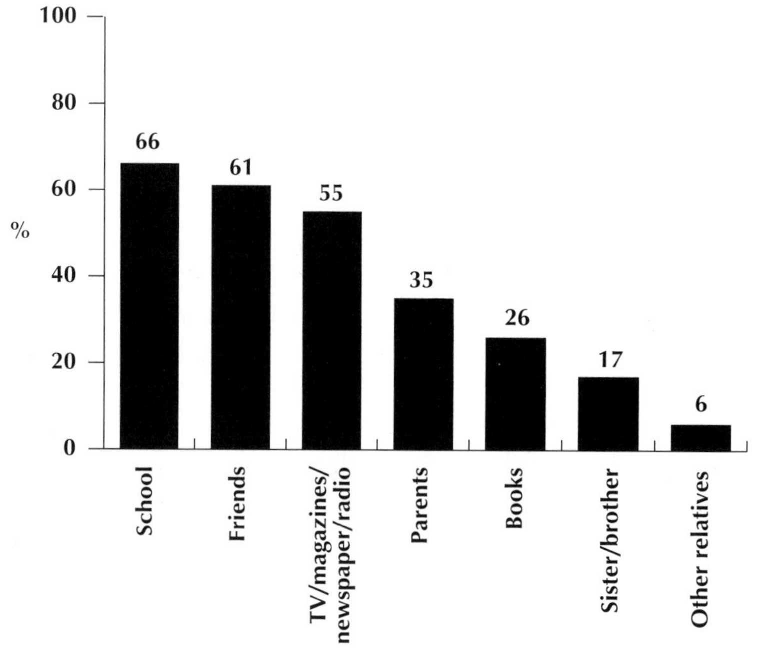

Base: all Years 10 and 11 (3993)

Two-thirds of young people in Years 10 and 11 said they got most of their information about sexual matters from school and a similar proportion (61%) said they got it from their friends. The media was also a useful source of information for young people, with over half (55%) receiving most of their information from this source. Parents were much less likely to be the main source of information on sexual matters. Girls were much more likely than boys to include their parents as a main source of information (41% compared with 29% of boys), and also friends (70% compared with 52% of boys) and the media (65% compared with 43% of boys) (Table 12d).

Table 12d   Main source of sexual information, by sex and school year (%)

	Total	Year 10		Year 11	
		Boys	Girls	Boys	Girls
Where get most information about sexual matters					
Parents	35	30	41	29	41
Sister/brother	17	14	18	18	19
Other relatives	6	5	7	6	9
Friends	61	49	66	55	74
School	66	62	65	70	66
TV/ magazines/ newspapers/radio	55	39	63	48	68
Books	26	25	24	27	29
Somewhere else	3	3	2	2	3
Not stated	7	12	6	7	3
Base	*3993*	*1009*	*1087*	*917*	*987*

Unweighted base: all in Years 10 and 11; multi-coding possible

12.4   KNOWLEDGE OF SEXUALLY TRANSMITTED INFECTIONS

The young people were asked if they had heard of a range of sexually transmitted infections, including a dummy infection, gonaditis. Nearly all young people had heard of HIV and AIDS but levels of knowledge about other sexually transmitted infections were much lower. Girls were more likely to have heard of all the infections; boys were more likely to claim to have heard of the dummy infection, gonaditis. Those in Year 11 were more likely than those in Year 10 to have heard of the infections (Table 12e).

Table 12e   Sexually transmitted infection knowledge, by sex and school year (%)

	Total	Year 10		Year 11	
		Boys	Girls	Boys	Girls
Gonorrhoea	39	24	38	40	53
Genital warts	57	38	61	55	75
Syphilis	33	22	28	40	45
Chlamydia	14	8	12	13	23
Gonaditis	10	9	6	16	8
HIV/AIDS	92	86	93	92	96
Herpes	51	37	47	56	68
Hepatitis B	60	48	58	64	71
NSU	11	8	9	15	12
Other	5	3	5	7	5
None of these	2	4	2	2	1
Not stated	5	9	4	5	2
Base	*3993*	*1009*	*1087*	*917*	*987*

Unweighted base: all in Years 10 and 11; multi-coding possible

Most young people (84%) said that using a condom would protect them against sexually transmitted infections, and 69% thought that not having sex would have the same effect. Over a quarter of young people (26%) said that the pill acted as a protection against sexually transmitted infections, and a similar proportion (28%) said the same about having a steady partner (Table 12f).

Table 12f   Beliefs about protection against sexually transmitted infections

	Yes	No	Don't know	Not stated
Not having sex	69	13	8	10
Taking the contraceptive pill	26	49	12	13
Using a condom	84	5	4	6
Using a female condom	60	13	16	10
Having a steady partner	28	43	18	12

Unweighted base: all young people in Years 10 and 11

Girls were more likely than boys to think not having sex, using a condom or using a female condom protected them against sexually transmitted infections whereas boys were more likely to think taking the pill or having a steady partner would protect them (Table 12g).

Table 12g   Beliefs about protection against sexually transmitted infections, by sex and school year (%)

	Total	Year 10		Year 11	
		Boys	Girls	Boys	Girls
Thought acted as a protection against sexually transmitted infections					
Not having sex	69	58	72	70	78
Taking the contraceptive pill	26	30	27	28	20
Using a condom	84	78	84	85	91
Using a female condom	60	54	61	57	70
Having a steady partner	28	31	25	32	24
Base	*3993*	*1009*	*1087*	*917*	*987*

Unweighted base: all in Years 10 and 11; multi-coding possible

12.5 CONTRACEPTION

The young people in Years 10 and 11 were also asked if they had heard of a number of methods of contraception.

Nearly all of the young people asked had heard of the condom (94%), contraceptive pill (90%) and the female condom (89%). There were varying degrees of knowledge about the other methods but generally girls were better informed than boys and, as would be expected, those in Year 11 were better informed than those in Year 10 (Table 12h).

Table 12h   **Knowledge of contraceptive methods, by sex and school year (%)**

	Total	Year 10		Year 11	
		Boys	Girls	Boys	Girls
Methods of contraception					
Condom	94	89	95	94	98
Female condom	89	81	91	91	95
Cap/diaphragm	78	59	81	82	89
Contraceptive pill	90	82	93	90	97
Emergency contraceptive pill	83	67	88	81	94
Coil/IUD	60	38	64	57	80
Barrier creams	52	40	54	53	63
Withdrawal	51	37	52	54	63
Rhythm method	47	34	51	43	58
Contraceptive sponge	37	31	35	36	46
Sterilisation	64	49	67	63	78
Injections/implants	51	42	52	46	62
Douching/washing	19	20	18	21	19
None of these	1	2	*	*	*
Not stated	5	9	4	5	2
Base	*3993*	*1009*	*1087*	*917*	*987*

Unweighted base: all in Years 10 and 11; multi-coding possible

12.6 ATTITUDES TO CONDOMS

Three-quarters (76%) of those in Years 10 and 11 agreed that 'a woman who carries condoms is sensible' and less than a quarter thought that it was 'the man's responsibility to carry condoms'. Two-thirds (65%) agreed that 'if they wanted to have sex they would stop if they did not have a condom' and three out of five (58%) thought 'using a condom shows people care for each other'. Only one in ten (11%) said they would be too embarrassed to suggest using a condom (Table 12i).

Table 12i   **Attitudes to condoms (%)**

	Agree strongly (100)	Agree (75)	Neither agree or disagree (50)	Disagree (25)	Disagree strongly (0)	Don't know	Not stated	Mean score
I would feel embarrassed buying condoms in shops	16	33	18	15	6	6	6	60.22
If I wanted to have sex I would stop if we didn't have a condom	33	31	11	9	5	5	6	71.75
Using a condom shows that people care for each other	22	37	22	7	2	4	6	68.97
It is the man's responsibility to carry condoms	7	16	28	30	10	3	6	44.46
I would be too embarrassed to suggest using a condom	3	8	18	39	22	4	6	30.59
A woman who carries condoms is sensible	32	45	10	3	1	3	6	78.32
I don't know enough about the risk of HIV/ AIDS to people like myself	7	17	23	24	11	10	7	45.58

Unweighted base: all in Years 10 and 11; multi-coding possible

Girls were more likely than boys to agree that if they wanted to have sex they would stop if they did not have a condom (72% compared with 56% of boys) and that 'a woman who carries a condom is sensible' (79% compared with 73% of boys). However, despite their agreement about the sensible nature of using condoms, they were more likely to 'feel embarrassed buying them in the shops' (52% of girls agreed this would be the case compared to 45% of boys), although girls in Year 11 were less likely to feel embarrassed than those in Year 10. Boys and girls were equally likely to agree that 'using a condom shows that people care for each other' (58%) and although only a minority of boys (29%) agreed that 'it was a man's responsibility to carry condoms', they were more likely to agree with this statement than girls (17%) (Tables 12i and 12j and Figure 32).

Figure 32   Attitudes to condoms

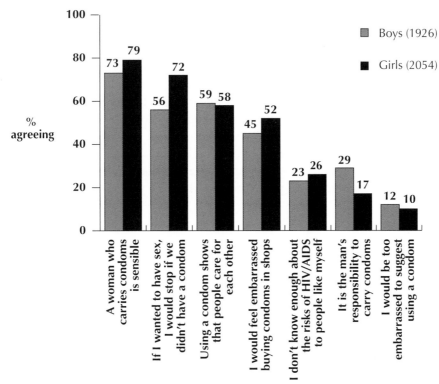

Base: all Years 10 and 11 (3993)

Table 12j   Agreement with statements about condoms, by sex and school year (%)

		Year 10		Year 11	
	Total	Boys	Girls	Boys	Girls
I would feel embarrassed buying condoms in shops	49	46	54	45	49
If I wanted to have sex I would stop if we didn't have a condom	64	55	72	57	71
Using a condom shows that people care for each other	58	57	58	60	57
It is the man's responsibility to carry condoms	23	30	21	28	13
I would be too embarrassed to suggest using a condom	11	13	11	11	8
A woman who carries condoms is sensible	76	70	75	77	84
I don't know enough about the risk of HIV/ AIDS to people like myself	25	25	29	21	23
Base	*3993*	*1009*	*1087*	*917*	*987*

Unweighted base: all in Years 10 and 11; multi-coding possible

12.7 COMPARISON WITH 1995 WAVE

The section of the 1997 questionnaire concerned with sexual health was greatly changed from the 1995 version. The 1995 questionnaire was more generally focused on health education, whereas in 1997 this section focused solely on sex education and attitudes to sexual health. The only comparable questions were those regarding ease of talking to various people about sexual matters. Table 12k shows that young people were slightly less likely to find their parents easy to talk to than in the previous wave (although this may be accounted for by the inclusion of step-parents in 1997, when these were previously asked about separately. However, young people seemed slightly more likely in 1997 than in 1995 to talk to other people about sexual matters. This was particularly true for girlfriends and boyfriends and professionals at family planning clinics (Table 12k).

Table 12k   Ease of discussing topics to do with sex with different people by sex – comparison with 1995 wave (%)

	1995 wave Year 11		1997 wave Year 11	
	Boys	Girls	Boys	Girls
Those who found it easy to discuss sex with				
Mother/stepmother	36	55	32	50
Father/stepfather	26	12	25	13
Older brother or sister	23	26	26	29
Teacher	13	14	11	14
Boyfriend or girlfriend	35	40	49	52
Friends of my age	58	80	64	85
Older friends	N/A	N/A	46	62
Doctor or GP	10	18	20	23
Family planning clinic	6	14	15	30
Base	*1001*	*855*	*917*	*987*

Unweighted base: all in Year 11; multi-coding possible

REFERENCES

1   Department of Health (1996) *The health of the nation – briefing pack*. London: HMSO.

2   Department of Health (1998). *Our healthier nation: a contract for health*. A consultation paper. London: The Stationery Office.

13 *Health risk behaviour*

Key findings

- There was a clear relationship between smoking, drinking alcohol and experimentation with drugs – smokers were more likely than non-smokers to drink alcohol, and drinkers were more likely than non-drinkers to smoke. (Section 13.1)

- Smokers and those who drank alcohol were more likely than non-smokers and non-drinkers to have tried drugs. (Section 13.1)

- Only 10% of current smokers saw themselves as 'very healthy' compared with 24% of those who had never smoked. (Section 13.2)

- Young people who indulged in one or more health risk behaviours were more likely to have experienced frequent symptoms of both physical and mental ill health. (Section 13.2)

- Smokers, drinkers and those who had experimented with drugs were less likely than those with healthier lifestyles to have eaten breakfast regularly, or indeed at all. (Section 13.3)

- Injuries were more common among young people who smoked, drank alcohol or had experimented with drugs. Young people who smoked, drank alcohol and had tried drugs were more likely to express negative feelings about school. (Section 13.4)

- Health behaviours such as smoking and drinking were good predictors of opinion – with the least positive attitudes being expressed by those whose behaviour may have brought them into conflict with teachers in their role as enforcers of school discipline. (Section 13.5)

- Half (50%) of those who currently smoked said they felt 'some' or 'a lot of pressure' from school work; in comparison, only a third (30%) of those who had never smoked felt this. (Section 13.6)

- Young people who smoked, drank alcohol or who had tried drugs were much more likely to spend time with friends after school. (Section 13.6)

- Although smokers and drinkers rated slightly more negatively in terms of self-esteem than those who did not indulge in these behaviours, there was very little difference between those who had experimented with drugs and those who had not. (Section 13.7)

- Those who had experimented with drugs were a little less likely to say they were very happy than those who had never tried them, but those who smoked, drank alcohol and, to a lesser extent, tried drugs were all more likely to have three or more friends than those who did not do these things. (Section 13.7)

> • There was very little difference between those involved in health risk behaviours and those not involved, in the number of half-hour or more moderate intensity activity sessions taken each week. (Section 13.8)
>
> • Comparisons with the 1995 wave of the survey showed similar relationships between drinking and smoking, with similar proportions of drinkers smoking. (Section 13.9)

So far this report has discussed a number of health behaviours in isolation. However, previous studies have found strong links between health risk behaviours, for example between smoking cigarettes and taking cannabis.[1] Secondary analysis work carried out on the 1995 HBSC data in England also found strong links between the risk behaviours. This chapter will look at the links between health risk behaviours and the type of young people indulging in them.

13.1 RELATIONSHIP BETWEEN DIFFERENT HEALTH RISK BEHAVIOURS

In terms of this report, health risk behaviours are defined as smoking, drinking and experimenting with drugs. There was a clear relationship between smoking and drinking alcohol. In each of the five year groups included in the sample those who were current smokers were more likely to drink alcohol. Pupils in Years 10 and 11 were also asked about drugs, and the link between smoking and trying drugs is even more evident: 68% of current smokers had tried drugs, compared with only 11% of those who had never smoked (Table 13a).

Table 13a Relationship between smoking and drinking by year (%)

		Smoking status		
		Current smoker	Lapsed smoker	Never smoked
Year 7	Drink alcohol	73	47	18
Year 8	Drink alcohol	81	48	22
Year 9	Drink alcohol	83	55	29
Year 10	Drink alcohol	89	67	42
Year 11	Drink alcohol	90	82	54

Unweighted base: all respondents

The drug most often tried – cannabis – is usually smoked, so the difference between smokers and non-smokers is perhaps understandable. However, the same pattern can be observed for all the other drugs listed in Table 13b, most of which are taken orally. This table also shows that 39% of Year 10 and 11 pupils who drank alcohol had tried cannabis compared with 9% of non-drinkers. In addition, in these two years, 47% of those who drank alcohol had tried at least one drug compared with just 14% of those who did not drink (Table 13b).

Table 13b   Having tried drugs – relationship between smoking, drinking and having tried drugs (%)

	Smoking			Drinking alcohol	
	Current	Lapsed	Never	Yes	No
Those who have tried at all					
Cannabis	63	23	5	39	9
Acid	16	4	2	10	2
Amphetamines	24	6	3	15	2
Ecstasy	8	2	2	5	2
Magic mushrooms	15	4	2	9	2
Amyl nitrite	13	5	1	9	1
Glue or solvents	23	8 ·	4	15	4
Gas/aerosols/butane/lighter fuel	27	6	3	16	3
Cocaine	8	2	2	5	2
Heroin	5	2	1	3	1
Tranquillisers	8	3	2	4	1
Crack	6	1	1	3	1
Anabolic steroids	5	2	1	3	1
Methadone	4	1	1	3	1
Nadropax	2	1	1	2	*
Base	*1294*	*1302*	*1373*	*2749*	*1212*

Unweighted base: all Years 10 and 11; multi-coding possible

Of those who had tried drugs, 32% had been drunk on ten or more occasions (compared with just 16% of all drinkers in Years 10 and 11). Twenty-six per cent of drinkers who currently smoked had been drunk more than ten times; indeed only 10% of these young people had never been really drunk. By contrast 33% of lapsed smokers who drank had never been really drunk and 46% of those who drank alcohol but had never smoked had never been drunk.

13.2   HEALTH RISK BEHAVIOUR AND SELF-REPORTED HEALTH

Only 10% of current smokers saw themselves as 'very healthy' compared with 24% of those who never smoked. At the other end of the scale 13% of smokers (twice the average proportion) saw themselves as 'not very healthy', as did 11% of those who had tried drugs and 8% of those who drank alcohol (Table 13c).

Table 13c   Self-assessment of health – relationship with health risk behaviour (%)

	Total	Current smoker	Drink alcohol	Tried drugs
Very healthy	20	10	18	15
Quite healthy	73	77	74	74
Not very healthy	6	13	8	11
Base	*10407*	*1979*	*5038*	*1472*

Unweighted base: all respondents

Young people who indulged in one or more health risk behaviours were also more likely to have experienced frequent symptoms of both physical and mental ill health – 56% of current smokers, 53% of those who had tried drugs and 48% of those who drank alcohol experienced irritability or bad temper at least once a week compared to just 42% of young people as a whole. Headaches were experienced at least once a week by four out of ten current smokers (40%) and a similar proportion of those who had tried drugs (39%) and about a third (34%) of those who drank alcohol. The overall proportion of young people experiencing headaches with this frequency was three in ten (30%) (Table 13d).

Table 13d   Symptoms experienced at least once a week and relationship with health risk behaviour (%)

	Total	Current smoker	Drink alcohol	Tried drugs
Irritability/bad temper	42	56	48	53
Difficulties in getting to sleep	31	39	34	37
Feeling low	28	41	32	37
Feeling nervous	31	34	32	32
Headache	30	40	34	39
Stomachache	19	24	20	20
Feeling dizzy	16	27	20	22
Backache	13	20	16	20
Base	*10407*	*1979*	*5038*	*1472*

Unweighted base: all respondents; multi-coding possible

Young people who indulged in one or more health risk behaviours were also more likely to have taken remedies for the specified ailments within the last month. The differences were particularly marked for headache (66% of those who had tried drugs, 64% of current smokers and 60% of those who drink alcohol had taken a tablet or medicine for headaches in the last month compared to 53% of young people overall) and stomachache remedies (33% of current smokers, 31% of those who had tried drugs and 26% of those who drank alcohol had taken a tablet or medicine for stomachache in the last month compared to 22% of young people overall (Table 13e).

Table 13e   Ailments for which tablets or medicine were taken in the last month – relationship with health risk behaviour (%)

	Total	Current smoker	Drink alcohol	Tried drugs
Headache	53	64	60	66
Difficulties in getting to sleep	5	6	6	6
Stomachache	22	33	26	31
Nervousness	3	4	4	4
Base	*10407*	*1979*	*5038*	*1472*

Unweighted base: all respondents; multi-coding possible

Young people who smoked or drank alcohol, or those who tried drugs (when compared to Years 10 and 11 as a whole), were more likely to report feeling tired in the mornings. More than one in three current smokers (36%) felt tired most school mornings compared with one in seven (15%) of those who had never smoked (Table 13f).

Table 13f   Frequency of feeling tired when setting off for school in the morning – relationship with health risk behaviour (%)

	Total	Current smoker	Drink alcohol	Tried drugs
Rarely or never	12	6	8	5
Occasionally	44	31	40	32
1–3 times a week	24	27	27	26
4 times a week	19	36	25	36
Not stated	1	*	1	1
Base	*10407*	*1979*	*5038*	*1472*

Unweighted base: all respondents; multi-coding possible

13.3 HEALTH RISK BEHAVIOUR AND EATING HABITS

The results of the survey also show a link between health risk behaviour and poor eating habits. Smokers, drinkers and those with experience of drugs were less likely than those with healthier lifestyles to have breakfast regularly, or indeed at all (in the case of drug experience, it should be kept in mind that these questions were asked only of pupils in Years 10 and 11, who were less likely to have breakfast anyway. Nevertheless there was a clear difference within Years 10 and 11 between those with and those without experience of drugs (Table 13g).

Table 13g   Frequency of eating breakfast before going to school – relationship with health risk behaviour (%)

		Base	Having breakfast every day	Never/hardly ever having breakfast
Total		(10407)	62	18
Smoker:	Current	(1979)	43	33
	Lapsed	(2983)	57	20
	Never	(5316)	72	12
Drink alcohol:	Yes	(5038)	55	23
	No	(5235)	69	14
Tried drugs:	Yes	(1472)	46	30
	No	(1095)	64	19

Unweighted base: all respondents

Smokers, drinkers and those who had experimented with drugs also tended to have eaten more snacks on the previous day than other young people (Table 13h). Smokers, drinkers and those who tried drugs all showed higher levels of concern about weight and a greater tendency to diet (Table 13i).

Table 13h   The frequency of eating snacks – relationship with health risk behaviours (%)

		Base	Having breakfast every day	Never/hardly ever having breakfast
Total		(10407)	28	38
Smoker:	Current	(1979)	27	41
	Lapsed	(2983)	27	39
	Never	(5316)	29	35
Drink alcohol:	Yes	(5038)	26	41
	No	(5235)	30	34
Tried drugs:	Yes	(1472)	28	40
	No	(1095)	29	36

Unweighted base: all respondents

Table 13i   Whether on a diet to lose weight – relationship with health risk behaviour (%)

		Base	Yes – on a diet	No – but should lose weight	No – because weight is fine
Total		(10407)	10	22	67
Smoker:	Current	(1979)	14	27	58
	Lapsed	(2983)	11	23	64
	Never	(5316)	7	20	71
Drink alcohol:	Yes	(8286)	12	24	63
	No	(1987)	8	20	71
Tried drugs:	Yes	(1472)	14	25	60
	No	(1095)	10	23	66

Unweighted base: all respondents

13.4   HEALTH RISK BEHAVIOUR AND INJURIES

Injuries were more common among young people who smoked, drank alcohol or experimented with drugs: 44% of current smokers, 42% of those who drank alcohol and 43% of those who tried drugs had been injured in the last 12 months compared with 38% of all respondents (Table 13j).

Table 13j   Number of injuries requiring treatment by a doctor or nurse in past 12 months – relationship with health risk behaviour (%)

	Total	Smoking status			Drink alcohol		Tried drugs	
		Current	Lapsed	Never	Yes	No	Yes	No
None	55	50	53	58	51	58	55	72
1	20	21	20	19	20	19	21	15
2	9	10	10	7	11	7	11	7
3 or more	9	13	10	7	11	7	12	5
Any injury	38	44	40	34	42	34	43	27
Not stated	8	6	7	8	7	8	2	1
Base	*10407*	*1979*	*2983*	*5316*	*5038*	*5235*	*1472*	*1095*

Unweighted base: all respondents; don't know/not stated answers not shown

13.5   HEALTH RISK BEHAVIOUR AND ATTITUDES TO SCHOOL

Further analysis shows that young people who smoked, drank alcohol or had tried drugs were more likely to express negative feelings about school. Only 10% of current smokers said they liked school 'a lot' compared with 34% of those who had never smoked, and the differences were even more marked in the younger age groups (in Year 7 15% of smokers said they liked school a lot compared to 46% of those who had never smoked). Similarly young people who did not drink alcohol were almost twice as likely as those who did drink alcohol to say they liked school 'a lot'. In Years 10 and 11, feelings about school were generally less positive, but negative views were more frequently expressed by those who had tried drugs (10% of those who had tried drugs liked school a lot compared with 23% of those who had not) (Table 13k).

Table 13k   Whether or not like school – relationship with health risk behaviour (%)

	Total	Smoking status			Drink alcohol		Tried drugs	
		Current	Lapsed	Never	Yes	No	Yes	No
Like it a lot	25	10	18	34	16	34	10	23
Like it a bit	47	39	52	47	47	47	41	52
Don't like it very much	18	27	20	13	22	13	28	19
Don't like it at all	9	23	8	4	14	5	20	6
Not stated	2	1	1	1	1	2	1	1
Base	*10407*	*1979*	*2983*	*5316*	*5038*	*5235*	*1472*	*1095*

Unweighted base: all respondents; don't know/not stated answers not shown

Attitudes towards school were explored in greater detail through a series of attitude statements with which respondents were invited either to agree or disagree. In the first set of general statements about school, young people who took risks with their health were less likely to agree that school was 'a nice place to be' and that school rules were fair than those who did not take risks (Table 13l).

Table 13l   **Attitude towards school and school rules – relationship with health risk behaviour (%)**

	Total	Smoking status			Drink alcohol		Tried drugs	
		Current	Lapsed	Never	Yes	No	Yes	No
I feel that I belong at this school	57	46	54	64	52	62	50	58
Our school is a nice place to be	48	32	43	57	40	56	35	47
The rules in this school are fair	54	35	48	64	44	64	36	52
The pupils are treated too severely/ strictly at this school	27	38	29	21	32	22	33	18
In our school the pupils take part in making rules	31	28	29	33	29	33	25	24
Base	*10407*	*1979*	*2983*	*5316*	*5038*	*5235*	*1472*	*1095*

Unweighted base: all respondents; multi-coding possible

A second set of statements focused more specifically on attitudes towards teachers. Health behaviours such as smoking and drinking were good predictors of opinion – with the least positive attitudes being expressed by those who indulged in health risk behaviour. Again it was the concept of fair treatment which showed the widest divergence between the views of those who did and did not take risks with their health (Table 13m).

Table 13m   **Attitude towards teachers – relationship with health risk behaviour (%)**

	Total	Smoking status			Drink alcohol		Tried drugs	
		Current	Lapsed	Never	Yes	No	Yes	No
When I need extra help I can get it	70	59	68	75	65	75	65	75
I am encouraged to express my own views in my class(es)	59	55	59	61	57	61	57	63
Our teachers treat us fairly	56	37	52	66	46	66	37	57
My teachers are interested in me as a person	39	30	36	43	34	43	33	42
Base	*10407*	*1979*	*2983*	*5316*	*5038*	*5235*	*1472*	*1095*

Unweighted base: all respondents; multi-coding possible

Attitudes towards teachers were, of course, very likely to be influenced by what the teachers thought of the pupil and his or her academic performance. Over half (56%) of current smokers said that their class teacher's assessment of their performance would be 'average' or 'below average' compared with only a quarter (26%) of those who had never smoked. Although not so marked, a similar pattern was apparent in relation to those indulging in other risk behaviours (Table 13n).

Table 13n   **Teacher's opinion of school performance – relationship with health risk behaviour (%)**

	Total	Smoking status			Drink alcohol		Tried drugs	
		Current	Lapsed	Never	Yes	No	Yes	No
Very good	18	8	13	24	13	23	9	23
Good	44	34	45	47	41	47	37	48
Average	31	43	36	24	36	26	40	25
Below average	4	13	4	2	7	2	12	2
Not stated	3	2	2	3	2	3	1	1
Base	*10407*	*1979*	*2983*	*5316*	*5038*	*5235*	*1472*	*1095*

Unweighted base: all respondents

There was also evidence from the survey that young people who adopted health risk behaviours were more likely to feel pressurised by school-work, and burdened by too high expectations from parents and teachers. In contrast their own expectations of continuing academic study once they reached school leaving age were below average (Table 13o).

Table 13o   **How pressured by school-work – relationship with health risk behaviour (%)**

	Total	Smoking status			Drink alcohol		Tried drugs	
		Current	Lapsed	Never	Yes	No	Yes	No
Not at all	16	10	14	20	12	21	8	9
A little	45	38	46	48	43	48	34	47
Some	22	26	24	20	25	19	29	26
A lot	14	24	14	10	18	9	27	17
Not stated	2	2	2	2	2	2	1	1
Base	*10407*	*1979*	*2983*	*5316*	*5038*	*5235*	*1472*	*1095*

Unweighted base: all respondents

Half (50%) of those who currently smoked said they felt 'some' or 'a lot of pressure' from school-work; in comparison to only a third (30%) of those who had never smoked. This is partly due to the fact that feeling pressure and smoking both increase with school year, but a substantial difference still remains even after this has been taken into account. Indeed, the difference between current smokers and those who had never smoked was more marked in the younger age groups, as by Year 11 most young people were feeling some pressure (Table 13o).

Similarly, around half of all smokers agreed that parents (51%) and teachers (53%) expected too much of them, compared with under a third of those who had never smoked. Those (30%) who drank alcohol were also more likely to say this. The differences can be observed within each year group, although they were most marked in Years 7, 8 and 9 (Table 13p).

Table 13p   Whether respondents feel too much was expected by parents and teachers – relationship with health risk behaviour (%)

Those agreeing that too much was expected		Base	By parents	By teachers
Total			37	39
Smoking:	Current	(1079)	51	53
	Lapsed	(2983)	39	42
	Never	(5316)	30	31
Drink alcohol:	Yes	(5038)	44	46
	No	(5235)	30	31
Tried drugs:	Yes	(1472)	49	51
	No	(1095)	34	39

Unweighted base: all respondents

Young people's expectations of what they would be doing once they reached age 16 also varied according to health risk behaviour. As shown in Table 13q, those who indulged in risky behaviour were less confident of doing A levels and more likely to expect that they would be leaving full-time education at 16 (Table 13q).

Table 13q   **Expectations for age 16 – relationship with health risk behaviour**

	Total	Smoking status			Drink alcohol		Tried drugs	
		Current	Lapsed	Never	Yes	No	Yes	No
At school/college doing A levels	50	38	49	55	46	54	43	55
At school/college doing some other course	15	21	17	12	17	13	22	21
Full-time job	7	9	8	6	8	6	8	4
Apprenticeship/ training	5	9	6	3	7	3	10	7
Unemployed	1	2	*	*	1	*	2	*
Employment training course	1	2	1	1	2	1	2	2
Don't know	16	15	15	18	14	18	10	9
Not stated	5	4	4	4	4	5	2	3
Base	*10407*	*1979*	*2983*	*5316*	*5038*	*5235*	*1472*	*1095*

Unweighted base: all respondents

A picture is gradually emerging of young smokers and those who drink alcohol who find the school environment less agreeable and more pressurised than young people who abstain from these behaviours. The next set of results reveal the extent to which their sense of alienation may perhaps have affected their relationships with other young people at school.

It is clear from the analysis presented in Chapter 3 that being bullied and bullying others were strongly associated. Here the relationships between being bullied, bullying other people and health risk behaviours are explored. The results are shown for each year individually to indicate the much greater divergence between risk-takers and other young people in the pre-GCSE years. Those who smoked and drank alcohol at an early age were, perhaps not surprisingly, a more extreme group in terms of behaviour (Table 13r).

Current smokers and those who drank alcohol were more likely than those who had not adopted these behaviours to bully others. Risk behaviour did not affect whether the pupils were bullied themselves (Table 13r).

Table 13r **Experience of bullying at school – relationship with health risk behaviour**

		Base	Ever been bullied at school	Ever bullies others at school
Total		10407	49	28
Year 7:	Smoker	86	52	50
	Non-smoker	1683	45	16
	Drinks alcohol	537	50	31
	Non-drinker	1617	46	17
Year 8:	Smoker	217	53	50
	Non-smoker	1249	47	17
	Drinks alcohol	736	49	37
	Non-drinker	1290	48	19
Year 9:	Smoker	370	54	50
	Non-smoker	986	50	18
	Drinks alcohol	1080	52	38
	Non-drinker	994	49	21
Year 10:	Smoker	631	55	45
	Non-smoker	783	49	20
	Drinks alcohol	1343	49	38
	Non-drinker	740	55	21
Year 11:	Smoker	663	49	47
	Non-smoker	590	50	21
	Drinks alcohol	1406	48	38
	Non-drinker	472	52	23

Unweighted base: all respondents

13.6 HEALTH RISK BEHAVIOUR AND RELATIONSHIPS WITH FAMILY AND FRIENDS

Young people taking risks with their health were less certain of parental support at school. The difference was fairly slight overall, as shown in Table 13s, although more substantial when examined within individual years. In particular, young risk-takers were less likely to believe that their parents would always be ready to help them if they had a problem at school.

Table 13s   **Parents' involvement with school – relationship with health risk behaviour (%)**

	Total	Smoking status			Drink alcohol		Tried drugs	
		Current	Lapsed	Never	Yes	No	Yes	No
Those saying 'always'								
My parents encourage me to do well at school	79	73	78	82	77	82	75	84
If I have a problem at school, my parents are ready to help	68	59	66	73	63	74	60	69
My parents are willing to come to school and talk to teachers	63	57	62	66	59	67	59	68
Base	*10407*	*1979*	*2983*	*5316*	*5038*	*5235*	*1472*	*1095*

Unweighted base: all respondents; multi-coding possible

It was clear that the young people with the least healthy behaviour were also those who found it most difficult to talk to parents – especially fathers. Of those in Years 10 and 11, 44% of smokers and 46% of those who had taken drugs said they found it difficult to talk to their fathers, compared to 37% of lapsed smokers and 40% of those who had not taken any drugs in the same year groups (Table 13t).

Table 13t   **Ease of talking to parents and friends about important things – relationship with health risk behaviour (%)**

	Total	Smoking status			Drink alcohol		Tried drugs	
		Current	Lapsed	Never	Yes	No	Yes	No
Those saying 'very easy'/'easy' to talk to								
Mother	77	68	78	81	74	81	70	79
Father	51	39	48	58	48	55	42	51
Friends of same sex	74	81	76	71	76	72	84	81
Friends of opposite sex	45	65	50	34	56	34	72	55
Base	*10407*	*1979*	*2983*	*5316*	*5038*	*5235*	*1472*	*1095*

Unweighted base: all respondents; multi-coding possible

Communication with friends did seem to be easier for young people whose behaviour was less healthy; although this was partly an age effect, age does not explain all of the difference. Of those in Years 10 and 11 who had experimented with drugs, 72% said they found it easy to talk to friends of the opposite sex about things that really bothered them, compared with 55% who had not (Table 13t).

The analysis by health behaviour also reveals some major, and extremely interesting, differences on friendship norms, with young people who smoked, drank alcohol or who had tried drugs all being much more likely to spend time with friends. Of those who had experimented with drugs, 54% went out with friends straight after school four or five times a week, and a similar proportion went out on at least five evenings. The equivalent figures for Years 10 and 11 combined who had never tried drugs were 32% and 23% respectively. Differences between smokers and non-smokers, and drinkers and non-drinkers in these years followed the same pattern, although for drinkers, they were not quite so extreme (Table 13u).

Table 13u   Spending time with friends – relationship with health risk behaviour (%)

		Smoking status			Drink alcohol		Tried drugs	
	Total	Current	Lapsed	Never	Yes	No	Yes	No
Spend time with friends after school								
4–5 days a week	38	57	40	29	45	30	54	32
5+ evenings a week	32	53	35	21	40	23	51	23
Base	*10407*	*1979*	*2983*	*5316*	*5038*	*5235*	*1472*	*1095*

Unweighted base: all respondents; multi-coding possible

13.7 HEALTH RISK BEHAVIOUR AND SELF-ESTEEM

It could be hypothesised that that there would be a negative relationship between risk-taking behaviours and indicators of self-esteem such as loneliness, happiness, confidence and helplessness – the ability to make friends and be at ease with others and oneself. In fact, although smokers and drinkers rated slightly more negatively on each of these scales than those who did not indulge in these behaviours, there was very little difference between those who had experimented with drugs and those who had not. Drugs experimenters were a little less likely to say they were very happy than those who had never tried them but those that smoked, drank alcohol and, to a lesser extent tried drugs, were all more likely to have three or more friends than those who did not engage in these behaviours (Table 13v).

Table 13v   **How happy pupils are, by health risk behaviour (%)**

	Total	Smoking status			Drink alcohol		Tried drugs	
		Current	Lapsed	Never	Yes	No	Yes	No
Feeling very happy	35	23	30	41	29	40	24	30
Never lonely	48	45	49	49	48	48	48	49
Always/often confident	56	49	55	59	54	57	56	56
Rarely/never helpless	63	58	64	65	62	64	64	65
3 or more close friends	74	78	76	72	78	71	80	79
Base	*10407*	*1979*	*2983*	*5316*	*5038*	*5235*	*1472*	*1095*

Unweighted base: all respondents; multi-coding possible

There is, however, strong evidence of links between satisfaction with one's own body and health risk behaviour. Over half of current smokers (57%), compared with a third (36%) of those who had never smoked, wanted some change and those who drank alcohol were also more likely to be dissatisfied with their bodies than non-drinkers (38% of those who did not drink alcohol wanted to change some aspect of their body compared to 50% of those who did drink alcohol). The difference in average age between smokers and non-smokers, and those who drink alcohol and those who do not, is of course at least part of the reason for this variation, since concern about personal appearance increased with school year. However, a substantial difference remained within each year group between smokers and non-smokers. Smokers, those who drank alcohol and those who had tried drugs were all more likely to think they were too fat (Tables 13w and 13x).

Table 13w   **Whether respondents want to change some aspect of their bodies (%)**

	Base	Wanting to change something
	10407	44
Total smoking:		
Current	1979	57
Lapsed	2983	50
Never	5316	36
Drink alcohol:		
Yes	5038	50
No	5235	38
Tried drugs:		
Yes	1472	60
No	1095	50

Unweighted base: all respondents

Table 13x **Satisfaction with physical appearance – relationship with health risk behaviour (%)**

Total		Base	Too thin	About right	Too fat	Don't think about it
		10407	13	47	29	5
Smoker:						
	Current	1979	13	40	38	5
	Lapsed	2983	13	45	32	5
	Never	5316	13	50	25	6
Drink alcohol:						
	Yes	5038	12	44	34	5
	No	5235	13	49	25	6
Tried drugs:						
	Yes	1472	13	43	38	5
	No	1095	13	47	35	5

Unweighted base: all respondents

13.8 HEALTH RISK BEHAVIOUR AND EXERCISE

There was very little difference between those involved in any health risk behaviour and the number of half-hour or more activity sessions taken each week (Table 13y).

Table 13y **Number of half-hour activity sessions participated in, by health risk behaviour (%)**

		Base	11+ half-hour sessions
Smoker:			
	Current	(1979)	35
	Lapsed	(2983)	38
	Never	(5316)	35
Drink alcohol:			
	Yes	(5038)	37
	No	(5235)	35
Tried drugs:			
	Yes	(1472)	33
	No	(1095)	32

Unweighted base: all respondents

13.9 COMPARISON WITH 1995 WAVE

Compared with the 1995 wave, the survey showed similar relationships between drinking and smoking, with similar proportions of drinkers smoking (Table 13z).

Table 13z   **Relationship between smoking and drinking, by year – comparison with 1995 wave (%)[†]**

		Smoking status	
		Current smoker	Never smoked
Year 7	Drink alcohol	61 (65)	18 (19)
Year 9	Drink alcohol	82 (81)	29 (30)
Year 11	Drink alcohol	90 (92)	54 (54)

Unweighted base: all respondents
[†]1995 figures appear in brackets

Similarly, the likelihood of current smokers and those who drank alcohol also taking drugs had changed very little. For some drugs, particularly cannabis and acid, a small drop in the overall proportion of young people who had tried the drug resulted in a similar drop in the proportion of current smokers who had tried cannabis (Table 13aa).

Table 13aa   **Year 11 having tried drugs – relationship with smoking and drinking – comparison with 1995 wave (%)[†]**

	Smoking status			Drinking alcohol	
	Current	Lapsed	Never	Yes	No
Those who have tried at all					
Cannabis	67 (75)	29 (32)	6 (7)	44 (47)	10 (13)
Acid	19 (33)	4 (7)	3 (1)	11 (18)	4 (3)
Amphetamines	30 (30)	9 (9)	3 (1)	18 (17)	3 (4)
Ecstasy	11 (27)	3 (9)	2 (2)	7 (15)	2 (6)
Magic mushrooms	15 (25)	5 (7)	3 (1)	10 (14)	3 (3)
Amyl nitrite	17 (18)	6 (6)	2 (1)	11 (11)	1 (2)
Glue or solvents	24 (14)	7 (2)	4 (1)	15 (11)	4 (2)
Cocaine	10 (8)	3 (3)	2 (*)	6 (7)	2 (2)
Heroin	5 (7)	1 (1)	2 (*)	3 (3)	2 (1)
Tranquillisers	8 (5)	2 (1)	2 (*)	5 (2)	2 (1)
Crack	8 (2)	* (*)	1 (*)	4 (1)	1 (*)
Nadropax (semeron)	3 (2)	* (*)	1 (*)	2 (1)	1(1)
1997 base	*663*	*626*	*590*	*1406*	*472*
(1995 base)	*(638)*	*(570)*	*(631)*	*(1397)*	*(457)*

Unweighted base: all Year 11; multi-coding possible
[†]1995 figures shown in brackets

REFERENCE

1 Hansbro, J., Bridgwood, A., Morgan, A. and Hickman, M. (1997) *Health in England 1996: what people know, what people think, what people do*. London: The Stationery Office.

Appendix
The questionnaire

52944 (1-5)   R.N.   (6-10) Card ① (11)

Assignment number [   ][   ][   ][   ] (12-16)   Date [   ] / [   ] / **9 7** (17-22)

Year [**7** | **8** | **9** | **10** | **11**] (23)
       1   2   3   4   5

YEARS 10–11

YOUNG PEOPLE'S HEALTH & LIFESTYLE
1997 QUESTIONNAIRE

Thank you for helping us with this survey. By answering these questions you will help us to find out more about the way that young people in England live.

Your answers will be looked at by the survey study team and by no one else. They will **NOT** be seen by your parents or teachers. There is no need to write your name on the questionnaire. After you have filled it in, you can put it in the envelope provided and seal it.

In most questions you will be asked to place a tick ☑ in the box that best fits your answer, for example:

Do you like football?   Yes ☐

                              No ☑

In other questions, a line is given where you can write your answer, for example:

✍   This is my answer

Some of the questions contain instructions telling you which question to answer next. Following these instructions means that you won't have to answer any questions that don't apply to you. For example:

Do you like Mondays?   Yes ☑ ☞ **Go to question 12**

                          No ☐ ☞ **Go on to question 18**

Take your time to read each question carefully in turn and answer it as best as you can. Please go on to the next question unless you are instructed otherwise.

Remember that we are only interested in your opinion – this is not a test.

ABOUT YOU

1. Are you a boy or a girl? (24)
Please tick one box

Boy ☐ 1

Girl ☐ 2

2. What month were you born? (25-26)
Please tick one box

Jan	Feb	Mar	Apr	May	Jun	Jul	Aug	Sep	Oct	Nov	Dec
☐	☐	☐	☐	☐	☐	☐	☐	☐	☐	☐	☐
01	02	03	04	05	06	07	08	09	10	11	12

3. What year were you born? (27)
Please tick one box

1980	1981	1982	1983	1984	1985	1986
☐ 1	☐ 2	☐ 3	☐ 4	☐ 5	☐ 6	☐ 7

4. What year are you in at school? (28)
Please tick one box

Year 7   (First year) ☐ 1

Year 8   (Second year) ☐ 2

Year 9   (Third year) ☐ 3

Year 10 (Fourth year) ☐ 4

Year 11   (Fifth year) ☐ 5

5. What kind of place do you live in? (29)
Please tick one box

City or very large town including suburbs ☐ 1

Town ☐ 2

Village ☐ 3

Countryside ☐ 4

212

HEALTH

6. How healthy do you think you are? (30)
Please tick one box

Very healthy ☐1

Quite healthy ☐2

Not very healthy ☐3

7. In general, how do you feel about your life at present? (31)
Please tick one box

I feel very happy ☐1

I feel quite happy ☐2

I don't feel very happy ☐3

I'm not happy at all ☐4

8. In the last 6 months, how often have you had the following?
Please tick one box for each line

	About every day	More than once a week	About every week	About every month	Rarely or never	
Headache	☐1	☐2	☐3	☐4	☐5	(32)
Stomach-ache	☐1	☐2	☐3	☐4	☐5	(33)
Backache	☐1	☐2	☐3	☐4	☐5	(34)
Feeling low	☐1	☐2	☐3	☐4	☐5	(35)
Irritability or bad temper	☐1	☐2	☐3	☐4	☐5	(36)
Feeling nervous	☐1	☐2	☐3	☐4	☐5	(37)
Difficulty in getting to sleep	☐1	☐2	☐3	☐4	☐5	(38)
Feeling dizzy	☐1	☐2	☐3	☐4	☐5	(39)

9. During the last *month*, have you taken any medicines or tablets for any of the following:
You may tick one box for each line

	No	Yes, once	Yes, more than once	
Headache	☐1	☐2	☐3	(40)
Stomach-ache	☐1	☐2	☐3	(41)
Difficulties in getting to sleep	☐1	☐2	☐3	(42)
Nervousness	☐1	☐2	☐3	(43)

10. How often do you feel tired when you go to school in the morning?
Please tick one box (44)

Rarely or never	☐1
Occasionally	☐2
1–3 times a week	☐3
4 or more times a week	☐4

11. How often do you brush your teeth? (45)
Please tick one box

More than once a day	☐1
Once a day	☐2
At least once a week, but not daily	☐3
Less than once a week	☐4
Never	☐5

EXERCISE

12. OUTSIDE SCHOOL HOURS: How OFTEN do you usually exercise in your free time so much that you get out of breath or sweat? (46)
Please tick one box

Every day	☐ 1
4–6 times a week	☐ 2
2–3 times a week	☐ 3
Once a week	☐ 4
Once a month	☐ 5
Less than once a month	☐ 6
Never	☐ 7

13. OUTSIDE SCHOOL HOURS: How many HOURS a week do you usually exercise in your free time so much that you get out of breath or sweat? (47)
Please tick one box

None	☐ 1
About half an hour	☐ 2
About 1 hour	☐ 3
About 2–3 hours	☐ 4
About 4–6 hours	☐ 5
7 hours or more	☐ 6

14. WALKING

How many days a week (including Saturdays and Sundays) do you usually do any walking that lasts for **at least 10 minutes**? (48)
Please include all types of walking. For example, walking to school, to a friend's house, to clubs, to the shops, dog walking, paper rounds or just going for a walk.
Please tick one box

None ☐ 0   ☞ **Go on to Question 16**

1 day a week	2 days a week	3 days a week	4 days a week	5 days a week	6 days a week	7 days a week
☐ 1	☐ 2	☐ 3	☐ 4	☐ 5	☐ 6	☐ 7

☞ **Go to Question 15**

15. On the days that you do some walking, about how long on average do you spend walking, **in total**, on each day? (49)
Please tick one box

Less than 15 minutes ☐ 1

At least 15 minutes but less than 30 minutes ☐ 2

At least 30 minutes but less than 1 hour ☐ 3

1 hour or more ☐ 4

16. CYCLING

How many days a week do you usually do any cycling that lasts for **at least 10 minutes**? (50)
Please include all types of cycling, for example, to or from school, to a friend's house, paper rounds, racing or just going out on your bike.
Please tick one box

None ☐ 0   ☞ **Go on to Question 18**

1 day a week	2 days a week	3 days a week	4 days a week	5 days a week	6 days a week	7 days a week
☐ 1	☐ 2	☐ 3	☐ 4	☐ 5	☐ 6	☐ 7

☞ **Go to Question 17**

17. On the days that you do some cycling, about how long on average do you spend cycling, **in total**, on each day? (51)
Please tick one box

Less than 15 minutes ☐ 1

At least 15 minutes but less than 30 minutes ☐ 2

At least 30 minutes but less than 1 hour ☐ 3

1 hour or more ☐ 4

18. SCHOOL P. E./GAMES LESSONS

How many P. E. or games lessons do you have in a week at school? (52)
Please write in the number, or if you do not have any, tick the box instead.

None ☐ 0 ☞ **Go on to Question 20**

OR

I have ✎ .... lesson(s) in a week   ☞ **Go to Question 19**

19. How long in **each** less do you spend actually doing P. E. or sport?　(53)
Do not include time spent getting changed, standing around etc.
Please tick one box

Less than 15 minutes ☐1

At least 15 minutes but less than 30 minutes ☐2

At least 30 minutes but less than 1 hour ☐3

1 hour or more ☐4

20. ACTIVITIES NOT IN SCHOOL LESSONS
Please read the following list of activities and tick any that you
do outside school lessons.　(54)
*Include activities that you do at break times, dinner time, before
school, after school or at weekends.*
You may tick more than one box

Swimming ☐1

Football, tennis, basketball, hockey,
netball or other ball games ☐2

Athletics, gymnastics, boxing, karate, judo ☐3

Aerobics, keep fit, jogging, running ☐4

Running about outdoors/Kicking a ball about ☐5 ☞ **If any of these, go to Question 21**

Roller skating, rollerblading, skateboarding
or iceskating ☐6

Dancing
(disco, rave, ballet, at home or at clubs) ☐7

Any other activities that make you at least
a bit out of breath or warmer than usual ☐8

None ☐9 ☞ **Go on to Question 23**

21. Thinking about all the things you've ticked at Question 20, on how many days a week do you do **any** of these activities? (55)
Please tick one box

Less than once a week ☐0 ☞ **Go on to Question 23**

1 day a week	2 days a week	3 days a week	4 days a week	5 days a week	6 days a week	7 days a week
☐1	☐2	☐3	☐4	☐5	☐6	☐7

☞ **Go to Question 22**

22. On the days that you do some of these activities, about how long on average do you spend **in total**, on each day? (56)
Please tick one box

Less than 15 minutes ☐1
At least 15 minutes but less than 30 minutes ☐2
At least 30 minutes but less than 1 hour ☐3
1 hour or more ☐4

RECREATION

23. On average, how many hours *a day* do you usually watch TV? (57)
Please tick one box

Not at all ☐1
Less than half an hour a day ☐2
Half an hour to 1 hour ☐3
2–3 hours ☐4
4 hours ☐5
More than 4 hours ☐6

24. How many hours *a week* do you usually play computer games? (58)
Please tick one box

Not at all ☐1
Less than 1 hour a week ☐2
1–3 hours ☐3
4–6 hours ☐4
7–9 hours ☐5
10 hours or more ☐6

25. How often do you spend time with your friends straight after school? (59)
Please tick one box

4–5 days a week ☐1

2–3 days a week ☐2

Once a week ☐3

Have no friends right now ☐4

26. On average, how many evenings a week do you usually spend out with your friends? (60)
Please tick one box

I am not allowed out in the evening ☐ x

None ☐ 0

1	2	3	4	5	6	7
evening a week	evenings a week	evenings a week	evenings a week	evenings a week	evenings a week	evenings a week
☐1	☐2	☐3	☐4	☐5	☐6	☐7

FOOD AND NUTRITION

27. Before going to school, how often do you have breakfast at home? (61)
Please tick one box

Every day ☐1

3–4 days a week ☐2

1–2 days a week ☐3

Hardly ever/never ☐4

28. Apart from your main meals (for example, breakfast, lunch, tea/dinner) how many times did you have a snack yesterday? (62)
Include things like chocolate, crisps, cake, biscuits and peanuts.
Please tick one box

None ☐1

Once ☐2

Twice ☐3

Three times ☐4

More than three times ☐5

Card 2	11②

(63-80)

29. How often do you drink or eat any of the following?
Please tick one box for each line

	More than once a day	Once a day	At least once a week but not daily	Rarely	Never	
Coffee	☐1	☐2	☐3	☐4	☐5	(12)
Fruit	☐1	☐2	☐3	☐4	☐5	(13)
Coke or other soft drinks that contain sugar	☐1	☐2	☐3	☐4	☐5	(14)
Sweets or chocolate	☐1	☐2	☐3	☐4	☐5	(15)
Raw vegetables or salad	☐1	☐2	☐3	☐4	☐5	(16)
Cooked vegetables	☐1	☐2	☐3	☐4	☐5	(17)
Peanuts	☐1	☐2	☐3	☐4	☐5	(18)
Crisps	☐1	☐2	☐3	☐4	☐5	(19)
Chips/fried potatoes	☐1	☐2	☐3	☐4	☐5	(20)
Hamburgers, hot dogs or sausages	☐1	☐2	☐3	☐4	☐5	(21)
Meat pies	☐1	☐2	☐3	☐4	☐5	(22)
Skimmed or semi-skimmed milk	☐1	☐2	☐3	☐4	☐5	(23)
Ordinary milk (full-fat)	☐1	☐2	☐3	☐4	☐5	(24)
Low-fat yoghurt or fromage frais	☐1	☐2	☐3	☐4	☐5	(25)
Fish (including fish fingers)	☐1	☐2	☐3	☐4	☐5	(26)
White bread	☐1	☐2	☐3	☐4	☐5	(27)
Wholemeal or rye bread	☐1	☐2	☐3	☐4	☐5	(28)
Cakes or biscuits	☐1	☐2	☐3	☐4	☐5	(29)
Pasta or rice	☐1	☐2	☐3	☐4	☐5	(30)

30. Please read the following statements about food and say if you agree or disagree.
Please tick one box for each line

	Agree strongly	Agree	Disagree	Disagree strongly	Don't know	
People of my age don't need to worry about the food they eat	☐1	☐2	☐3	☐4	☐5	(31)
Experts never agree which foods are good for you	☐1	☐2	☐3	☐4	☐5	(32)
I find healthy foods too boring	☐1	☐2	☐3	☐4	☐5	(33)
As you are reasonably active you can eat what you like	☐1	☐2	☐3	☐4	☐5	(34)
I don't know enough about which foods are good for you	☐1	☐2	☐3	☐4	☐5	(35)
I just eat the food I like and I don't worry about whether it's healthy or not	☐1	☐2	☐3	☐4	☐5	(36)

31. Are you thinking of changing what you eat to make it more healthy? (37)
Please tick one box

Yes ☐1 ☞ **If Yes**, please say what changes you are thinking of

✍ .... (38) (39)

....

....

No ☐2

32. Are you on a diet to lose weight? (40)
Please tick one box

No, because my weight is fine ☐1

No, but I do need to lose weight ☐2

Yes ☐3

ALCOHOL

33. Have you ever tasted an alcoholic drink? (That means beer, cider, alcoholic 'soft' drinks (eg alcoholic lemonade), wine, sherry, spirits like whisky, gin and vodka, or cocktails/mixers) (41)
Please tick one box

Yes ☐1

No ☐2

34. Thinking just about alcoholic drinks, which of these best describes (42)
your drinking habits?
Please tick one box

I do not drink alcohol at all ☐₁ ☞ **Go on to Question 37**

- -

I hardly drink alcohol at all ☐₂

I drink a little alcohol ☐₃

I drink a moderate amount of alcohol ☐₄ ☞ **Go on to Question 35**

I drink quite a lot of alcohol ☐₅

I drink heavily ☐₆

35. At present, how often do you drink anything alcoholic, such as cider,
wines, alcoholic 'soft' drinks, spirits, cocktails or beer? Try to include
even those times when you only drink a small amount.
Please tick one box for each line

	Every day	Every week	Every month	Less than once a month	Never	
High/extra-strength lager	☐₁	☐₂	☐₃	☐₄	☐₅	(43)
Normal-strength lager	☐₁	☐₂	☐₃	☐₄	☐₅	(44)
High/extra-strength beer	☐₁	☐₂	☐₃	☐₄	☐₅	(45)
Normal-strength beer	☐₁	☐₂	☐₃	☐₄	☐₅	(46)
Spirits, liqueurs, or cocktails/mixers (cocktails/mixers are mixtures of spirits with soft drinks or fruit juices)	☐₁	☐₂	☐₃	☐₄	☐₅	(47)
Sherry or martini (including port, vermouth, Cinzano, Dubonnet)	☐₁	☐₂	☐₃	☐₄	☐₅	(48)
Wine, Babycham or champagne	☐₁	☐₂	☐₃	☐₄	☐₅	(49)
Cider	☐₁	☐₂	☐₃	☐₄	☐₅	(50)
Alcoholic 'soft' drinks (alcoholic lemonades, alcoholic colas etc) like Hooch, Two Dogs etc	☐₁	☐₂	☐₃	☐₄	☐₅	(51)

36. Have you ever had so much alcohol that you were really drunk?   (52)
Please tick one box

No, never ☐1

Yes, once ☐2

Yes, 2–3 times ☐3

Yes, 4–10 times ☐4

Yes, more than 10 times ☐5

TO BE COMPLETED BY EVERYONE

37. Please read all these statements carefully and say whether you agree or disagree with each one.
Please tick one box for each line

	Agree	Disagree	Don't know
Life is more fun when you have a drink	☐1	☐2	☐3 (53)
Drinking is only dangerous if you get addicted to it	☐1	☐2	☐3 (54)
I feel more confident when I have a drink	☐1	☐2	☐3 (55)
Young people don't know enough about the dangers of drinking	☐1	☐2	☐3 (56)
I enjoy the taste of alcoholic drinks	☐1	☐2	☐3 (57)
I like soft drinks more than alcoholic drinks	☐1	☐2	☐3 (58)
I sometimes worry about the amount I drink	☐1	☐2	☐3 (59)
I sometimes feel pressurised into having an alcoholic drink by my friends, even if I don't really want to	☐1	☐2	☐3 (60)
There is no point drinking if you don't get drunk	☐1	☐2	☐3 (61)

SMOKING

38. Have you ever smoked at least one cigarette?
Please tick one box

Yes ☐1 (62)

No ☐2

How old were you when you first smoked a cigarette?

✍ I was .... years old   (63-64)

223

39. Now read all the following sentences carefully and tick the box next to the **one** which you think you are the **most** like? (65)
Please tick one box

I have never smoked ☐1

I only ever tried smoking once ☐2

I used to smoke sometimes, but I never smoke cigarettes now ☐3

I sometimes smoke cigarettes now, but not as many as one a week ☐4

I smoke at least once cigarette a week, but I don't smoke every day ☐5

I smoke every day ☐6

40. How many cigarettes do you usually smoke in a week?
If you do not smoke cigarettes, please tick the box instead

I do not smoke cigarettes ☐xx ☞ **Go on to Question 43**

OR I usually smoke about ✍ .... cigarettes a week (66-67)
☞ **Go to Question 41**

41. Would you like to give up smoking? (68)
Please tick one box

Yes ☐1

No ☐2

42. Have you ever tried to give up smoking? (69)
Please tick one box

Yes ☐1

No ☐2

TO BE COMPLETED BY EVERYBODY

43. And what do you think about smoking?
(We are interested in your opinion even if you do not smoke yourself.)
Please tick one box for each line

	Agree	Disagree	Don't know	
Smoking makes you look more grown up	☐1	☐2	☐3	(70)
Smoking can help to calm you down	☐1	☐2	☐3	(71)
Smoking helps to give you confidence	☐1	☐2	☐3	(72)
Smoking can put you in a better mood	☐1	☐2	☐3	(73)
Smoking can help you to stay slim	☐1	☐2	☐3	(74)
Smoking can help you to make friends more easily	☐1	☐2	☐3	(75)
Smokers have more fun than people who don't smoke	☐1	☐2	☐3	(76)
Smokers are more likely to have boyfriends or girlfriends than people who don't smoke	☐1	☐2	☐3	(77)
Smokers are more boring than people who don't smoke	☐1	☐2	☐3	(78)
Smokers tend to be more rebellious than people who don't smoke	☐1	☐2	☐3	(79)
Sometimes it is difficult to say "no" when people offer you cigarettes	☐1	☐2	☐3	(80)

Card 3	11③

ABOUT SCHOOL

44. How do you feel about school at present (12)
Please tick one box

I like it a lot ☐1
I like it a bit ☐2
I don't like very much ☐3
I don't like it all ☐4

45. IN YOUR OPINION: What does your class teacher(s) think about   (13)
your school performance compared to your classmates?
Please tick one box
He/she thinks I am:

Very good ☐1
Good ☐2
Average ☐3
Below average ☐4

46. Please tick one box for each of the statements about your teachers in
general. If you only have one teacher, think of this person when you
answer the questions.
Please tick one box on each line

	Agree strongly	Agree	Neither agree or disagree	Disagree	Disagree strongly	
I am encouraged to express my own views in my class(es)	☐1	☐2	☐3	☐4	☐5	(14)
Our teachers treat us fairly	☐1	☐2	☐3	☐4	☐5	(15)
When I need extra help, I can get it	☐1	☐2	☐3	☐4	☐5	(16)
My teachers are interested in me as a person	☐1	☐2	☐3	☐4	☐5	(17)

47. Please tick one box for each statement about the pupils in your class(es).
Please tick one box for each line

	Always	Often	Sometimes	Rarely	Never	
The pupils in my class(es) enjoy being together	☐1	☐2	☐3	☐4	☐5	(18)
Most of the pupils in my class(es) are kind and helpful	☐1	☐2	☐3	☐4	☐5	(19)
Other pupils accept me as I am	☐1	☐2	☐3	☐4	☐5	(20)

48. How often do you think that going to school is boring?   (21)
Please tick one box

Very often ☐1
Often ☐2
Sometimes ☐3
Rarely ☐4
Never ☐5

49. How often does it happen that other pupils don't want to spend (22)
time with you at school and you end up being alone?
Please tick one box

It hasn't happened this term ☐1

Once or twice ☐2

Sometimes ☐3

About once a week ☐4

Several times a week ☐5

50. How many days did you skip classes or school this term? (23)
Please tick one box

None this term ☐1

1 day ☐2

2 days ☐3

3 days ☐4

4 or more days ☐5

51. How often do you feel safe at school? (24)
Please tick one box

Always ☐1

Often ☐2

Sometimes ☐3

Rarely ☐4

Never ☐5

52. How much do you agree or disagree with each of the following
statements?
Please tick one box for each line

	Agree strongly	Agree	Neither agree or disagree	Disagree	Disagree strongly	
My *parents* expect too much of me at school	☐1	☐2	☐3	☐4	☐5	(25)
My *teachers* expect too much of me at school	☐1	☐2	☐3	☐4	☐5	(26)

53. How pressured do you feel by the school work you have to do?
Please tick the box which fits the best for you personally. (27)
Please tick one box

Not at all ☐1
A little ☐2
Some ☐3
A lot ☐4

54. Please read each statement about your school carefully.
Please tick one box for each line

	Agree strongly	Agree	Neither agree or disagree	Disagree	Disagree strongly	
In our school the pupils take part in making rules	☐1	☐2	☐3	☐4	☐5	(28)
The pupils are treated too severely/strictly in this school	☐1	☐2	☐3	☐4	☐5	(29)
The rules in this school are fair	☐1	☐2	☐3	☐4	☐5	(30)
Our school is a nice place to be	☐1	☐2	☐3	☐4	☐5	(31)
I feel I belong at this school	☐1	☐2	☐3	☐4	☐5	(32)

55. What do you think you will be doing when you are 16? (33)
If you are 16, answer for what you think you will be doing next year
Please tick one box

Doing A levels, either at school (6th form) or at college ☐1
Doing some other course at school (6th form) or at college ☐2
Getting a full-time job ☐3
Getting an apprenticeship/training ☐4
Be unemployed ☐5
Going on an employment training course ☐6
Don't know ☐7

Here are some questions about bullying. We say a pupil is BEING BULLIED when another pupil, or group of pupils, or group of pupils, say or do nasty and unpleasant things to him or her. It is also bullying when a pupil is teased repeatedly in a way he or she doesn't like. But it is NOT BULLYING when two pupils of about the same strength quarrel or fight.

56. Have you ever been bullied at school? (34)
(This could be at any school)
Please tick one box

Yes ▢₁ ☞ **Go to Question 57**

No ▢₂ ☞ **Go on to Question 58**

57. How often have you been bullied in school this term? (35)
(This could be at school)
Please tick one box

I haven't been bullied in school this term ▢₁

Once or twice ▢₂

Sometimes ▢₃

About once a week ▢₄

Several times a week ▢₅

58. Have you ever bullied other people at school? (36)
(This could be at any school)
Please tick one box

Yes ▢₁ ☞ **Go to Question 59**

No ▢₂ ☞ **Go on to Question 60**

59. How often have you taken part in bullying other pupils in school this term? (37)
Please tick one box

I haven't bullied others in school this term ▢₁

Once or twice ▢₂

Sometimes ▢₃

About once a week ▢₄

Several times a week ▢₅

FAMILY AND FRIENDS

60. How many other people do you live with at home, apart from yourself? If your mother and father live in different places, answer for the home where you live *most* of the time.

I live with ✍ .... other people (not including myself) (38-39)

61. Please say whether or not the following people **live with you** at your home. *If your mother and father live in different places, answer for the home where you live most of the time.*
Please tick one box for each line

	Yes – lives with me	No – doesn't live with me/I don't have one	
Mother	☐1	☐2	(40)
Stepmother	☐1	☐2	(41)
Father	☐1	☐2	(42)
Stepfather	☐1	☐2	(43)

62. Please write in *how many* of the following people **live with you** at your home. *If your mother and father live in different places, answer for the home where you live most of the time. If you do not have that person living at your home please write in "0".*

Brothers or stepbrothers ✍ .... (44)

Sisters or stepsisters ✍ .... (45)

Grandparents ✍ .... (46)

Other people who live with you (not including parents/step-parents) ✍ .... (47)

230

63. What are your parents' jobs?
Please describe exactly what they do, for example, shop assistant, farm worker, lorry driver, dentist, hairdresser, teacher. You can write down "don't know" or "has no paid job at the moment" or "unemployed", if that is the right answer.

✐ My father: .... (48)

....

64.
✐ My mother: .... (49)

....

65. Please tick *one* box to show which of these best describes you.
I am ... (50)

White ☐ 1

Black – Caribbean ☐ 2

Black – African ☐ 3

Black – other (write in) ✐ .... ☐ 4

Indian ☐ 5

Pakistani ☐ 6

Bangladeshi ☐ 7

Chinese ☐ 8

Mixed race ☐ 9

Any other group (write in) ✐ .... ☐ 0 (51)

66. Do you have your own bedroom for yourself? (52)
Please tick one box

Yes ☐ 1

No ☐ 2

67. How well off do you think your family is? (53)
Please tick one box

Very well off ☐ 1

Quite well off ☐ 2

Average ☐ 3

Not very well off ☐ 4

Not at all well off ☐ 5

68. During the past year, how many times did you travel away on holiday with your family? (54)
Please tick one box

Not at all ☐1

Once ☐2

Twice ☐3

More than twice ☐4

69. Thinking about the house or flat you live in at the moment, does your family own it or is it rented? *If your mother and father live in different places, answer for the home where you live most of the time.*
If your family are buying their home on a mortgage, tick 'owned'. (55)
Please tick one box

Owned ☐1

Rented ☐2

Don't know ☐3

70. How much money do you usually get each week (including pocket money and money you earn yourself)? Do NOT include any money you may be given for travel or school dinners.

£.............. . ... (56-59)

71. Does anyone you live with have a car or van? (60)
Please tick one box

No ☐1

Yes, one ☐2

Yes, two or more ☐3

72. How often do you use a seat belt when you sit in a car? (61)
Please tick one box

Usually there is no seat belt where I sit ☐1

Always ☐2

Often ☐3

Sometimes ☐4

Rarely or never ☐5

I hardly ever travel by car ☐6

73. How often do you wear a helmet when you ride a bicycle? (62)
Please tick one box

Always ☐1

Often ☐2

Sometimes ☐3

Rarely or never ☐4

I do not ride bicycles ☐5

74. Please tick one box for each statement about your parents. *If your mother and father live in different places, answer for the home where you live **most** of the time.*
Please tick one box for each line

	Always	Often	Sometimes	Rarely	Never	
If I have a problem at school, my parents are ready to help	☐1	☐2	☐3	☐4	☐5	(63)
My parents are willing to come to school and talk to teachers	☐1	☐2	☐3	☐4	☐5	(64)
My parents encourage me to do well at school	☐1	☐2	☐3	☐4	☐5	(65)

75. How easy is it for you to talk to the following people about things that really bother you?
Please tick one box for each line

	Very easy	Easy	Difficult	Very difficult	Don't have or see this person	
Father	☐1	☐2	☐3	☐4	☐5	(66)
Stepfather	☐1	☐2	☐3	☐4	☐5	(67)
Mother	☐1	☐2	☐3	☐4	☐5	(68)
Stepmother	☐1	☐2	☐3	☐4	☐5	(69)
Elder brother(s)	☐1	☐2	☐3	☐4	☐5	(70)
Elder sister(s)	☐1	☐2	☐3	☐4	☐5	(71)
Friends of the same sex	☐1	☐2	☐3	☐4	☐5	(72)
Friends of the opposite sex	☐1	☐2	☐3	☐4	☐5	(73)

76. How many close friends do you have? (74)
Please tick one box

None ☐1
One ☐2
Two ☐3
Three or more ☐4

(75-80)

| Card 4 | 11④ |

77. Do you ever feel lonely? (12)
Please tick one box

Yes, very often ☐1
Yes, rather often ☐2
Yes, sometimes ☐3
No ☐4

78. How often do you feel...

	Always	Often	Sometimes	Rarely	Never	
...left out of things?	☐1	☐2	☐3	☐4	☐5	(13)
...helpless?	☐1	☐2	☐3	☐4	☐5	(14)
...confident in yourself?	☐1	☐2	☐3	☐4	☐5	(15)

Please tick one box for each line

79. How often in the last term has someone done any of these things to you?
Please tick one box for each line

	Not this term	Once or twice	Sometimes	About once a week	More than once a week	
Made fun of you because of your religion or race	☐1	☐2	☐3	☐4	☐5	(16)
Made fun of you because of your looks or the way you talk	☐1	☐2	☐3	☐4	☐5	(17)
Hit, slapped or pushed you	☐1	☐2	☐3	☐4	☐5	(18)
Spread rumours or mean lies about you	☐1	☐2	☐3	☐4	☐5	(19)

80. Is it easy or difficult for you to make new friends? (20)
Please tick one box

Very easy ☐1

Easy ☐2

Difficult ☐3

Very difficult ☐4

ABOUT YOURSELF

81. Is there anything about your body you would like to change?
Please tick one box

Yes ☐1 (21) ☞ **If Yes,** what would you change?

✍ ....

.... (22) (23)

No ☐2

82. Do you think your body is: (24)
Please tick one box

Much too thin ☐1

A bit too thin ☐2

About the right size ☐3

A bit too fat ☐4

Much too fat ☐5

I don't think about it ☐6

83. Do you think you are: (25)
Please tick one box

Very good-looking ☐1

Quite good-looking ☐2

About average ☐3

Not very good-looking ☐4

Not at all good-looking ☐5

I don't think about my looks ☐6

ACCIDENTS AND INJURIES

Many young people get hurt or injured at places such as the street, at home, playing sports, or during a fight with others. Injuries can also include being poisoned or burned. They do NOT include diseases such as measles, the flu or chicken pox. The following questions are about injuries you may have had **DURING THE PAST 12 MONTHS.**

84. During the PAST 12 MONTHS, how many times were you injured, (26) so much that you *had to be treated by a doctor or nurse*? *Please tick one box*

I was *not* treated by a doctor or nurse for an injury ☐1 ☞ **Go to to Question 94**

1 time ☐2

2 times ☐3

3 times ☐4

4 or more times ☐5

85. We would like you think about just **one** of these injuries and **no others** when you answer Questions 85 to 93.
You should think about **the most serious** injury to happen to you in the last 12 months – that is, the one that **took the most time to get better.**
If you only had ONE injury in the last 12 months, just think about that injury.

Please describe this injury (eg broken arm, hit over head etc)

✍ .... (27-28)

....

86. STILL THINKING OF YOUR MOST SERIOUS INJURY (from Question 85)
What were you doing at the time of the injury?
(eg riding a bicycle, playing hockey, running around etc)

✍ .... (29-30)

....

87. STILL THINKING OF YOUR MOST SERIOUS INJURY
(from Question 85)
How did the accident happen?
(eg I was hit by a car, I was hit with a hockey stick, I tripped and fell etc)

✍ .... (31-34)

....

88. STILL THINKING OF YOUR MOST SERIOUS INJURY
(from Question 85)
Where were you when this injury happened? (35-36)
Please tick the box which BEST DESCRIBES this place

At home (yours or someone else's) ☐ 01

At school (including school grounds) ☐ 02

At a sports facility or field (not at school) ☐ 03

In the street/road ☐ 04

In some other place (please tick box and write in where) ☐ 05

✍ ....

---

89. STILL THINKING OF YOUR MOST SERIOUS INJURY
(from Question 85)
Did this injury cause you to miss at least **one full day** of school
or other usual activities?
Please tick one box

If 'yes', how many days did you miss?

Yes ☐ 1 (37)

✍ I missed .... days (38-39)

No ☐ 2

---

90. STILL THINKING OF YOUR MOST SERIOUS INJURY
(from Question 85)
Which of the following happened as a result of this injury? (40)
You may tick more than one box

Had a cast put on ☐ 1

Had stitches ☐ 2

Needed crutches or a wheelchair ☐ 3

Had an operation ☐ 4

Stayed in hospital overnight ☐ 5

NONE OF THE ABOVE ☐ 6

91. STILL THINKING OF YOUR MOST SERIOUS INJURY
(from Question 85)
What were the results of this injury? (41)
You may tick more than one box

Bone was broken, dislocated or out of joint ☐ 1

Sprain, strain or pulled muscle ☐ 2

Cuts, puncture or stab wounds ☐ 3

Concussion or other head or neck injury, knocked out, whiplash ☐ 4

Bruises, black and blue marks or internal bleeding ☐ 5

Burns ☐ 6

Other results (please tick box and write in what) ☐ 7 (42)

✍ ....

NONE OF THE ABOVE ☐ 8

92. STILL THINKING OF YOUR MOST SERIOUS INJURY
(from Question 85)
In what month did this injury happen? (43-44)
Please tick one box

Jan	Feb	Mar	Apr	May	Jun	Jul	Aug	Sep	Oct	Nov	Dec
☐	☐	☐	☐	☐	☐	☐	☐	☐	☐	☐	☐
01	02	03	04	05	06	07	08	09	10	11	12

93. STILL THINKING OF YOUR MOST SERIOUS INJURY
(from Question 85)
Did this injury occur because someone meant to hurt you? (45)
Please tick one box

Yes ☐ 1

No ☐ 2

238

TO BE COMPLETED BY EVERYONE

94. Some injuries are *not* treated by a *doctor or nurse*.　(46)
During the past 12 months, how many times were you injured
so much that you missed *at least one full day* of school or other usual
activities, but were *not* treated by a doctor or nurse?
Please tick one box

None ☐1
1 time ☐2
2 times ☐3
3 times ☐4
4 or more times ☐5

(47-80)

Card 5	11⑤

SEXUAL HEALTH

95. Have you had any classes at school which have given information an
or discussed the following topics?
Please tick one box for each line

	No	Yes, once	Yes, a few times	Yes many times	
Sexual relationships	☐1	☐2	☐3	☐4	(12)
Sexual feelings and emotions	☐1	☐2	☐3	☐4	(13)
How our bodies develop	☐1	☐2	☐3	☐4	(14)
Pregnancy and having a baby	☐1	☐2	☐3	☐4	(15)
Contraception or birth control	☐1	☐2	☐3	☐4	(16)
How to use a condom	☐1	☐2	☐3	☐4	(17)
Abortion	☐1	☐2	☐3	☐4	(18)
HIV/AIDS	☐1	☐2	☐3	☐4	(19)
Other sexually transmitted infections	☐1	☐2	☐3	☐4	(20)
Homosexuality (men who have sex with men)	☐1	☐2	☐3	☐4	(21)
Lesbianism (women who have sex with women)	☐1	☐2	☐3	☐4	(22)

96. And which, if any, of these topics do you feel your school has *not* given you enough information about? (23)
Please tick as many boxes as apply

Sexual relationships ☐1
Sexual feelings and emotions ☐2
How our bodies develop ☐3
Pregnancy and having a baby ☐4
Contraception or birth control ☐5
How to use a condom ☐5
Abortion ☐6
HIV/AIDS ☐7
Other sexually transmitted infections ☐8
Homosexuality (men who have sex with men) ☐9
Lesbianism (women who have sex with women) ☐0
NONE OF THESE ☐x

97. How difficult is it for you to discuss topics to do with sex with the following people?
Tick one box for each line

	Very easy	Fairly easy	Fairly difficult	Very difficult	Don't know	Don't have or see this person	
Mother/stepmother	☐1	☐2	☐3	☐4	☐5	☐6	(24)
Father/stepfather	☐1	☐2	☐3	☐4	☐5	☐6	(25)
Older brother or sister	☐1	☐2	☐3	☐4	☐5	☐6	(26)
Teacher	☐1	☐2	☐3	☐4	☐5	☐6	(27)
Boyfriend or girlfriend	☐1	☐2	☐3	☐4	☐5	☐6	(28)
Friends of my age	☐1	☐2	☐3	☐4	☐5	☐6	(29)
Older friends	☐1	☐2	☐3	☐4	☐5	☐6	(30)
Doctor or GP	☐1	☐2	☐3	☐4	☐5	☐6	(31)
Family planning clinic	☐1	☐2	☐3	☐4	☐5	☐6	(32)

98. Which of the following sexually transmitted infections have you heard of?
Tick all those that you have heard of

Gonorrhoea ☐ 1   (33)

Genital warts ☐ 2

Syphilis ☐ 3

Chlamydia ☐ 4

Gonaditis ☐ 5

HIV/AIDS ☐ 6

Herpes ☐ 7

Hepatitis B ☐ 8

NSU (Non-Specific Urethritis) ☐ 9

Other (Please tick box and write in what) ☐ 0   (34)

✍ ....

NONE OF THESE ☐ x

99. Which of the following do you think could protect you against sexually transmitted infections?
Tick one box for each line

	Yes	No	Don't know	
Not having sex	☐1	☐2	☐3	(35)
Taking the contraceptive pill	☐1	☐2	☐3	(36)
Using a condom	☐1	☐2	☐3	(37)
Using a female condom (Femidom)	☐1	☐2	☐3	(38)
Having a steady partner	☐1	☐2	☐3	(39)

100. Which of the following forms of contraception or protection have you *heard of*?
Tick all those that you have heard of

Condom ☐ 1 (40)

Female condom (Femidom) ☐ 2

Cap/Diaphragm ☐ 3

Contraceptive pill ☐ 4

Emergency contraception ("Morning after" pill) ☐ 5

Coil/IUD ☐ 6

"Barrier" creams (Foam tablets/Jelly/Creams/ Suppositories/Pessaries/Aerosol foams) ☐ 7

Withdrawal ☐ 8

Rhythm method/safe period ☐ 9

Contraceptive sponge ☐ 1 (41)

Sterilisation ☐ 2

Injections/Implants ☐ 3

Douching/Washing ☐ 4

NONE OF THESE ☐ 5

101. How much do you agree or disagree with each of the following statements?
Please tick one box for each line

	Strongly agree	Agree	Neither agree nor disagree	Disagree	Strongly disagree	Don't know
I would feel embarrassed buying condoms in shops	☐1	☐2	☐3	☐4	☐5	☐6 (42)
If I wanted to have sex, I would stop if we didn't have a condom	☐1	☐2	☐3	☐4	☐5	☐6 (43)
Using a condom shows that people care for each other	☐1	☐2	☐3	☐4	☐5	☐6 (44)
It is the man's responsibility to carry condoms	☐1	☐2	☐3	☐4	☐5	☐6 (45)
I would be too embarrassed to suggest using a condom	☐1	☐2	☐3	☐4	☐5	☐6 (46)
A woman who carries condoms is sensible	☐1	☐2	☐3	☐4	☐5	☐6 (47)
I don't know enough about the risk of HIV/AIDS to people like myself	☐1	☐2	☐3	☐4	☐5	☐6 (48)

102. Where do you get *most* of your information about sexual matters?
You may tick more than one box

Parents ☐ 1   (49)

Sister/Brother ☐ 2

Other relative(s) ☐ 3

Friends ☐ 4

School ☐ 5

TV/Magazines/Newspapers/Radio ☐ 6

Books ☐ 7

Somewhere else (Please tick box and write in what) ☐ 8   (50)

✎ ....

DRUGS

103. Have you ever used any of the following drugs?
Please tick one box for each line

	Never	Once or twice	Three times or more	
Amphetamines (Speed, Uppers, Whizz, Sulphate, Billy)	☐1	☐2	☐3	(51)
Cannabis (Marijuana, Dope, Pot, Blow, Hash, Black, Grass, Draw, Ganja, Spliffs, Joints)	☐1	☐2	☐3	(52)
Cocaine (Coke, Charlie)	☐1	☐2	☐3	(53)
Crack (Rock, Sand, Stone, Pebbles)	☐1	☐2	☐3	(54)
Ecstasy ('E', Dennis the Menace)	☐1	☐2	☐3	(55)
Heroin (Morphine, Smack, Skag, 'H')	☐1	☐2	☐3	(56)
Acid (LSD, Tabs, Trips)	☐1	☐2	☐3	(57)
Magic Mushrooms (Psilocybin)	☐1	☐2	☐3	(58)
Methadone/Physeptone (Dolls, Dollies, Mud, Phyamps, Red Rock, Tootsie Roll)	☐1	☐2	☐3	(59)
Nadropax (Pax)	☐1	☐2	☐3	(60)
Tranquillisers (Downers, Barbiturates, Blues, Temazies, Jellies, Tranx) **without** a prescription	☐1	☐2	☐3	(61)
Amyl Nitrites (Nitrites, Poppers)	☐1	☐2	☐3	(62)
Anabolic Steroids (Steroids) **without** a prescription	☐1	☐2	☐3	(63)
Glues or solvents (to sniff or inhale)	☐1	☐2	☐3	(64)
Gas/Aerosols/Butane/Lighter fuel (to sniff or inhale)	☐1	☐2	☐3	(65)
Something else	☐1	☐2	☐3	(66)

If something else, please write down what: (67)

✍ ....

IF YOU HAVE *NEVER USED ANY* OF THE DRUGS LISTED IN THE LAST QUESTION, *MOVE ON TO QUESTION 106*

104. If you have ever taken one of these drugs, how old were you the first time and which drug did you take?

I was about ✍ .... years old   (68-69)

and the first drug that I took was ✍ .... (70-71)

	(72-80)
Card 6	11⑥

105. During the *last four weeks*, how often have you used any of the following drugs?
Please tick one box on each line

	Not in the last 4 weeks	Once or twice	Three times or more	
Amphetamines (Speed, Uppers, Whizz, Sulphate, Billy)	☐1	☐2	☐3	(12)
Cannabis (Marijuana, Dope, Pot, Blow, Hash, Black, Grass, Draw, Ganja, Spliffs, Joints)	☐1	☐2	☐3	(13)
Cocaine (Coke, Charlie)	☐1	☐2	☐3	(14)
Crack (Rock, Sand, Stone, Pebbles)	☐1	☐2	☐3	(15)
Ecstasy ('E', Dennis the Menace)	☐1	☐2	☐3	(16)
Heroin (Morphine, Smack, Skag, 'H')	☐1	☐2	☐3	(17)
Acid (LSD, Tabs, Trips)	☐1	☐2	☐3	(18)
Magic Mushrooms (Psilocybin)	☐1	☐2	☐3	(19)
Methadone (Dolls, Dollies, Mud, Phyamps, Red Rock, Tootsie Roll)	☐1	☐2	☐3	(20)
Nadropax (Pax)	☐1	☐2	☐3	(21)
Tranquillisers (Downers, Barbiturates, Blues, Temazies, Jellies, Tranx) **without** a prescription	☐1	☐2	☐3	(22)
Amyl Nitrites (Nitrites, Poppers)	☐1	☐2	☐3	(23)
Anabolic Steroids (Steroids) **without** a prescription	☐1	☐2	☐3	(24)
Glues or solvents (to sniff or inhale)	☐1	☐2	☐3	(25)
Gas/Aerosols/Butane/Lighter fuel (to sniff or inhale)	☐1	☐2	☐3	(25)
Something else	☐1	☐2	☐3	(27)

If something else, please write down what: (28)

✍ ....

106. How harmful do you think the following are to someone's health if taken on a regular basis?
Tick one box for each line

	Very harmful	Fairly harmful	Not harmful	Not at all harmful	Don't know	
Heroin	☐1	☐2	☐3	☐4	☐5	(29)
Amyl nitrite	☐1	☐2	☐3	☐4	☐5	(30)
Ecstasy	☐1	☐2	☐3	☐4	☐5	(31)
Caffeine	☐1	☐2	☐3	☐4	☐5	(32)
Crack	☐1	☐2	☐3	☐4	☐5	(33)
Cannabis	☐1	☐2	☐3	☐4	☐5	(34)
Tranquillisers	☐1	☐2	☐3	☐4	☐5	(35)
Cigarettes	☐1	☐2	☐3	☐4	☐5	(36)
Amphetamines	☐1	☐2	☐3	☐4	☐5	(37)
Glue sniffing	☐1	☐2	☐3	☐4	☐5	(38)
Magic mushrooms	☐1	☐2	☐3	☐4	☐5	(39)
Acid	☐1	☐2	☐3	☐4	☐5	(40)
Alcohol	☐1	☐2	☐3	☐4	☐5	(41)
Cocaine	☐1	☐2	☐3	☐4	☐5	(42)

107. Please read the following statements about drugs and say if you agree or disagree with each one.
Tick one box for each statement

	Agree strongly	Agree slightly	Disagree slightly	Disagree strongly	Don't know	
Taking drugs is exciting	☐1	☐2	☐3	☐4	☐5	(43)
Taking drugs is OK if it makes you feel good	☐1	☐2	☐3	☐4	☐5	(44)
Most young people will try out drugs at some time	☐1	☐2	☐3	☐4	☐5	(45)
People take drugs to relax	☐1	☐2	☐3	☐4	☐5	(46)
It's OK to use soft drugs like cannabis, but I'd never touch hard drugs like heroin	☐1	☐2	☐3	☐4	☐5	(47)
Drugs are not as harmful as people say they are	☐1	☐2	☐3	☐4	☐5	(48)

(49-80)

☺ THE END ☺

THANK YOU VERY MUCH FOR YOUR HELP

Please put your questionnaire into the envelope you have been given and seal it.

If you finish early you may wish to have a go at this puzzle. How many of the words listed below can you find in the grid? They may be vertical, horizontal or diagonal, up or down. An example is shown on the grid.

E	C	A	R	R	R	E	T	S	I	S	A	K	S
K	A	O	T	E	E	W	S	W	I	S	E	R	M
E	N	B	M	Y	O	H	A	E	U	R	V	O	U
R	T	I	U	P	F	E	F	I	T	A	E	W	S
O	E	C	R	L	U	A	K	G	I	R	N	E	M
E	E	Y	B	D	L	T	A	H	G	E	I	M	R
D	N	C	R	E	I	Y	E	T	O	H	N	O	O
I	L	L	T	N	F	T	R	R	D	T	G	H	F
V	L	E	H	S	U	R	B	H	T	O	O	T	H
E	A	A	A	B	A	A	I	K	O	R	E	O	T
G	B	L	R	E	R	E	L	E	H	B	U	E	X
E	T	L	A	O	G	A	F	E	N	R	I	T	I
T	O	T	E	R	M	A	I	N	S	D	E	L	S
A	O	M	E	A	I	L	L	N	E	S	S	M	T
B	F	E	R	S	R	C	H	A	L	K	O	O	C
L	N	E	H	E	E	N	W	O	N	K	T	N	I
E	L	A	O	M	E	D	I	C	I	N	E	E	S
S	P	A	W	A	L	K	I	N	G	D	A	Y	U
E	C	A	F	G	N	A	G	Y	G	K	L	I	M

BICYCLE	FALL	LEARNING	SMOKING
BRAIN	FEAST	LESSONS	SUMS
BREAKFAST	FOOTBALL	MEDICINE	SWEAT
BROTHER	FRIENDS	MILK	SWEET
BULLY	GAMES	MONEY	TERM
CANTEEN	GANG	MORAL	TOOTHBRUSH
CHALK	GREEN	MUSIC	TREK
COMPUTER	HOMEWORK	RACE	VEGETABLES
DIET	HOTDOG	SALT	VIDEO
DRINK	HOURS	SHAPE	WALKING
EVENING	ILLNESS	SISTER	WEIGHT
FACE	KNOW	SIXTH FORM	WHEAT